The Missing Bootstrap 5 Guide

Customize and extend Bootstrap 5 with Sass and JavaScript to create unique website designs

Jeppe Schaumburg Jensen

BIRMINGHAM—MUMBAI

The Missing Bootstrap 5 Guide

Associate Group Product Manager: Pavan Ramchandani

Publishing Product Manager: Kushal Dave

Senior Editor: Mark Dsouza

Content Development Editor: Divya Vijayan

Technical Editor: Joseph Aloocaran

Copy Editor: Safis Editing

Project Coordinator: Rashika Ba

Proofreader: Safis Editing

Indexer: Manju Arasan

Production Designer: Alishon Mendonca

Marketing Coordinators: Anamika Singh and Marylou De Mello

First published: August 2022

Production reference: 1290722

Published by Packt Publishing Ltd.

Livery Place

35 Livery Street

Birmingham

B3 2PB, UK.

ISBN 978-1-80107-643-2

www.packt.com

To Maja, who supported me and gave me time to write this book during the last year.

– Jeppe Schaumburg Jensen

Contributors

About the author

Jeppe Schaumburg Jensen is an experienced frontend developer with a deep interest in teaching Bootstrap and other UI frameworks. He holds a master of science degree in information technology with a specialization in interaction design and user experience. Over the last few years, he has been successful in establishing himself as an independent Instructor by creating online courses on different frontend development topics for various online course providers. On Udemy, his courses on Bootstrap have achieved the "Bestseller" and "Highest rated" badges, with more than 25,000 students so far. Besides teaching, Jeppe is a Senior Software Engineer on the Design System Team at Siteimprove, a multinational and industry-leading **Software-as-a-Service (SaaS)** company.

I want to thank the whole team at Packt Publishing for working with me throughout the creation of this book from the very beginning to the very end. Thank you for asking me to write this book and for trusting and supporting me in the whole process.

About the reviewer

Bello Ololade is a freelance frontend developer and product designer based in Nigeria. He broke into the tech industry two years ago when he was studying for his bachelor's degree in zoology at Olabisi Onabanjo University, Ago Iwoye, Ogun State, Nigeria.

Since then, he has worked with many clients and startups in many countries, providing solutions through tech and design. Throughout his years of experience, he has worked with many technologies to bring forward the best experience for clients and their users.

Guust Nieuwenhuis is a Full Stack Web Wizard with experience in a wide range of technologies. Over the last couple of years, he's been involved in projects for various clients including the European Commission, NSHQ (NATO), Adobe, AS Adventure Group, NS (Dutch Railways), CZ Groep, Proximus, Avery Dennison, and Mediagenix.

In his free time, he plays the double bass and drums, crosses the forest on his mountain bike, and coaches the youth at his local football club. He likes spending time with his wife and two kids or meeting friends for a chat, game, or drink.

When he still has some time left, he mainly spends it behind his computer to fulfil his hunger for the latest trends in IT.

Thank you to my wife, Joke, and my kids, Seppe and Saar.

Table of Contents

3

Downloading and Exploring the Bootstrap 5 Sass Files

4

Bootstrap 5 Global Options and Colors

5

Customizing Various Bootstrap 5 Elements

6

Understanding and Using the Bootstrap 5 Utility API

Part Two – Creating a Unique-Looking Website Based on Bootstrap 5 and Customization

7

Creating the Website Using Default Bootstrap 5 Elements

8

Customizing the Website Using Bootstrap 5 Variables, Utility API, and Sass

9

Improving the Website
with Interactive Features Using JavaScript

Part Three – Advanced Topics Related to Bootstrap 5

10

Using Bootstrap 5 with Advanced Sass and CSS Features

11

Using Bootstrap 5 with Advanced JavaScript Features

12

Optimizing Bootstrap 5 CSS and JavaScript Code

Index

Other Books You May Enjoy

Preface

Bootstrap is one of the world's most popular frontend UI toolkit and comes with easy-to-use and off-the-shelf solutions for building responsive websites with the use of components, utilities, JavaScript plugins, and more. You can customize Bootstrap 5 with Sass to achieve a unique-looking layout that stands out from the crowd. Learning how to customize Bootstrap 5 enables a developer to create something unique that doesn't look like Bootstrap.

Who this book is for

The book is intended for UI designers and developers who are familiar with HTML and already have some experience with using Bootstrap version 4 or 5. This includes frontend as well as backend developers using Bootstrap who don't know how to code CSS but know enough about HTML.

Experienced users of the default Bootstrap files can also benefit from this book by learning all about customization and other advanced features.

This book won't teach the basics of how to code a user interface with default Bootstrap 5 components. Instead, this book is about customization of Bootstrap 5 in various ways.

What this book covers

Chapter 1, *Why and How to Customize Bootstrap*, explores why we would want to customize Bootstrap 5, what can be customized (what the most important parts to customize are), and how that's done.

Chapter 2, *Using and Compiling Sass*, covers what Sass is, and we will learn about its features and benefits, how to use it, how to compile it into regular CSS, and the Sass features used by Bootstrap 5.

Chapter 3, *Downloading and Exploring the Bootstrap 5 Sass Files*, shows how to download Bootstrap 5 and then takes a closer look at the Bootstrap 5 Sass files and Sass variables, including how they are structured.

Chapter 4, *Bootstrap 5 Global Options and Colors*, delves into how to import the Bootstrap 5 Sass partials individually, how to change the global options, and how to customize the colors.

Chapter 5, *Customizing Various Bootstrap 5 Elements*, explores how to customize the visual style of the Bootstrap 5 elements: layout, content, forms, components, helpers, and utilities.

Chapter 6, *Understanding and Using the Bootstrap 5 Utility API*, examines how to use the utility API to generate and add new simple and complex utilities, as well as overwrite, modify, and remove existing utilities.

Chapter 7, Creating the Website Using Default Bootstrap 5 Elements, takes a closer look at the website we will create, including a description of the page setup, a description of global modules, and a description of the page types.

Chapter 8, Customizing the Website Using Bootstrap 5 Variables, Utility API, and Sass, shows how to customize our website by setting some global options, defining our own colors, changing the styling of various Bootstrap 5 elements, and using the utility API.

Chapter 9, Improving the Website with Interactive Features Using JavaScript, covers customizing the *feel* of our website by adding different interactive features, using the JavaScript-based components of Bootstrap 5 as well as custom JavaScript.

Chapter 10, Using Bootstrap 5 with Advanced Sass and CSS Features, looks at advanced Sass and CSS features related to Bootstrap 5, including how to use Sass mixins, functions, and extends, how to use CSS custom properties, and how to use the RFS plugin.

Chapter 11, Using Bootstrap 5 with Advanced JavaScript Features, examines the advanced JavaScript features that can be used with the interactive components of Bootstrap 5, including initialization, options, methods, and events.

Chapter 12, Optimizing Bootstrap 5 CSS and JavaScript Code, delves into how to optimize the compiled CSS by specifying the components we use and removing unused helpers and utilities, and how to use a module bundler to optimize JavaScript and minify both the compiled CSS and bundled JavaScript.

To get the most out of this book

You need to have some experience with creating user interfaces using Bootstrap 5 (or maybe Bootstrap 4). This means that you should know how to create various Bootstrap 5 components using HTML and all the right Bootstrap 5 classes and attributes, or at least know how this all works.

Software/hardware covered in the book	Operating system requirements
Bootstrap 5 (latest version – v5.2.0)	Windows, macOS, or Linux
Sass	A modern browser (for example, Chrome, Firefox, or Safari). Internet Explorer is not supported.
Scout-App and Live Sass Compiler (briefly)	A text editor (for example, Visual Studio Code)
Node.js, NPM, and Laravel Mix (briefly)	

If you are using the digital version of this book, we advise you to type the code yourself or access the code from the book's GitHub repository (a link is available in the next section). Doing so will help you avoid any potential errors related to the copying and pasting of code.

Download the example code files

You can download the example code files for this book from GitHub at `https://github.com/PacktPublishing/The-Missing-Bootstrap-5-Guide`. If there's an update to the code, it will be updated in the GitHub repository.

We also have other code bundles from our rich catalog of books and videos available at `https://github.com/PacktPublishing/`. Check them out!

Download the color images

We also provide a PDF file that has color images of the screenshots and diagrams used in this book. You can download it here: `https://packt.link/yXP75`.

Conventions used

There are a number of text conventions used throughout this book.

`Code in text`: Indicates code words in text, database table names, folder names, filenames, file extensions, pathnames, dummy URLs, user input, and Twitter handles. Here is an example: "We are first importing some configuration files so that we can use the `$spacer` variable as a value for the other variables, which we will set right after."

A block of code is set as follows:

```
// Required
@import "../bootstrap/scss/functions";
@import "../bootstrap/scss/variables";
@import "../bootstrap/scss/maps";
@import "../bootstrap/scss/mixins";
@import "../bootstrap/scss/root";
```

When we wish to draw your attention to a particular part of a code block, the relevant lines or items are set in bold:

```
// Modified variables
$breadcrumb-bg: $gray-300;
$breadcrumb-border-radius: $spacer;
$breadcrumb-padding-y: $spacer;
$breadcrumb-padding-x: $spacer;
$breadcrumb-item-padding-x: $spacer;
$breadcrumb-divider: quote("·");
```

Any command-line input or output is written as follows:

```
npm install bootstrap
```

Bold: Indicates a new term, an important word, or words that you see onscreen. For instance, words in menus or dialog boxes appear in **bold**. Here is an example: "The Page title global module is used on all pages except for the **Home** page and **Product** page."

> **Tips or Important Notes**
> Appear like this.

Get in touch

Feedback from our readers is always welcome.

General feedback: If you have questions about any aspect of this book, email us at customercare@packtpub.com and mention the book title in the subject of your message.

Errata: Although we have taken every care to ensure the accuracy of our content, mistakes do happen. If you have found a mistake in this book, we would be grateful if you would report this to us. Please visit www.packtpub.com/support/errata and fill in the form.

Piracy: If you come across any illegal copies of our works in any form on the internet, we would be grateful if you would provide us with the location address or website name. Please contact us at copyright@packt.com with a link to the material.

If you are interested in becoming an author: If there is a topic that you have expertise in and you are interested in either writing or contributing to a book, please visit authors.packtpub.com.

Share Your Thoughts

Once you've read *The Missing Bootstrap 5 Guide*, we'd love to hear your thoughts! Scan the QR code below to go straight to the Amazon review page for this book and share your feedback.

https://packt.link/r/180107643X

Your review is important to us and the tech community and will help us make sure we're delivering excellent quality content.

Part One –
Customizing Bootstrap 5
with Sass

In this part, we will first learn why and how to customize Bootstrap. Then, we will learn how to use and compile Sass, with a special focus on the Sass features used by Bootstrap 5. After that, we take a deep dive into the Bootstrap 5 Sass files and learn how to change the global options, define a color palette, customize various Bootstrap 5 elements, and use the utility API in various ways.

This part comprises the following chapters:

- *Chapter 1, Why and How to Customize Bootstrap*
- *Chapter 2, Using and Compiling Sass*
- *Chapter 3, Downloading and Exploring the Bootstrap 5 Sass Files*
- *Chapter 4, Bootstrap 5 Global Options and Colors*
- *Chapter 5, Customizing Various Bootstrap 5 Elements*
- *Chapter 6, Understanding and Using the Bootstrap 5 Utility API*

1

Why and How to Customize Bootstrap

Bootstrap is an open source, frontend framework used to quickly design, develop, and customize responsive, mobile-first websites. It has a flexible grid system, a great variety of prebuilt accessible and interactive components, and many useful helpers and utilities.

Bootstrap comes with predefined CSS styles for all its components. These styles cover everything from typography and colors to sizes and spacing, as well as breakpoints, options for the grid system, and more. Bootstrap 5 can be used with the default styles out of the box, but it is also possible to customize this in different ways.

In this chapter, you will learn when you would want to customize Bootstrap, what can be customized (and what the most important parts to customize are), and how it is done. Learning about this is important before you start customizing Bootstrap without any prior knowledge, since you will be better prepared to customize the right elements and pick the right method for customization.

In this chapter, we're going to cover the following main topics:

- When we should customize Bootstrap
- What elements can be customized?
- How we can customize Bootstrap 5
- Examples of a component customized with three different methods
- Examples of user interfaces with a customized version of Bootstrap 5

> **Bootstrap Versions**
>
> This book is written with the latest version of Bootstrap in mind: *v5.2.0*, generally referred to as Bootstrap 5 throughout the book. Some of the features and techniques described in this book might also work with Bootstrap 4 but probably not Bootstrap 3.

Technical requirements

- A code editor and browser to preview the examples

You can find the code files of the chapter on GitHub at `https://github.com/PacktPublishing/The-Missing-Bootstrap-5-Guide`

When we should customize Bootstrap

When Bootstrap is used with a precompiled style sheet, it has all the default colors, typography, spacing, and more that people associate with Bootstrap. When using these styles for your own project, it will inevitably look like Bootstrap unless you change these styles. This might not be a problem if you are creating a personal project or one for internal use. But if you have specific brand guidelines that your customers or users recognize you by, you will likely need to change these styles to match the style of your brand. Since Bootstrap is so immensely popular and widespread across the internet, some people might recognize the default Bootstrap styles unless you change them. That might have a bad impact on user experience, so for professional use cases, it is highly recommended to customize the default Bootstrap styles.

What elements can be customized?

Bootstrap 5 is easily customizable in many ways. You can customize various options for typography, color, spacing, sizing, border radius, box shadow, and more across all components, as well as customize all the different components individually. You can also customize the helpers and utilities in many different ways. The most important elements to customize are, without doubt, the color palette and typography so that they will match that of your brand. The other aspects can then be further customized to align with your current brand guidelines or just to differentiate your user interface from all the websites that make use of the default Bootstrap styles.

> **JavaScript Behavior Can Be Customized Too**
>
> You generally want to customize the styles of Bootstrap, as described previously; however, the behavior of JavaScript-enabled components can also be changed from the default values. While this is not that important for the perception of your brand, it might be something to consider changing as well.

How we can customize Bootstrap 5

Bootstrap 5 can be customized using three different methods:

- Editing the compiled Bootstrap **CSS** directly
- Overwriting the Bootstrap **CSS** with your own custom styles
- Customizing the default styles using **Sass**

We will now see a short description of each of these methods.

> **What Is Sass?**
>
> **Syntactically Awesome Style Sheets** (**Sass**) is a preprocessor scripting language that is interpreted and compiled into **Cascading Style Sheets** (**CSS**). Sass extends the default capabilities of CSS with variables, nesting, partials, functions, and more. We will learn more about Sass in *Chapter 2, Using and Compiling Sass*.

Method 1 – editing the compiled Bootstrap CSS directly

It is possible to simply edit the compiled Bootstrap CSS directly to achieve the styles you want. This can be rather complex, depending on what you want to change, but most importantly, this will make it hard to update Bootstrap, since you will need to make all your changes again if you want to update to a newer version of it. This approach is not recommended.

Method 2 – overwriting the Bootstrap CSS with your own custom styles

You may choose to simply override the Bootstrap CSS with your own custom styles, but it will increase the size of the total CSS code and might take a lot of work if you want to change many aspects of the default styles. When updating to a newer version of Bootstrap 5, it is easier to maintain than the aforementioned first approach, but if new components or utilities are added to Bootstrap 5, these will have to be overridden manually according to your design needs. This approach might work for you if you simply need to change the color palette or – for some reason – cannot use a Sass compiler to work with the original source code of Bootstrap. For this book, though, we will learn how to customize Bootstrap 5 using Sass.

Method 3 – customizing the default styles using Sass

If you want maximum control and possibilities, you should customize Bootstrap using Sass. This requires a Sass compiler, some knowledge of the Sass language, and knowledge of the Bootstrap Sass files. All of this will be explained and demonstrated in the next two chapters.

Some of the advantages of using Sass are that you can change global settings, modify the used color palette and typography in only one place, and easily customize components. It is also a lot easier and quicker to work with, and on top of that, the compiled file size can be optimized to reflect the actual elements and features being used. For these reasons, this is the recommended approach to customize Bootstrap 5.

Now that we have looked at the various ways in which we can customize Bootstrap, let's look at an example component, customized using each of the three different methods mentioned previously.

Examples of a component customized with the three different methods

In this section, we will see how we can get the same visual style using the three different methods explained in the previous section. We will customize the default **Breadcrumb** component from Bootstrap that looks like this:

Figure 1.1 – The default Breadcrumb component

We will add a gray background color, a border radius on all corners, and padding on all sides. We will also increase the horizontal padding on the breadcrumb items and change the divider. The customized version of the Breadcrumb component will then look like this:

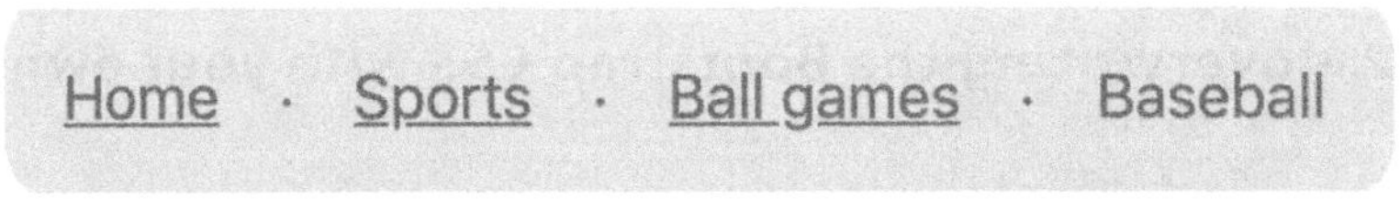

Figure 1.2 – The customized Breadcrumb component

The HTML for this component is mostly the same, irrespective of the methods you use to customize the style. The HTML is as follows:

```
<nav aria-label="Breadcrumb">
  <ol class="breadcrumb">
    <li class="breadcrumb-item"><a href="#">Home</a></li>
    <li class="breadcrumb-item"><a href="#">Sports</a></li>
    <li class="breadcrumb-item"><a href="#">Ball games</a>
    </li>
    <li class="breadcrumb-item active"
      aria-current="page">Baseball</li>
```

```
    </ol>
  </nav>
```

The first two methods use plain CSS and should not require any further explanation. The last example is based on Sass and might not make much sense to you if you are not familiar with Sass. It is, however, included in this chapter to show you the difference in terms of what code is required to achieve the same style using each of these three methods. In the next chapter, I will give a general introduction to Sass and how it is used by Bootstrap.

Method 1 – editing the compiled Bootstrap CSS directly

In the following, we see a slightly edited version of the CSS for the Breadcrumb component found in the compiled and un-minified Bootstrap CSS file (bootstrap.css – line 4494-4525). The changes we need to make to that code to get the specific style that we want are highlighted with a + symbol for new properties and * for changes to a property:

---

part-1/chapter-1/customization-methods/editing-css/css/bootstrap.css

```
.breadcrumb {
  --bs-breadcrumb-padding-x: 0;
  --bs-breadcrumb-padding-y: 0;
  --bs-breadcrumb-margin-bottom: 1rem;
  --bs-breadcrumb-bg: ;
  --bs-breadcrumb-border-radius: ;
  --bs-breadcrumb-divider-color: #6c757d;
  --bs-breadcrumb-item-padding-x: 0.5rem;
  --bs-breadcrumb-item-active-color: #6c757d;
  display: flex;
  flex-wrap: wrap;
  padding: var(--bs-breadcrumb-padding-y)
           var(--bs-breadcrumb-padding-x);
  margin-bottom: var(--bs-breadcrumb-margin-bottom);
  font-size: var(--bs-breadcrumb-font-size);
  list-style: none;
* background-color: var(--bs-gray-300);
* border-radius: 1rem;
+ padding: 1rem;
}
```

```css
.breadcrumb-item + .breadcrumb-item {
* padding-left: 1rem;
}
.breadcrumb-item + .breadcrumb-item::before {
  float: left;
* padding-right: 1rem;
  color: var(--bs-breadcrumb-divider-color);
* content: var(--bs-breadcrumb-divider, "•");
}
.breadcrumb-item.active {
  color: var(--bs-breadcrumb-item-active-color);
}
```

The divider for the Breadcrumb component is added with the ::before pseudo-element and the content property, as seen in the preceding. We will change the fallback value that comes after the --bs-breadcrumb-divider CSS custom property, since this is not defined by Bootstrap. Alternatively, we could have changed the divider by defining the CSS custom property in the HTML, like so:

```html
<nav aria-label="Breadcrumb"
  style="--bs-breadcrumb-divider: '·';">
```

It's also possible to simply add our new divider directly as the value of the content property, like so:

```css
content: '·';
```

We will learn more about how to use CSS custom properties in *Chapter 10, Using Bootstrap 5 with Advanced Sass and CSS Features*.

Method 2 – overwriting the Bootstrap CSS with your own custom styles

Here, we see the custom CSS that we would need to add to our page after the Bootstrap CSS to overwrite the same property values shown in the previous example:

part-1/chapter-1/customization-methods/overwriting-css/css/style.css

```css
.breadcrumb {
  background-color: var(--bs-gray-300);
  border-radius: 1rem;
```

```
  padding: 1rem;
}
.breadcrumb-item + .breadcrumb-item {
  padding-left: 1rem;
}
.breadcrumb-item + .breadcrumb-item::before {
  padding-right: 1rem;
  content: '·';
}
```

If you compare this example with the previous example, you will see that we are adding/overwriting the exact same properties/values as we added/changed before.

For this to work, remember to reference your own style sheet after the Bootstrap style sheet in your `<head>` of the HTML file, like this:

part-1/chapter-1/customization-methods/overwriting-css/index.html

```
<link rel="stylesheet" href="../../../../bootstrap/dist/css/
bootstrap.min.css">
<link rel="stylesheet" href="css/style.css">
```

Method 3 – customizing the default styles using Sass

Now, we will see the recommended approach to customizing Bootstrap, where we compile the Sass styles with new values for certain Bootstrap variables. This will then give us the visual output we want.

We are first importing some configuration files so that we can use the `$spacer` variable as a value for the other variables, which we will set right after.

After setting these variables, we will import some other necessary Bootstrap files in the default order, and finally, we will import the Breadcrumb component. We will not be able to use other Bootstrap components, utilities, and so on with the generated style sheet, since we are just focusing on the absolutely necessary files to include for this example:

part-1/chapter-1/customization-methods/using-sass/scss/bootstrap.scss

```
// Required
@import "../../../../../bootstrap/scss/functions";
@import "../../../../../bootstrap/scss/variables";
@import "../../../../../bootstrap/scss/maps";
```

```scss
@import "../../../../../bootstrap/scss/mixins";
@import "../../../../../bootstrap/scss/root";

// Modified variables
$breadcrumb-bg: $gray-300;
$breadcrumb-border-radius: $spacer;
$breadcrumb-padding-y: $spacer;
$breadcrumb-padding-x: $spacer;
$breadcrumb-item-padding-x: $spacer;
$breadcrumb-divider: quote("·");

// Optional Bootstrap CSS
@import "../../../../../bootstrap/scss/reboot";
@import "../../../../../bootstrap/scss/breadcrumb";
```

This Sass needs to be compiled by a preprocessor, and we will learn how to do this in the next chapter.

If we compare the code for the three different methods, we can see that method 3 is the most simple and easiest to understand. We are simply declaring the values for some easy-to-understand variables and do not have to use any CSS selectors to do this. This can be used for future versions of Bootstrap as well. Method 1 requires you to edit the compiled Bootstrap CSS again every time you want to use a newer version of Bootstrap 5, while with method 2, the code might need to be changed for future versions of Bootstrap if the class names or HTML structure are changed.

Examples of user interfaces with a customized version of Bootstrap 5

In this section, we will see four examples of user interfaces using a customized version of Bootstrap 5. For each example, we will first see a screenshot of the user interface using the default Bootstrap 5 styles and then a screenshot of the user interface using a customized version of Bootstrap 5. This will then be followed by a list of what has been customized. We will start with a simple example of one UI element, where we can better see the actual changes, and then have a look at three different full-page examples. All screenshots, as well as the complete customized examples, can be found in the accompanying code for this book in the following folder: part-1/chapter-1/example-user-interfaces/. I recommend that you look at those while going through these examples and the lists of what has been customized to have a better understanding of the actual changes.

The card component

The following is the first example, which is a Bootstrap 5 `card` component. Inside of the component, we're using the `nav` and `list group` components as well:

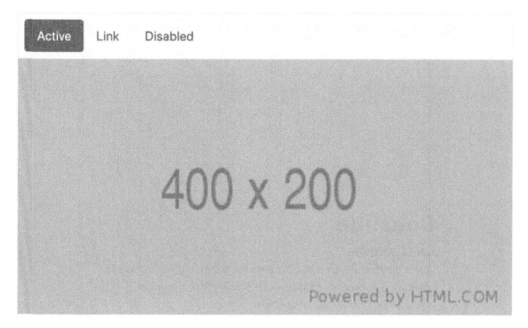

Figure 1.3 – The card component using the default Bootstrap 5 styles

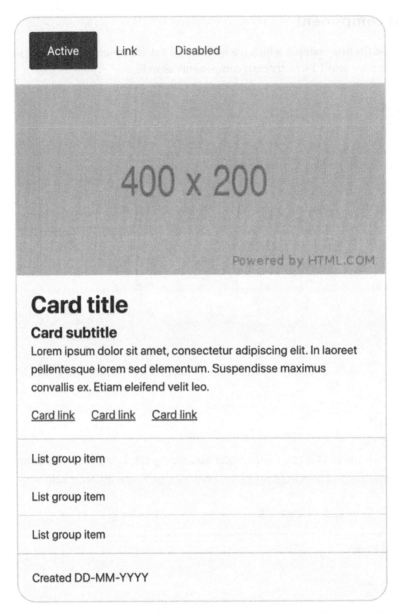

Figure 1.4 – The card component using a customized version of Bootstrap 5

In this example, the following Bootstrap 5 customizations have been made:

- Changed the global settings for the primary color, base font size, headings, and font weight
- Changed the color, background color, font size, padding, margin, border width, and border radius for the card component

- Changed the padding for the nav component
- Changed the color, background color, and padding for the list group component

Forum

The following is the second example, which is a common forum UI taken from an *online forum template*. It's created with the use of tables and various Bootstrap 5 components, including buttons, a breadcrumb, badges, dropdowns, and pagination.

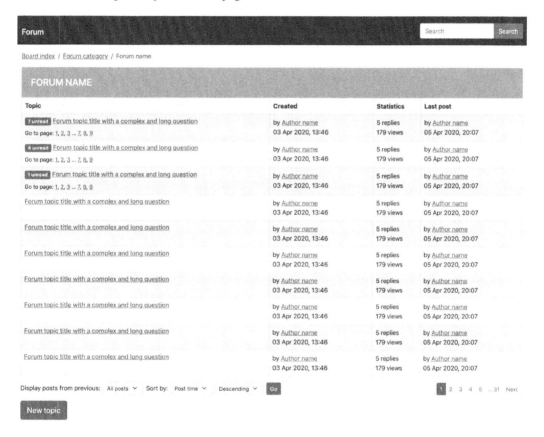

Figure 1.5 – A forum UI using the default Bootstrap 5 styles

Figure 1.6 – A forum UI using a customized version of Bootstrap 5

In this example, the following Bootstrap 5 customizations have been made:

- Changed global settings for primary, info, and body background colors
- Removed the underline from links
- Removed all border radiuses
- Changed the background color of input elements
- Changed the color, padding, and borders of tables
- Changed the horizontal padding for buttons

- Changed the horizontal padding for paginations
- Changed the padding for and added text-transform to badges

The contact page

The following is the third example, which is a contact page taken from a *Small Business Website* template. It features various Bootstrap 5 form elements, including input groups, text inputs, dropdowns, textarea, and buttons. It also uses the ratio helper class to embed a Google Maps map with the right aspect ratio.

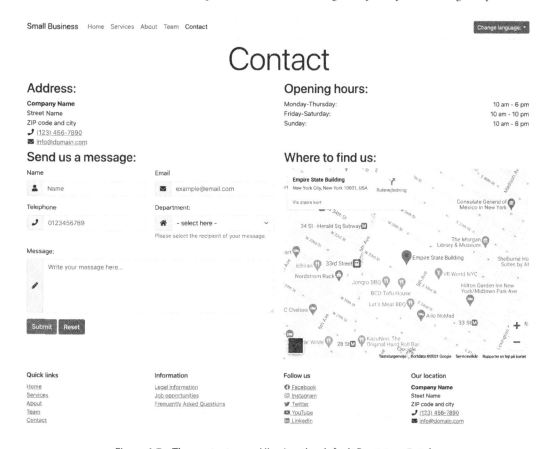

Figure 1.7 – The contact page UI using the default Bootstrap 5 styles

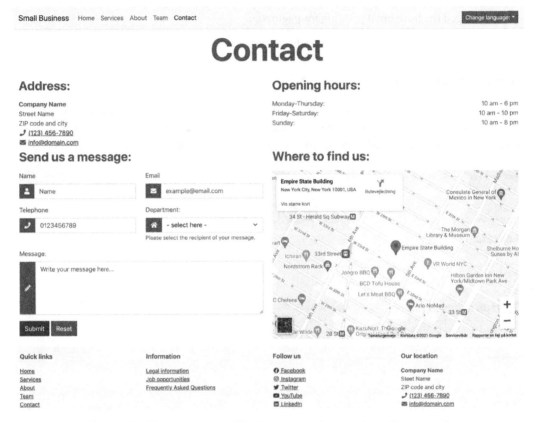

Figure 1.8 – The contact page UI using a customized version of Bootstrap 5

In this example, the following Bootstrap 5 customizations have been made:

- Changed global settings for primary and body text colors
- Removed the border radius on buttons, dropdowns, select elements, and input elements
- Changed the color for input group addons
- Changed the "4x3" ratio helper to "3x2"
- Changed the font weight and margin for headings

Portfolio

The following is the fourth and final example, which is a portfolio item page taken from a *Portfolio* template. It features a carousel, image thumbnails, and various kinds of typography.

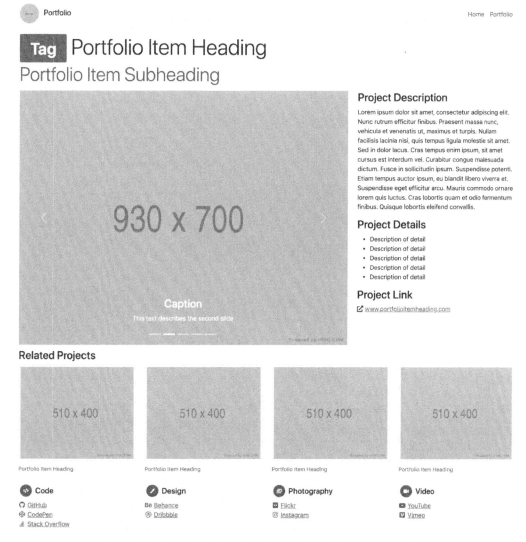

Figure 1.9 – A portfolio item UI using the default Bootstrap 5 styles

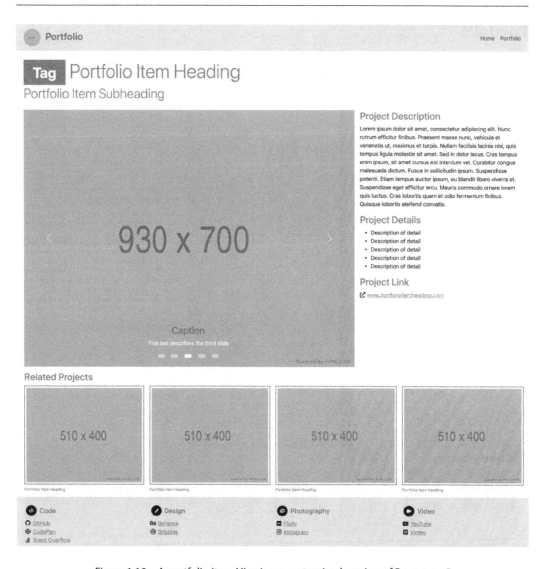

Figure 1.10 – A portfolio item UI using a customized version of Bootstrap 5

In this example, the following Bootstrap 5 customizations have been made:

- Changed global settings for primary and light colors
- Generated a darker variant of the primary color using a Bootstrap 5 color function
- Disabled the border radius on all elements using the global option
- Increased the container maximum width for the `xxl` breakpoint
- Decreased the grid gutter width

- Changed the colors of headings and muted text

- Changed the font size used for small text

- Changed the color and font size of the navbar

- Changed the indicators of the carousel

- Changed the image thumbnail borders

- Changed the color and font size of the figure caption

Further customizations in this book

The four preceding examples only showed the visual impact of different customizations and a brief description of the changes. In *Chapter 3, Downloading and Exploring the Bootstrap 5 Sass Files*, we will learn about the code needed to make similar changes. Later, in *Part 2* of this book, we will create a fully customized example of a complete website project.

Summary

In this chapter, we have learned when we should consider customizing Bootstrap, what elements we can customize, and ways in which this can be done. We have also seen four different examples of Bootstrap 5 customization. We are now better prepared to customize the right elements and pick the right method for customization.

In the next chapter, you will learn about Sass. You will learn about its features and benefits, how to use it, and last but not least, how to compile it into regular CSS that can be parsed by the browser.

2
Using and Compiling Sass

This chapter is an introduction to **Sass**. If you're new to Sass, you should definitely go through this chapter to learn the basics of Sass, which is the language the Bootstrap styles are written in. If you're already familiar with Sass, you can skip this chapter, but I will still suggest you take a look at the *Sass features used by Bootstrap* and *Most important Sass features for Bootstrap developers* sections. This will prepare you before starting the next chapter about customizing Bootstrap.

In this chapter, we're going to cover the following main topics:

- What is Sass?
- Sass syntax
- Sass features
- Sass features used by Bootstrap
- Most important Sass features for Bootstrap developers
- Compiling Sass

Technical requirements

- To preview the examples, you will need a code editor
- To compile Sass to CSS, you will need either of the following:

    - **Node.js**, if you prefer a **command-line interface (CLI)** using Terminal (Mac) or Command Prompt (Windows)
    - **Scout-App**, if you prefer a **graphical user interface (GUI)**
    - **Visual Studio Code**, if you prefer to use an extension from the Visual Studio Code Marketplace

I will explain all these approaches in this chapter.

You can find the code files of the chapter on GitHub at `https://github.com/PacktPublishing/The-Missing-Bootstrap-5-Guide`.

What is Sass?

Sass is an abbreviation of **Syntactically Awesome Style Sheets**. It is a special kind of stylesheet language known as a preprocessor scripting language that extends the default capabilities of CSS. This enables you to use JavaScript-like logic and features in the code, such as **variables**, **nesting**, **mixins**, **inheritance**, **partials**, **functions**, **mathematical operations**, and more. All of this helps you write more robust and maintainable code by automating repetitive tasks, reducing the number of errors, creating reusable code snippets, and more. Sass has a syntax similar to CSS, but the Sass files need to be compiled to regular CSS before they can be rendered in browsers. This can be done using different tools, which we will learn more about later in this chapter.

Sass was first released in 2006 and is still being actively supported and developed by a large community. It is by far the most popular and used CSS preprocessor, with **Less** and **Stylus** being two other established CSS preprocessors in the market.

In the following section, we will take a look at the Sass syntax.

Sass syntax

Sass supports two different syntaxes: the original indented Sass syntax and the **SCSS** syntax, which is basically a superset of regular **CSS**. The SCSS syntax is the easiest one for beginners, the most popular one, and the one used for the Bootstrap styles. It's also the one that I will be using throughout this book. However, both of these different syntaxes support the same features of Sass.

Comparison between the original Sass syntax and the modern Sass syntax

The original syntax uses the `.sass` file extension. It uses indentation instead of curly braces to separate code blocks, and *newline* characters (every time you hit the *Enter* key) to separate rules within a code block.

The indented syntax looks like this:

```
.link
  background-color: #aaa
  &:hover
    text-decoration: underline
  &__icon
    color: #fff
```

The modern syntax uses the .scss file extension. **SCSS** is an abbreviation for **Sassy CSS**. It uses curly braces to separate code blocks, and semicolons to separate rules within a code block.

The SCSS syntax looks like this:

```
.link {
  background-color: #aaa;
  &:hover { text-decoration: underline;}
  &__icon {
    color: #fff;
  }
}
```

Both types of syntaxes will output the following CSS:

```
.link {
  background-color: #aaa;
}
.link:hover {
  text-decoration: underline;
}
.link__icon {
  color: #fff;
}
```

As you can see, they're similar. But SCSS allows you more options to format your code as long as you use semicolons and curly braces in the same way as in CSS, while the original Sass syntax requires stricter formatting because of its reliance on indentation and line breaks.

Parent selector

With Sass, you can use a parent selector with the ampersand symbol, &. This special selector is invented by Sass and used in nested selectors to refer to the parent selector. The ampersand will be replaced by the parent selector, no matter how many levels you are nesting (nesting will be described later in this section). You can use this in different ways, and we will now go through some examples.

Adding an extra class

If you want to create a more specific selector with two classes, you can use the ampersand as follows:

```
.class-one {
  &.class-two {
    color: red;
  }
}
```

This will generate the following output:

```
.class-one.class-two {
  color: red;
}
```

Adding pseudo-classes

To write common pseudo-classes for a certain selector, you can do the following:

```
.link {
  &:visited {}
  &:hover {}
  &:active {}
}
```

This compiles to the following:

```
.link:visited {}
.link:hover {}
.link:active {}
```

Qualifying based on another selector

You can qualify a selector by using the ampersand after another selector. So, if you, for example, want to change the styling of an element when it's being used inside of another element, you can do it like so:

```
.heading {
  .alert & {}
}
```

This compiles to the following:

```
.alert .heading {}
```

This style rule will only apply to a `.heading` class when it's a child of a `.alert` class.

Modifying the ampersand

The ampersand can be modified by adding a string of text right after it. Consider the following example for different button styles:

```
.button {
  &-small {}
  &-medium {}
  &-large {}
}
```

This will compile to the following:

```
.button-small {}
.button-medium {}
.button-large {}
```

This is very helpful when using a naming methodology that, instead of combined selectors, uses dashes and underscores to create child selectors or modifier selectors.

Now that we have learned about the two different syntaxes for Sass and the special parent selector, we can move on to learn about the different Sass features.

Sass features

In this section, we will take a look at some of the most used features of Sass. This will just be a brief introduction to get familiar with Sass code and not a detailed guide, as we're not going to write much Sass code during the course of this book.

Variables

Sass variables can be used to store any kind of CSS value that you want to reuse. Variables are, for example, helpful to use for colors when you need to implement a consistent color scheme across many components and potentially need to change one or more of the colors later in the process. This can then be done simply by updating the value of the variable. To create a variable, you simply assign a value to a name that begins with the $ symbol. Here is an example of creating and using a variable:

```
$color-primary: blue;

.button {
  background-color: $color-primary;
}
```

When the Sass file is processed, it takes the values of the variables and places them in the regular CSS. The generated CSS will look like this:

```
.button {
  background-color: blue;
}
```

Default values

If you assign a value to a variable that already has a value, it will be overwritten. But it is also possible to use the !default flag to only assign a new value to a variable if that variable is not already defined or the value is null. This is useful when creating Sass libraries such as Bootstrap, where you want to allow the users to configure the variables before generating the CSS. If the user does not configure any variables, the default value set by the library will be used.

Here's an example with the normal use of variables that will be overridden:

```
$color-primary: blue;
$color-primary: red;

.button {
  background-color: $color-primary;
}
```

This compiles to the following:

```
.button {
  background-color: red;
}
```

The background color of the button becomes red since the value of the $color-primary variable has been overridden.

If you instead use the !default flag, it will work like this:

```
$color-primary: blue;
$color-primary: red !default;

.button {
  background-color: $color-primary;
}
```

This compiles to the following:

```
.button {
  background-color: blue;
}
```

As we can see, the background color of the button will now remain blue, since the !default flag won't change the value of the $color-primary variable.

Nesting

With Sass, you can nest your CSS selectors and achieve the same visual hierarchy as your HTML. While nesting CSS selectors, having many levels is generally considered a bad practice; using carefully nested CSS selectors is a good way to make your code more readable.

Take, for example, this navigation component created with an unordered list of links:

```
<nav>
  <ul>
    <li>
      <a>Menu item</a>
    </li>
    <li>
      <a>Menu item</a>
    </li>
    <li>
      <a>Menu item</a>
    </li>
</nav>
```

To get a better overview in our code, we can nest the CSS selectors in the following way to reflect the structure of our HTML:

```
nav {
  ul {
    margin: 0;
    padding: 0;
    list-style: none;
    li {
      display: inline-block;
      a {
        text-decoration: none;
      }
    }
  }
}
```

This compiles to the following:

```
nav ul {
  margin: 0;
  padding: 0;
  list-style: none;
}
nav ul li {
  display: inline-block;
}
nav ul li a {
  text-decoration: none;
}
```

Partials and import

Partials are small files with Sass code that you can import into other Sass files. This is useful for organizing your code into different parts and modules for a better overview of your project. A Sass partial file begins with the underscore character (_), which will prevent it from being generated into its own CSS file. To import a Sass partial into another file, you should use the @import rule. You don't need to include the file extension and you can omit the leading underscore character.

Since the Sass @import rule is handled during compilation – unlike the regular CSS @import rule, which requires multiple HTTP requests – you get access to mixins, functions, and variables.

In the following example, we will have two Sass partials, _button.scss and _link.scss, and one main file, styles.scss, that imports them:

First partial's filename: _button.scss

```scss
$color-primary: red;
.button {
  background-color: $color-primary;
}
```

Second partial's filename: _link.scss

```scss
$color-link: blue;
.link {
  color: $color-link;
}
```

Main file: styles.scss

```scss
@import 'button';
@import 'link';
// other SCSS code here
```

This will compile to the following:

```css
.button {
  background-color: red;
}
.link {
  color: blue;
}
// other CSS code here
```

> **Import is being deprecated**
>
> The use of the @import rule is discouraged by the Sass team. It will be phased out during the following years and eventually removed completely. Instead, the @use rule should be used. Bootstrap uses the @import rule in their Sass code, and that is why I'm using it here instead of @use.

Mixins

With mixins, you can group together CSS declarations that you want to reuse across your project. Mixins can also receive arguments allowing them to be customized for each time they are being used. They are defined using the `@mixin` rule and are included in the code using the `@include` rule. Mixins copy the styles into the place they are being used.

Simple mixin

Here's an example of a simple mixin with no arguments. It's a so-called `clearfix` mixin, which is taken directly from the Bootstrap 5 Sass code and also used for its `clearfix` helper utility:

```
@mixin clearfix {
  &::after {
    display: block;
    content: "";
    clear: both;
  }
}


.parent-with-floated-child-elements {
  @include clearfix;
}
```

This compiles to the following:

```
.parent-with-floated-child-elements::after {
  display: block;
  content: "";
  clear: both;
}
```

Mixin with argument

In this example, we see a mixin for a simple grid. It has the `$grid` argument with the `true` default value. After the definition of the mixin, we include it for two elements. The first one will use the default argument to get the `display` value (`grid`) and the other will use `false` as an argument to get the `display` value (`flex`):

```
@mixin grid($grid: true) {
  @if $grid {
```

```
      display: grid;
  } @else {
      display: flex;
  }
}

.row-grid {
  @include grid;
}

.row-flex {
  @include grid(false);
}
```

This will compile to the following:

```
.row-grid {
    display: grid;
}

.row-flex {
    display: flex;
}
```

Extend

Extends are another method of reusing CSS declarations in Sass. With this method, you can share the styles of one selector in another selector. When you extend a class selector to another selector, the result is equal to adding that class to the HTML element. Extending a selector does not copy any styles as mixins do, but instead, updates the style rule of the *extended* selector to also contain the *extending* selector.

Here's an example of a simple .alert class with border and padding. Nested inside this is a modified parent selector that generates the .alert-success class, which will extend the .alert class plus add a background color:

```
.alert {
    border: 1px solid black;
    padding: 1rem;
```

```
  &-success {
    @extend .alert;
    background-color: green;
  }
}
```

This compiles to the following:

```
.alert, .alert-success {
  border: 1px solid black;
  padding: 1rem;
}
.alert-success {
  background-color: green;
}
```

As you can see, the `.alert-success` class is now added to the style declaration for the `.alert` class. So, to clarify, when one class selector extends another, the styles belonging to the extended selector will now also be available for the extending selector.

Operators

With **operators**, you can do basic mathematical calculations with different values in your CSS. Besides the basic mathematical calculations such as addition, subtraction, multiplication, and division, you can check for relation and equality for various values, and more.

Here are some examples of basic mathematical calculations for both numbers and strings:

```
.addition {
    margin: 10px + 5px;
    content: "Hello " + "world!";
}

.subtraction {
    margin: 25px - 10px;
}

.multiplication {
    margin: 3 * 5px;
}
```

```
.division {
    margin: (30 / 2) * 1px;
}
```

This compiles to the following:

```
.addition {
  margin: 15px;
  content: "Hello world!";
}

.subtraction {
  margin: 15px;
}

.multiplication {
  margin: 15px;
}

.division {
  margin: 15px;
}
```

> **Division with / is deprecated**
>
> Division with / in Sass is deprecated since it's being used as a separator in CSS. Instead, a division should be done using the built-in `math.div()` math module function of Sass like so: `math.div(30, 2)`, which equals `15`.

Functions

You can create your own functions for specific operations that you need to reuse in your project. They are created with the `@function` rule and return a value using the `@return` rule. They are called using the normal CSS function syntax. Just like mixins, functions can receive arguments, allowing the behavior to be customized for each time they are called. The arguments are available within the function as variables.

Here's a simple function that adds two values together and returns the result. It can be either numbers or strings, but in this example, it will be two numbers:

```
@function add($a, $b) {
    @return $a + $b;
}


.ordered-item {
    order: add(1, 2);
}
```

This compiles to the following:

```
.ordered-item {
  order: 3;
}
```

You must specify the correct number of arguments when calling the function unless you make any of them optional by defining a default value for it.

Here's how to make the second argument optional by giving it the default value of 2:

```
@function add($a, $b: 2) {
    @return $a + $b;
}


.ordered-item {
    order: add(1);
}
```

This compiles to the following:

```
.ordered-item {
  order: 3;
}
```

Special values

Sass supports many kinds of values. Most of them come from CSS, while some of them are specific to Sass. Maps are an example of a special Sass value and are used to associate keys and values in a list. Maps are not valid CSS values, so they can't be used on their own. However, Sass provides various functions to work with maps.

Here's a simple example that first defines a `$font-size` map with three key/value pairs, and then gets the value of the third key by using the `map-get()` function with the name of the map and the key for the requested value as arguments:

```
$font-size: (
    "small": 12,
    "default": 16,
    "large": 20
);

.lead-paragraph {
    font-size: map-get($font-size, "large");
}
```

This compiles to the following:

```
.lead-paragraph {
  font-size: 20;
}
```

Built-in modules

Sass provides built-in modules containing various functions and mixins. These functions were originally globally available, but should now be loaded via the `@use` rule (with few exceptions). Among the more useful functions are functions for manipulating color values and working with list- and map-based values.

Here's an example of how to fluidly scale a color property using the `color.scale()` function from the built-in color module. In this example, the function is used to increase the lightness of the color by 25%, and you can see that this even works when using a named color as the argument:

```
@use "sass:color";
$color-primary: blue;

.button {
  color: $color-primary;
  background-color: color.scale($color-primary,
                                $lightness: 25%);
}
```

This compiles to the following:

```
.button {
  color: blue;
  background-color: #4040ff;
}
```

Now that we have had a look at some of the features of Sass, let's take a look at which features are being used by Bootstrap.

Sass features used by Bootstrap

This is just a quick overview of the Sass features used by Bootstrap. We will dive deeper into how Bootstrap is built in the next chapter.

Syntax

As already mentioned, the Bootstrap Sass code is written using the SCSS syntax. It also uses the & parent selector for pseudo-classes and states, together with attribute selectors.

Partials

The Sass code for Bootstrap 5 is divided into 81 partials and five folders. These partials are then imported through other partials or regular SCSS files. This creates a good overview of all the various parts making up Bootstrap.

Variables

Variables are used extensively by Bootstrap. They are used to maintain visual consistency across components regarding colors, spacing, and more, but they are also used in such a way that they can easily be configured by a user before the generation of the CSS.

Maps

Maps are often used in Sass libraries and design systems. In Bootstrap, they are used primarily for configuring the values used by the utilities.

Mixins

Mixins are used a lot throughout the Bootstrap Sass code. They are used for layout, components, helpers, utilities, and other visual styling.

Built-in modules

Bootstrap uses the color and map modules of Sass. It uses functions from the color module (as well as other included color functions) to work with the visual style regarding colors, and it uses functions from the map module to work with map values that are used to generate utilities.

We now know how Bootstrap utilizes the various features of Sass. But, what features are most important for developers working with customization of Bootstrap? Let's take a look at that now.

Most important Sass features for Bootstrap developers

Here's a quick overview of what Sass features you will use the most when customizing Bootstrap.

Variables for customization

The ability to use variables with Sass is the most important feature to understand when customizing Bootstrap. Most changes that you would want to make require you to overwrite a variable already used by Bootstrap.

Maps for the utility API

The special map value that comes with Sass is used together with the utility API to generate various utility classes. This can be used to modify or remove existing utilities or add your own. We will learn all about how to use the utility API in the next chapter.

> **The utility API**
>
> The utility API is a built-in tool of Bootstrap 5 that is used to generate the different utility classes. Sass maps are used to provide settings and options for the utility API.

Mixins and extend for semantic code

Bootstrap has a lot of mixins used by different Bootstrap elements, but these mixins can also be used in your own code. Mixins and the extend feature of Sass can both be used to write more semantic code, which we will take a closer look at in *Chapter 8, Customizing the Website Using Bootstrap 5 Variables, Utility API, and Sass*.

We have just seen how to use some of the features of Sass, and we will now learn how to compile Sass code to regular CSS.

Compiling Sass

There are various ways that you can compile your Sass code. If you are new to Sass and want to experiment with the syntax and features, you can use **Sassmeister** and get started right away. If you want to incorporate Sass compilation into your development workflow, there are several ways to do this. I will show you three different ways of doing this. The first way requires you to use **Node.js** and the Terminal or Command Prompt, the second way uses a free application called **Scout-App**, and the third way uses an extension for the **Visual Studio Code** code editor.

Experimenting with Sass using Sassmeister

Sassmeister, which can be visited at sassmeister.com, is a free tool to experiment with Sass in a playground environment. You can use either the Sass or SCSS syntax, select between different Sass compilers, define the CSS output, and more. All the examples in this chapter can be seen in action using Sassmeister.

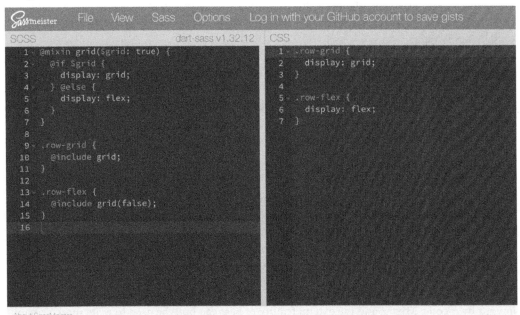

Figure 2.1 – Sassmeister Sass playground on sassmeister.com

Incorporating Sass compilation into a development workflow

In the next three subsections, I will describe different ways of incorporating Sass compilation into a development workflow. For all these approaches, we will use the same HTML file and SCSS file. You will have to create these files yourself and place them in a project folder.

The HTML file should contain the following code:

index.html

```html
<!DOCTYPE html>
<html lang="en">
  <head>
    <meta charset="utf-8">
    <meta name="viewport" content="width=device-width,
      initial-scale=1">
    <link rel="stylesheet" href="style.css">
    <title>Compiling Sass</title>
  </head>
  <body>
    <h1>Hello world!</h1>
  </body>
</html>
```

This is basic code for an HTML file, including a `<link>` tag to a stylesheet that doesn't exist until it has been compiled from the source Sass code. If you open this file in a browser before any compilation, it will simply display an **H1** heading with the default black text color and the text `Hello world!`.

The SCSS file should contain the following code:

style.scss

```scss
$color-primary: blue;
h1 {
  color: $color-primary;
}
```

First, we have the blue color stored in the $color-primary variable. Then, we use that variable to set the text color of h1 elements. After compiling our Sass, we get a new CSS file with the following code:

style.css

```
h1 {
    color: blue;
}
```

After reloading the HTML file in the browser, we will see that the text color of the heading is now blue. This shows that the Sass compilation is working as expected and the referenced CSS file has now been generated.

Continue reading the next sections to learn different ways of incorporating Sass compilation into a development workflow.

Using Node.js

Step 1: Download and install Node.js

This method requires you to download and install Node.js. To do this, you simply go to the official website at nodejs.org and download it from there. npm is the default package manager that's automatically installed together with Node.js.

Step 2: Navigate to your project folder with the Terminal or Command Prompt

Now, open the Terminal (macOS) or Command Prompt (Windows) and use the following command to navigate to your project folder:

```
cd [project-folder-path]
```

The square brackets should not be used, so, for example, like this:

```
cd projects/bootstrap/example
```

> **Drag your folder from Finder on macOS**
>
> If you're using macOS, you can simply type cd   (remember the space in the end) and then drag your folder from Finder to the Terminal. This will insert the right folder path. Now, you just have to hit *Enter*.

> **Type cmd in File Explorer on Windows**
>
> If you're using Windows, you can type the cmd shortcut in the search bar of a **File Explorer** window. Hitting *Enter* will open up the folder in the Command Prompt.

Step 3: Initialize a new npm project

Then, to initialize a new npm project, we enter one of the following two commands:

```
npm init
npm init -y
```

If you use the first option (*without* the -y flag), you will be asked to type in the information for the project. Each step can be skipped simply by hitting *Enter*, and all of it can be edited afterward as well.

If you choose the second option (*with* the -y flag), it will automatically answer these questions. This can also be edited at a later point.

After running the npm init command, a package.json file will be generated with basic information about your npm project. It will look something like this:

```
{
  "name": "[the name of your folder]",
  "version": "1.0.0",
  "description": "",
  "main": "index.js",
  "scripts": {
    "test": "echo \"Error: no test specified\" && exit 1"
  },
  "keywords": [],
  "author": "",
  "license": "ISC"
}
```

Step 4: Install Sass globally

We will now install the Sass npm package globally on the machine so it will be available for this and other future projects. This package is used to compile your Sass code to CSS. Type in the following command:

```
npm install sass -g
```

To check that you have successfully installed Sass, you can enter the following command:

```
sass --version
```

You will see something like the following in your terminal:

```
1.43.4 compiled with dart2js 2.14.4
```

If you're using the Terminal on macOS and are getting errors regarding file permission when trying to install Sass, you can try to add the `sudo` command so that the full command will be as follows:

```
sudo npm install sass -g
```

If you're experiencing similar problems on Windows, you can try to run the Command Prompt as an administrator.

Step 5: Compile Sass to CSS

Now, it's time to compile your Sass code. To do this, you use the `sass` command followed by the path to your input file (your Sass source file) and your output file (the CSS file you want to use for your website), as well as any optional settings:

```
sass [input-path] [output-path]
```

or

```
sass [input-path] [output-path] [settings]
```

Please note that in the preceding commands, the square brackets should not be used.

The most useful settings are as follows:

- `--style=expanded` – Generates a compressed and minified CSS file.
- `--no-source-map` – Prevents the generation of a source map file. This file maps the transformed source to the original source so that the browser can show the original in the debugger.
- `--watch` – Watches for any changes in your file and recompiles automatically.

Remember to add spaces in between each of the settings, if you're adding more than one.

To compile the SCSS file that comes with the starter template, you will type the following command:

```
sass style.scss style.css
```

This will compile the Sass code found in `style.scss` to CSS and create the new `style.css` file as well as the `style.css.map` source map file in the same folder.

You are now able to view the starter template in a browser with the compiled Bootstrap CSS.

Using Scout-App

If you prefer to use a GUI when compiling Sass, you can use the free app, **Scout-App**. It can be downloaded from `scout-app.io` and there's a version for macOS, Windows, and Linux.

There's a great *Getting Started* video on the front page that I suggest you watch to learn how the app works. The video can also be accessed directly on YouTube via the following link: `https://youtu.be/6zA78zMsH9w`.

Figure 2.2 – Screenshot of the front page of the official Scout-App website

Using Live Sass Compiler extension for Visual Studio Code

If you're using Visual Studio Code as your code editor, you can install the **Live Sass Compiler** extension, which can watch and compile your Sass code. Simply open the **Extensions** tab in the Activity Bar and search for `Live Sass Compiler` by Glenn Marks and then click **Install**:

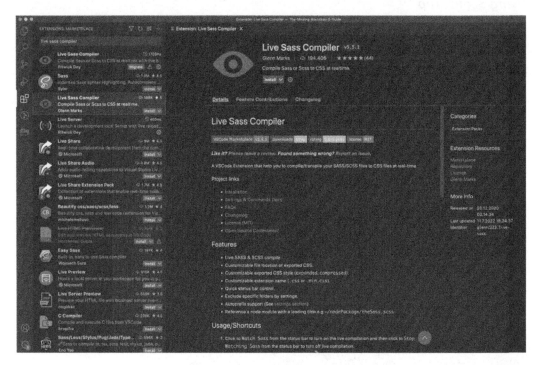

Figure 2.3 – Screenshot of the Live Sass Compiler extension
opened in the Extensions tab of Visual Studio Code

You can also find the extension on the Visual Studio Marketplace via this link:

```
https://marketplace.visualstudio.com/items?itemName=glenn2223.
live-sass
```

After successfully installing the extension, you now need to click **Watch Sass** in the Status Bar when you have a SCSS or SASS file open to activate the live Sass compiler. When done working you simply click the same button again to deactivate it.

Summary

This chapter was an introduction to Sass for people with no prior experience. We have learned about the syntax and features in general, and also about which features are used by Bootstrap as well as which features are the most important ones for Bootstrap developers. Finally, we also learned about various ways to compile Sass, either for simple experimentation or for incorporating Sass compilation into a development workflow.

In the next chapter, we will learn how to customize Bootstrap 5 with Sass. If you have read this chapter, you are now well prepared to dive into the Sass code of Bootstrap 5.

3

Downloading and Exploring the Bootstrap 5 Sass Files

In this chapter, we will first see two different ways to download the Bootstrap 5 source code, and then we will take a closer look at the Bootstrap 5 Sass files in that source code. We will learn how the Sass code is divided into various files, how these files are structured, and what that structure means.

After that, we will learn how to import the default Bootstrap 5, and finally, we will learn about the Bootstrap 5 Sass variables.

It's useful to be familiar with the Bootstrap 5 Sass files and variables before customizing the styling, as you will know where to search and look for specific variables for your needs. You will also know about the dependency between certain variables and files.

In this chapter, we're going to cover the following topics:

- Downloading the Bootstrap 5 source code
- Exploring the Bootstrap 5 Sass files
- Importing the default Bootstrap 5
- Exploring the Bootstrap 5 variables

Technical requirements

- To preview the examples, you will need a code editor and a browser.
- You will need a Sass compiler to compile the Bootstrap 5 Sass files to CSS. Please see *Chapter 2, Using and Compiling Sass*, for different ways to do this.

You can find the code files of the chapter on GitHub at `https://github.com/PacktPublishing/The-Missing-Bootstrap-5-Guide`

Downloading the Bootstrap 5 source code

You can download Bootstrap 5 in different ways. Here, I'll show you three.

From the website

From the official Bootstrap website at `getbootstrap.com`, you can download the Bootstrap files from the **Download** page in the **Getting started** section of **Docs**: `getbootstrap.com/docs/5.2/getting-started/download`.

From that **Download** page, you can download a compiled version of the Bootstrap 5 CSS and JavaScript files or you can download the source files, which contain all the Sass code, JavaScript code, and documentation files. We want the source files, so you should click the purple **Download source** button to download a ZIP file containing everything we need.

From GitHub

The source code for Bootstrap 5 can be downloaded from the official GitHub repository at `github.com/twbs/bootstrap`. To download it from there, you first click the green **Code** button to expand a popover. From there, you can get the URL to clone it using Git with the following command:

```
git clone https://github.com/twbs/bootstrap.git
```

Or, you can simply download a ZIP file containing all the source code.

From NPM

If you're using NPM in your development setup, you can download and install the latest version of Bootstrap 5 with the following command:

```
npm install bootstrap
```

It will now be downloaded to the `node_modules` folder of your project. We will see how we can set up a build process using Node.js, NPM, and Laravel Mix in *Chapter 12, Optimizing Bootstrap 5 CSS and JavaScript Code*.

Now that we have downloaded Bootstrap 5, it's time to take a look at the Sass files.

Exploring the Bootstrap 5 Sass files

In this section, we will explore the Bootstrap 5 Sass files. These files are located in the `scss` folder of the downloaded Bootstrap 5 files. We will go through the contents of this folder and its subfolders.

Root folder

In the root of the scss folder, we have a total of 41 files, of which 37 are Sass partials because they start with an underscore, and the remaining 4 files are regular SCSS files. Here's an overview with a comment next to each file:

```
_accordion.scss (component)
_alert.scss (component)
_badge.scss (component)
_breadcrumb.scss (component)
_button-group.scss (component)
_buttons.scss (component)
_card.scss (component)
_carousel.scss (component)
_close.scss (component)
_containers.scss (layout)
_dropdown.scss (component)
_forms.scss (imports partials from the "forms" folder)
_functions.scss (various custom Bootstrap 5 functions)
_grid.scss (layout)
_helpers.scss (imports partials from the "helpers" folder)
_images.scss (content)
_list-group.scss (component)
_maps.scss (Sass maps for customization)
_mixins.scss (imports partials from the "vendor" and
              "mixins" folder)
_modal.scss (component)
_nav.scss (component)
_navbar.scss (component)
_offcanvas.scss (component)
_pagination.scss (component)
_placeholders.scss (component)
_popover.scss (component)
_progress.scss (component)
_reboot.scss (normalization of HTML elements)
_root.scss (CSS custom properties)
_spinners.scss (component)
```

```
_tables.scss (content)
_toasts.scss (component)
_tooltip.scss (component)
_transitions.scss (global transitions)
_type.scss (content)
_utilities.scss (settings for utilities)
_variables.scss (Sass variables for customization)
bootstrap-grid.scss (main SCSS file that imports grid and
                     flex utilities only)
bootstrap-reboot.scss (main SCSS file that imports reboot
                       styles only)
bootstrap-utilities.scss (main SCSS file that imports
                          utilities only)
bootstrap.scss (main SCSS file that imports everything)
```

As you can see from my comments, most of the files relate to styling for individual parts of Bootstrap 5: layout, content, and components. Here's a quick explanation of the other files.

_forms.scss

This file imports all the Sass partial files from the forms folder; it is used to provide styling for various form elements.

_functions.scss

This file contains various custom Bootstrap 5 functions. It is primarily used for evaluating source code across variables, maps, and mixins, but among other things, you will also find the tint-color() and shade-color() color functions, which we will get back to later in this chapter.

_helpers.scss

This file imports all the Sass partial files from the helpers folder; it is used to provide styling for the various helper classes.

_maps.scss

This file contains re-assigned Sass maps, which can be used for customization by overriding the default Sass maps. This will then automatically update utilities, and more.

_mixins.scss

This file imports all the Sass partial files from the `vendor` and `mixins` folders. The `vendor` folder contains the styling for the **Responsive Font Sizes** (**RFS**) Sass plugin, and the `mixins` folder contains many useful mixins, which are used elsewhere by other files. We will learn more about how to make full use of the RFS Sass plugin and the Bootstrap 5 mixins in *Chapter 10, Using Bootstrap 5 with Advanced Sass and CSS Features*.

_reboot.scss

This file contains code to normalize the styling of common HTML elements. It's not targeting any classes, but only HTML elements directly. It's a fork of **Normalize.css**, where some code has been removed while some other code has been added. Normalize.css is a reset stylesheet that makes browsers render all elements more consistently. Learn more about it on the official website: `necolas.github.io/normalize.css/`.

_root.scss

This file is used to generate various CSS custom properties for root elements, which, in this case, means colors and basic typography. It is mostly used in the `_reboot.scss` file, but some are also used elsewhere.

_transitions.scss

This file contains styling for transitions used by various components.

_utilities.scss

This file contains all the settings for the utilities. These settings are used by the utility API to generate utility classes. You will learn much more about the utility API in *Chapter 6, Understanding and Using the Bootstrap 5 Utility API*.

_variables.scss

This file contains a long list of variables used across Bootstrap 5. You will learn much more about this file in *Chapter 4, Bootstrap 5 Global Options and Colors*, and *Chapter 5, Customizing Various Bootstrap 5 Elements*.

Main SCSS files

After all the Sass partial files, we have four main SCSS files, which are used to import different versions of Bootstrap 5. Here's a quick overview of each of them and what they import:

- `bootstrap-grid.scss`: The grid system and the flex utilities only
- `bootstrap-reboot.scss`: The reboot styles only

- `bootstrap-utilities.scss`: The helpers and utilities only
- `bootstrap.scss`: Everything

Of these four, we will only use `bootstrap.scss` to import everything, but we will also use a modified version of the code inside `bootstrap.scss` to be able to make specific customizations and optimizations.

The `scss` folder also contains the following subfolders: `forms`, `helpers`, `mixins`, `utilities`, and `vendor`. These folders contain more Sass partial files. I have already referred to these folders when describing the Sass partial files in the root folder, so I won't go into further details. Generally, all the Sass partial files should be left untouched, unless you have very advanced and specific requirements. We customize Bootstrap 5 in our own files and import the Bootstrap 5 files as they are.

Importing the default Bootstrap 5

In the previous chapter, we learned how to compile Sass to CSS. To import the default Bootstrap 5 without any customizations, we simply need to import the `bootstrap.scss` file into our own SCSS file as follows:

part-1/chapter-3/import-compile-default-bootstrap/scss/bootstrap.scss

```
@import "../../../../bootstrap/scss/bootstrap";
```

In the next chapter, we will learn how to import a more advanced customized version of Bootstrap 5, where we import the individual SCSS files of Bootstrap 5, instead of the main file as in the preceding code.

Before learning how to customize Bootstrap 5 in different ways, we will take a closer look at the `bootstrap.scss` file.

Exploring bootstrap.scss

The `bootstrap.scss` file contains all the code that will import the individual Sass partial files for the various elements. Let's now see what this file contains:

bootstrap.scss

```
@import "mixins/banner";
@include bsBanner("");


// scss-docs-start import-stack
// Configuration
```

```
@import "functions";
@import "variables";
@import "maps";
@import "mixins";
@import "utilities";

// Layout & components
@import "root";
@import "reboot";
@import "type";
@import "images";
@import "containers";
@import "grid";
@import "tables";
@import "forms";
@import "buttons";
@import "transitions";
@import "dropdown";
@import "button-group";
@import "nav";
@import "navbar";
@import "card";
@import "accordion";
@import "breadcrumb";
@import "pagination";
@import "badge";
@import "alert";
@import "progress";
@import "list-group";
@import "close";
@import "toasts";
@import "modal";
@import "tooltip";
@import "popover";
@import "carousel";
@import "spinners";
```

```
@import "offcanvas";
@import "placeholders";

// Helpers
@import "helpers";

// Utilities
@import "utilities/api";
// scss-docs-end import-stack
```

As you can see from the preceding code, the bootstrap.scss file will import all the Sass partial files from the root scss folder, while some of these files will import the Sass partial files in the subfolders. For some customizations, it's enough to import this file after defining the custom changes, but for other customizations, we need to import the Bootstrap 5 partials individually and add our own custom changes in between these imports. In the following chapters, I will show you when you need to either import the whole bootstrap.scss file or the Bootstrap 5 partials individually.

Let's talk a bit about the Bootstrap 5 variables next.

Exploring the Bootstrap 5 variables

To customize any element of Bootstrap 5, you will start by looking at the _variables.scss file. This file contains all the variables used by Bootstrap 5, including variables for global options, colors, layout, content (including typography), forms, components, helpers, and utilities. So, for example, to know which part of a component can be customized, you simply need to search for the component name within the _variables.scss file. Then, you will find all the relevant variables with their default values grouped together. You now need to use these same variable names in your own Sass file to change it. You will learn exactly how to do this in the next chapter.

The variables have been carefully ordered by the team behind Bootstrap since some variables reference other variables. The order in which the variables for different components appear is not alphabetical, so my best suggestion to find them is to scroll through the file or search for the component name.

There's a total of 886 variables used by Bootstrap 5, and some of these are Sass maps that contain multiple values. All these variables and their values are used to build the different elements of Bootstrap 5, and they can all be customized.

We won't see examples of how to customize all elements of Bootstrap 5 (be it layout, content, forms, components, helpers, or utilities), but we will go through enough examples from each category to learn how to change everything else.

> **An alternative way to find variable names**
>
> You can also find variable names for various elements of Bootstrap 5 by looking in the partial files in the root of the `scss` folder. If you, for example, go into the `_breadcrumb.scss` file, you can see the variables being used in the different CSS declarations for that component. There, you can see what property the variable is being used as a value for, but in general, it should be easiest, quickest, and adequate to just look up variables in the `_variables.scss` file.

Default values with the !default flag

All the Bootstrap 5 variables use the `!default` flag. The function of this flag is described in the previous chapter under the *Default values* subsection. In brief, the `!default` flag is used so that the variable values can be set in advance before importing the Bootstrap 5 Sass files. This is the way Bootstrap 5 customization works.

Null value default variables

Forty-four of the 886 variables have the `null` value. When these variables are used in a CSS declaration elsewhere in the Bootstrap 5 source code, that declaration won't compile. This is a smart way of providing even more customization options for the user without bloating the code base with unnecessary styles. If the user chooses to define the value of one of these variables before importing the Bootstrap 5 files, then the `null !default` value will be overwritten and the CSS declaration will compile.

Take, for example, the `$headings-font-style` variable on line 591 that has a `null !default` value. This variable is used in the `_reboot.scss` file for some general styling of headings as follows:

```
font-style: $headings-font-style;
```

This CSS declaration will not compile when the value is `null`. If, however, we give the variable a value, the declaration *will* compile. In this way, the headings won't have any specific font style, but they can easily be given one since the `$headings-font-style` variable is already available for the developer to use.

Summary

You have now learned how to download the Bootstrap 5 source code from the official website or from NPM. You have also learned about the Bootstrap 5 Sass files and variables in the `scss` folder and its subfolders, and how those files and variables are related to each other. Finally, you have learned how to import and compile Bootstrap 5.

In the next chapter, we will start customizing the Bootstrap 5 styles by focusing on the global options and color palette.

4

Bootstrap 5 Global Options and Colors

In this chapter, we will start customizing Bootstrap 5. After some important information about the code examples, we will learn how we can change the global options, and then how we can customize the colors.

Changing global options and customizing colors will have an effect on many elements of Bootstrap 5, so it's useful to know these kinds of customizations since they can save you a lot of time.

In this chapter, we're going to cover the following topics:

- Importing the Bootstrap 5 files individually
- Changing the global options
- Customizing the colors

Technical requirements

- To preview the examples, you will need a code editor and a browser.
- You will also need a Sass compiler to compile the Sass files to CSS. Please see *Chapter 2, Using and Compiling Sass* for different ways to do this.

You can find the code files of the chapter on GitHub at `https://github.com/PacktPublishing/The-Missing-Bootstrap-5-Guide`.

About the code examples

Throughout this chapter, I will provide code examples taken from the Bootstrap 5 Sass files. I will include the filename and the line number so it will be easier for you to find the specific code.

I have made the following changes to the code from Bootstrap 5 to give you a better overview:

- Comments in the original Bootstrap 5 source code have been left out
- Excess spaces in between variable names and their values have been deleted in some cases, but not all, to accommodate the layout of this book and keep most of them on one line

Empty lines have been kept, so it's easier to find the code examples in the Bootstrap 5 source code.

Importing the Bootstrap 5 files individually

In the previous chapter, we saw how to import the default Bootstrap 5. This way of importing Bootstrap 5 is sufficient when changing the global options or overriding any default variables (and not needing any of the functions). However, to have more granular control and be able to customize Bootstrap 5 in more advanced ways, we need to import the Bootstrap 5 partials individually (some of them in the correct order) and our customization code at the appropriate places in between the Bootstrap 5 partials.

The full list of the individual Bootstrap 5 partials together with comments for where to place our own customization code is as follows:

style.scss

```
// Required
@import "../../../../../bootstrap/scss/functions";


// Default variable overrides


// Required
@import "../../../../../bootstrap/scss/variables";


// Variable value using existing variable


// Required
@import "../../../../../bootstrap/scss/maps";
@import "../../../../../bootstrap/scss/mixins";
@import "../../../../../bootstrap/scss/root";
```

```scss
// Optional Bootstrap CSS
@import "../../../../../bootstrap/scss/reboot";
@import "../../../../../bootstrap/scss/type";
@import "../../../../../bootstrap/scss/images";
@import "../../../../../bootstrap/scss/containers";
@import "../../../../../bootstrap/scss/grid";
@import "../../../../../bootstrap/scss/tables";
@import "../../../../../bootstrap/scss/forms";
@import "../../../../../bootstrap/scss/buttons";
@import "../../../../../bootstrap/scss/transitions";
@import "../../../../../bootstrap/scss/dropdown";
@import "../../../../../bootstrap/scss/button-group";
@import "../../../../../bootstrap/scss/nav";
@import "../../../../../bootstrap/scss/navbar";
@import "../../../../../bootstrap/scss/card";
@import "../../../../../bootstrap/scss/accordion";
@import "../../../../../bootstrap/scss/breadcrumb";
@import "../../../../../bootstrap/scss/pagination";
@import "../../../../../bootstrap/scss/badge";
@import "../../../../../bootstrap/scss/alert";
@import "../../../../../bootstrap/scss/progress";
@import "../../../../../bootstrap/scss/list-group";
@import "../../../../../bootstrap/scss/close";
@import "../../../../../bootstrap/scss/toasts";
@import "../../../../../bootstrap/scss/modal";
@import "../../../../../bootstrap/scss/tooltip";
@import "../../../../../bootstrap/scss/popover";
@import "../../../../../bootstrap/scss/carousel";
@import "../../../../../bootstrap/scss/spinners";
@import "../../../../../bootstrap/scss/offcanvas";
@import "../../../../../bootstrap/scss/placeholders";

// Helpers
@import "../../../../../bootstrap/scss/helpers";

// Utilities
```

```
@import "../../../../../bootstrap/scss/utilities";


// Utilities API
@import "../../../../../bootstrap/scss/utilities/api";
```

> **The utility API and own custom styles**
>
> The preceding list will be extended a bit when we want to use the utility API and include our own custom styles. We will see exactly how to do that in *Chapter 6, Understanding and Using the Bootstrap 5 Utility API*, and *Chapter 8, Customizing the Website Using Bootstrap 5 Variables, Utility API and Sass*, respectively.

In those customization examples that require us to import the Bootstrap 5 partials individually, I have reduced the long list of Bootstrap 5 imports grouped under the // Optional Bootstrap CSS comment. This is done so that the code examples won't take up too much space. Here's what the shortened list looks like:

style.scss

```
// Optional Bootstrap CSS
@import "../../../../../bootstrap/scss/reboot";
@import "../../../../../bootstrap/scss/type";
@import "../../../../../bootstrap/scss/images";
// The long list of imports have been reduced here.
```

Later in this book, we will also see how we can optimize our CSS code by only including the exact Bootstrap 5 Sass partial files that we need.

Now that we are aware of these changes to the code examples, we will start customizing Bootstrap 5.

Changing the global options

Bootstrap 5 comes with a set of variables to enable or disable different global options for styles and behavior. Most of these variables can be found grouped together in the _variables.scss file, on lines 337-352, except for the $spacer variable, which can be found on line 374.

Here's an overview of the different available options. They are listed here in the same order as they appear in the `_variables.scss` file:

- Caret

- Rounded (border-radius)

- Shadows (box-shadow)

- Gradients

- Transitions

- Reduced motion

- Smooth scroll

- Grid classes

- Container classes

- CSS grid

- Button pointers

- Responsive Font Sizes (RFS)

- Validation icons

- Negative margins

- Deprecation messages

- Important utilities

- Spacer

We will now run through each of the options and see their variable name, their default value, where they are defined, what they look like or do, and how they can be changed. For each option, there will be a code example in the `part-1/chapter-4/options/` folder and the content of each example's Sass file is shown in the following section.

Caret

Variable name: `$enable-caret`

Default value: `true`

Defined: `_variables.scss`, line `337`

This option enables a caret placed in a pseudo element on the toggle button for the dropdown component.

Here you can see an example of what enabling or disabling this option will look like:

Figure 4.1 – Dropdown button with the caret option enabled (default)

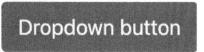

Figure 4.2 – Dropdown button with the caret option disabled (changed)

To disable the caret option, use the following Sass code:

part-1/chapter-4/options/caret/scss/style.scss

```
$enable-caret: false;
@import "../../../../../bootstrap/scss/bootstrap.scss";
```

Rounded

Variable name: $enable-rounded

Default value: true

Defined: _variables.scss, line 338

This option enables predefined border-radius styles on various components.

Here you can see a few different examples of what enabling or disabling this option will look like:

Figure 4.3 – Button with the rounded option enabled (default)

Figure 4.4 – Button with the rounded option disabled (changed)

Figure 4.5 – Text input with the rounded option enabled (default)

Figure 4.6 – Text input with the rounded option disabled (changed)

Figure 4.7 – Alert component with the rounded option enabled (default)

Figure 4.8 – Alert component with the rounded option disabled (changed)

To disable the rounded option, use the following Sass code:

part-1/chapter-4/options/rounded/scss/style.scss

```
$enable-rounded: false;
@import "../../../../../bootstrap/scss/bootstrap.scss";
```

Shadows

Variable name: $enable-shadows

Default value: false

Defined: _variables.scss, line 339

This option enables predefined decorative box-shadow styles on various components.

Here you can see a few different examples of what enabling or disabling this option will look like:

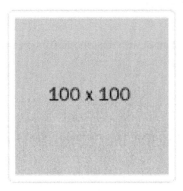

Figure 4.9 – Image thumbnail with the shadows option disabled (default)

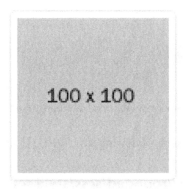

Figure 4.10 – Image thumbnail with the shadows option enabled (changed)

Select option	⌄

Figure 4.11 – Select with the shadows option disabled (default)

Select option	⌄

Figure 4.12 – Select with the shadows option enabled (changed)

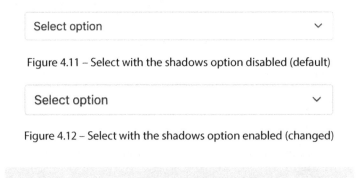

Figure 4.13 – Progress component with the shadows option disabled (default)

Figure 4.14 – Progress component with the shadows option enabled (changed)

To enable the shadows option, use the following Sass code:

part-1/chapter-4/options/shadows/scss/style.scss

```
$enable-shadows: true;
@import "../../../../../bootstrap/scss/bootstrap.scss";
```

Gradients

Variable name: $enable-gradients

Default value: false

Defined: _variables.scss, line 340

This option enables predefined gradients via background-image styles on various components. This visual effect is very subtle and might be hard to see. However, the following CSS will be used on most of the compatible components to create the gradient effect on top of the background color:

```
background-image: linear-gradient(180deg,
   rgba(255,255,255,0.15), rgba(255,255,255,0));
```

On the carousel component, the following CSS will be used instead:

```
.carousel-control-prev {
  background-image: linear-gradient(90deg,
    rgba(0,0,0,0.25), rgba(0,0,0,0.001));
}
.carousel-control-next {
  background-image: linear-gradient(270deg,
    rgba(0,0,0,0.25), rgba(0,0,0,0.001));
}
```

Here you can see a few different examples of what enabling or disabling this option will look like:

Figure 4.15 – Alert component with the gradients option disabled (default)

Figure 4.16 – Alert component with the gradients option enabled (changed)

Figure 4.17 – Button with the gradients option disabled (default)

Figure 4.18 – Button with the gradients option enabled (changed)

Figure 4.19 – Carousel component with the gradients option disabled (default)

Figure 4.20 – Carousel component with the gradients option enabled (changed)

To enable the gradients option, use the following Sass code:

---

part-1/chapter-4/options/gradients/scss/style.scss

```
$enable-gradients: true;
@import "../../../../../bootstrap/scss/bootstrap.scss";
```

Transitions

Variable name: $enable-transitions

Default value: true

Defined: _variables.scss, line 341

This option enables predefined transitions on various components.

No examples can be shown here in print, but the transitions are applied to accordions, carousels, modals, progress bars, floating labels, and more.

To disable the transitions option, use the following Sass code:

---

part-1/chapter-4/options/transitions/scss/style.scss

```
$enable-transitions: false;
@import "../../../../../bootstrap/scss/bootstrap.scss";
```

Reduced motion

Variable name: $enable-reduced-motion

Default value: true

Defined: _variables.scss, line 342

This option enables a prefers-reduced-motion media query, which will remove or change certain animations and transitions based on users' preferences.

This option applies to the progress and spinner components, and to see the effect, you need to change some settings on your computer.

To disable the reduced motion option, use the following Sass code:

part-1/chapter-4/options/reduced-motion/scss/style.scss

```
$enable-reduced-motion: false;
@import "../../../../bootstrap/scss/bootstrap.scss";
```

Smooth scroll

Variable name: $enable-smooth-scroll

Default value: true

Defined: _variables.scss, line 343

This option enables smooth scroll behavior globally, except for users who prefer reduced motion.

To disable the smooth scroll option, use the following Sass code:

part-1/chapter-4/options/smooth-scroll/scss/style.scss

```
$enable-smooth-scroll: false;
@import "../../../../bootstrap/scss/bootstrap.scss";
```

Grid classes

Variable name: $enable-grid-classes

Default value: true

Defined: _variables.scss, line 344

This option enables the generation of CSS classes used for the grid system. This includes `.row`, `.col`, and other related classes.

To disable the grid classes option, use the following Sass code:

---

part-1/chapter-4/options/grid-classes/scss/style.scss

```scss
$enable-grid-classes: false;
@import "../../../../../bootstrap/scss/bootstrap.scss";
```

Container classes

Variable name: `$enable-container-classes`

Default value: `true`

Defined: `_variables.scss`, line `345`

This option enables the generation of CSS classes used for layout containers. This includes `.container`, `.container-fluid`, and other related classes.

To disable the container classes option, use the following Sass code:

---

part-1/chapter-4/options/container-classes/scss/style.scss

```scss
$enable-container-classes: false;
@import "../../../../../bootstrap/scss/bootstrap.scss";
```

CSS grid

Variable name: `$enable-cssgrid`

Default value: `false`

Defined: `_variables.scss`, line `346`

This option is used to enable a separate grid system that's built on a CSS grid.

If you want to enable this, you should disable the default grid system using the grid classes option mentioned earlier.

To enable the CSS grid option, use the following Sass code:

part-1/chapter-4/options/css-grid/scss/style.scss

```scss
$enable-grid-classes: false;
$enable-cssgrid: true;
@import "../../../../bootstrap/scss/bootstrap.scss";
```

Button pointers

Variable name: $enable-button-pointers

Default value: true

Defined: _variables.scss, line 347

This option adds a pointer cursor to non-disabled button elements and button components (with the .btn class).

Here you can see an example of what enabling or disabling this option will look like:

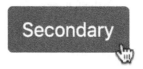

Figure 4.21 – Button with the button pointers option enabled (default)

Figure 4.22 – Button with the button pointers option disabled (changed)

To disable the button pointers option, use the following Sass code:

part-1/chapter-4/options/button-pointers/scss/style.scss

```scss
$enable-button-pointers: false;
@import "../../../../bootstrap/scss/bootstrap.scss";
```

Responsive Font Sizes

Variable name: $enable-rfs

Default value: true

Defined: _variables.scss, line 348

This option enables RFS globally. You will learn more about RFS and how to use it in *Chapter 10, Using Bootstrap 5 with Advanced Sass and CSS Features*.

To disable the RFS option, use the following Sass code:

---

part-1/chapter-4/options/responsive-font-sizes/scss/style.scss

```
$enable-rfs: false;
@import "../../../../../bootstrap/scss/bootstrap.scss";
```

Validation icons

Variable name: $enable-validation-icons

Default value: true

Defined: _variables.scss line 349

This option enables background-image icons within textual inputs and some custom forms for validation states.

Here you can see an example of what enabling or disabling this option will look like:

Valid feedback text

Figure 4.23 – Valid text input with the validation icons option enabled (default)

Valid feedback text

Figure 4.24 – Valid text input with the validation icons option disabled (changed)

Invalid feedback text

Figure 4.25 – Invalid text input with the validation icons option enabled (default)

Invalid feedback text

Figure 4.26 – Invalid text input with the validation icons option disabled (changed)

To disable the validation icons option, use the following Sass code:

part-1/chapter-4/options/validation-icons/scss/style.scss

```
$enable-validation-icons: false;
@import "../../../../../bootstrap/scss/bootstrap.scss";
```

Negative margins

Variable name: $enable-negative-margins

Default value: false

Defined: _variables.scss, line 350

This option enables the generation of negative margin utilities.

To enable the negative margins option, use the following Sass code:

part-1/chapter-4/options/negative-margins/scss/style.scss

```
$enable-negative-margins: true;
@import "../../../../../bootstrap/scss/bootstrap.scss";
```

Deprecation messages

Variable name: $enable-deprecation-messages

Default value: true

Defined: `_variables.scss`, line 351

This option enables Sass warning messages for deprecated mixins or functions. Currently, no mixins or functions have been deprecated, so you won't encounter this warning message with this version of Bootstrap 5.

To disable the deprecation messages option, use the following Sass code:

---

part-1/chapter-4/options/deprecation-messages/scss/style.scss

```
$enable-deprecation-messages: false;
@import "../../../../../bootstrap/scss/bootstrap.scss";
```

The code example for this option has an HTML file without any content since this option will only show Sass warning messages for any future deprecated mixins or functions.

Important utilities

Variable name: `$enable-important-utilities`

Default value: `true`

Defined: `_variables.scss`, line 352

This option enables the `!important` suffix in utility classes. So, this option controls whether the value of the CSS declaration for utility classes will have `!important` added at the end and thus override all previous styling for an element.

Here's an example that shows the difference:

```
// Important utilities enabled
.text-center {
  text-align: text-center !important;
}
// Important utilities disabled
.text-center {
  text-align: text-center;
}
```

To disable the important utilities option, use the following Sass code:

part-1/chapter-4/options/important-utilities/scss/style.scss

```scss
$enable-important-utilities: false;
@import "../../../../../bootstrap/scss/bootstrap.scss";
```

Spacer

Variable name: $spacer

Default value: 1rem

Defined: _variables.scss, line 374

This variable specifies the default spacer value used by many other component variables in the _variables.scss file (as well as a few other places). It's also used to programmatically generate the spacer utilities.

Here you can see an example of what changing this variable to 2rem will look like:

Secondary alert!

Figure 4.27 – Alert component with spacer set to 1rem (default)

Secondary alert!

Figure 4.28 – Alert component with spacer set to 2rem (changed)

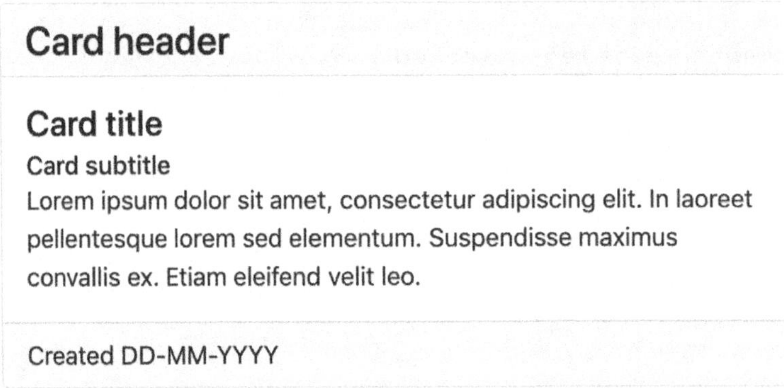

Card header

Card title
Card subtitle
Lorem ipsum dolor sit amet, consectetur adipiscing elit. In laoreet pellentesque lorem sed elementum. Suspendisse maximus convallis ex. Etiam eleifend velit leo.

Created DD-MM-YYYY

Figure 4.29 – Card component with spacer set to 1rem (default)

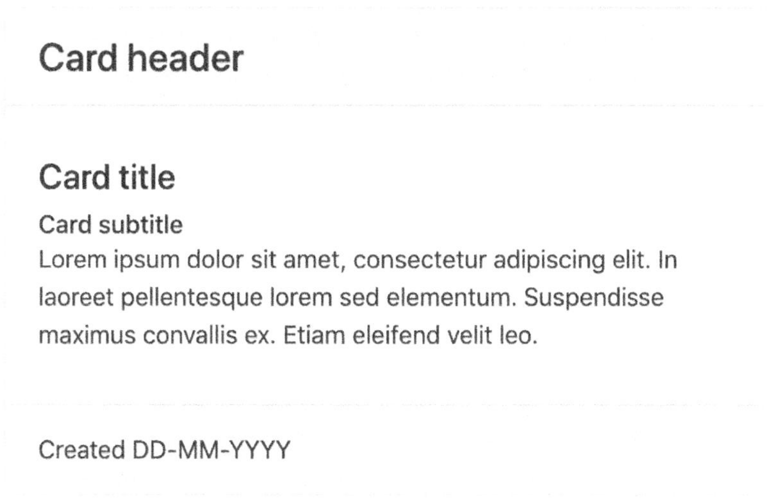

Card header

Card title
Card subtitle
Lorem ipsum dolor sit amet, consectetur adipiscing elit. In laoreet pellentesque lorem sed elementum. Suspendisse maximus convallis ex. Etiam eleifend velit leo.

Created DD-MM-YYYY

Figure 4.30 – Card component with spacer set to 2rem (changed)

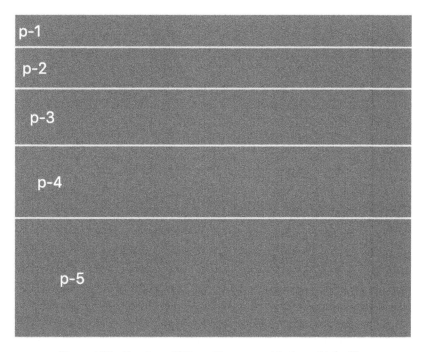

Figure 4.31 – Spacing utilities with spacer set to 1rem (default)

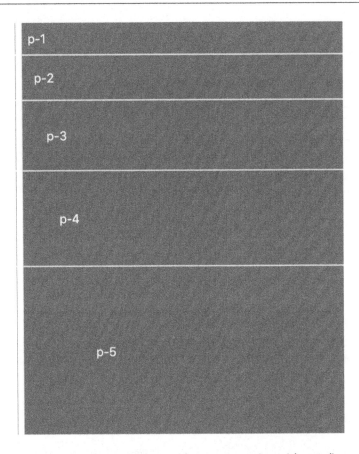

Figure 4.32 – Spacing utilities with spacer set to 2rem (changed)

To change the value of this variable to 2rem, use the following Sass code:

part-1/chapter-4/options/spacer/scss/style.scss

```
$spacer: 2rem;
@import "../../../../../bootstrap/scss/bootstrap.scss";
```

Now that we have learned all about how to change the global options of Bootstrap 5, we will move on to learn about customizing the colors.

Customizing the colors

Bootstrap 5 has an advanced color system that provides the correct styling for all elements. This color system is based on color variables, which can be customized in different ways to match your brand or design.

In this section, we're going to cover the following topics:

- Overview of the color variables
- Generating color classes
- Adding color to theme colors
- Removing color from theme colors

Overview of the color variables

The first of many variables in the `_variables.scss` file are color variables. They can be found on lines 9-321.

The color system is ordered and grouped in the following way:

- Grays
- Regular colors
- Tints and shades of colors
- Theme colors

In each of these groups, the individual colors are first assigned to different variables, and these variables are then assigned to keys in a Sass map, grouping these related colors together. The Sass maps are used to easily loop over a list of colors. You can add, remove, or modify values in the Sass maps, which will be reflected in many of the components. We will see some examples of this later in this section.

But first, we will go through the different groups of colors listed previously and learn more about their color values, the variables, and the Sass maps.

Grays

First, we have nine tints and shades of gray, plus white and black. The line numbers, variable names, and default values are as follows:

bootstrap/scss/_variables.scss

```
 9 $white:    #fff !default;
10 $gray-100: #f8f9fa !default;
11 $gray-200: #e9ecef !default;
12 $gray-300: #dee2e6 !default;
13 $gray-400: #ced4da !default;
14 $gray-500: #adb5bd !default;
```

```
15 $gray-600: #6c757d !default;
16 $gray-700: #495057 !default;
17 $gray-800: #343a40 !default;
18 $gray-900: #212529 !default;
19 $black:    #000 !default;
```

These color values represent the following actual colors:

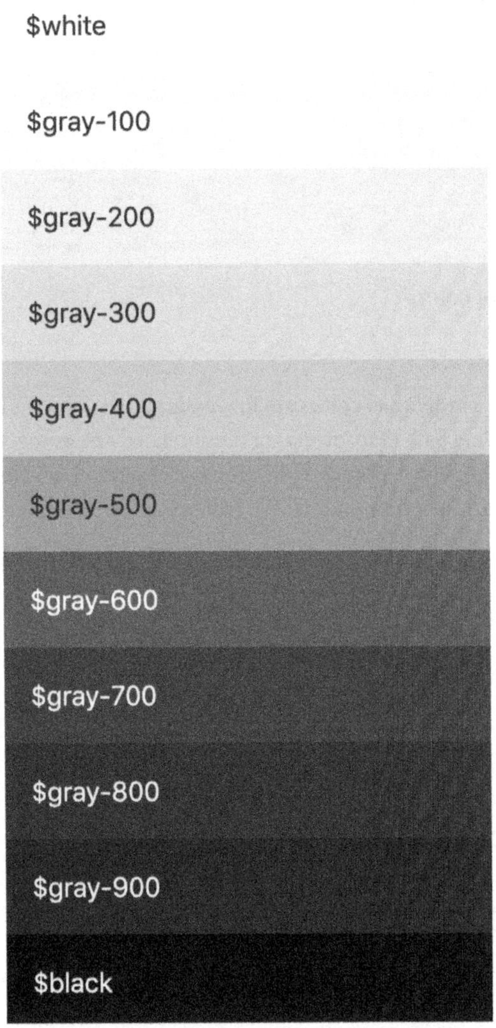

$white

$gray-100

$gray-200

$gray-300

$gray-400

$gray-500

$gray-600

$gray-700

$gray-800

$gray-900

$black

Figure 4.33 – Gray colors plus white and black

These variables (excluding $white and $black) are then grouped into the $grays Sass map:

bootstrap/scss/_variables.scss

```
24 $grays: (
25   "100": $gray-100,
26   "200": $gray-200,
27   "300": $gray-300,
28   "400": $gray-400,
29   "500": $gray-500,
30   "600": $gray-600,
31   "700": $gray-700,
32   "800": $gray-800,
33   "900": $gray-900
34 ) !default;
```

Regular colors

Then, we have 10 different regular colors. The line numbers, variable names, and default values are as follows:

bootstrap/scss/_variables.scss

```
39 $blue:    #0d6efd !default;
40 $indigo:  #6610f2 !default;
41 $purple:  #6f42c1 !default;
42 $pink:    #d63384 !default;
43 $red:     #dc3545 !default;
44 $orange:  #fd7e14 !default;
45 $yellow:  #ffc107 !default;
46 $green:   #198754 !default;
47 $teal:    #20c997 !default;
48 $cyan:    #0dcaf0 !default;
```

These color values represent the following actual colors:

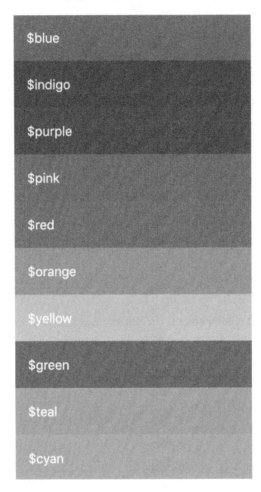

Figure 4.34 – Regular colors

These 10 regular color variables plus $black, $white, $gray-600, and $gray-800 are then grouped into the $colors Sass map:

bootstrap/scss/_variables.scss

```
52 $colors: (
53    "blue":        $blue,
54    "indigo":      $indigo,
55    "purple":      $purple,
```

```
56    "pink":        $pink,
57    "red":         $red,
58    "orange":      $orange,
59    "yellow":      $yellow,
60    "green":       $green,
61    "teal":        $teal,
62    "cyan":        $cyan,
63    "black":       $black,
64    "white":       $white,
65    "gray":        $gray-600,
66    "gray-dark":   $gray-800
67 )  !default;
```

Tints and shades of colors

After the regular colors, we have a long list of individual color variables for all tints and shades of the regular colors, followed by a list of Sass maps that group all these together.

The individual tints and shades of a regular color are generated using custom color functions to either tint (lighten) or shade (darken) a color (see the next source code). These custom color functions that are built into Bootstrap 5 use the mix() color function of Sass to create the desired colors.

As an example, we will look at the tints and shades of the blue color. The line numbers, variable names, and default values are as follows:

bootstrap/scss/_variables.scss

```
79 $blue-100: tint-color($blue, 80%) !default;
80 $blue-200: tint-color($blue, 60%) !default;
81 $blue-300: tint-color($blue, 40%) !default;
82 $blue-400: tint-color($blue, 20%) !default;
83 $blue-500: $blue !default;
84 $blue-600: shade-color($blue, 20%) !default;
85 $blue-700: shade-color($blue, 40%) !default;
86 $blue-800: shade-color($blue, 60%) !default;
87 $blue-900: shade-color($blue, 80%) !default;
```

In the preceding code, you can see that the middle value, $blue-500, is assigned to the $blue color. The lighter values above that are then tinted, and the darker values below that are shaded using the custom color functions.

This list is followed by similar lists for the other colors (indigo, purple, pink, red, orange, yellow, green, teal, and cyan), and starting at line 179, we have the Sass maps for these colors. In case of the blue color, the Sass map looks like this:

bootstrap/scss/_variables.scss

```
179 $blues: (
180   "blue-100": $blue-100,
181   "blue-200": $blue-200,
182   "blue-300": $blue-300,
183   "blue-400": $blue-400,
184   "blue-500": $blue-500,
185   "blue-600": $blue-600,
186   "blue-700": $blue-700,
187   "blue-800": $blue-800,
188   "blue-900": $blue-900
189 ) !default;
```

Theme colors

Finally, we have selected colors from the groups of grays and regular colors, which are now assigned to eight different theme color variables. These are often also referred to as *contextual colors*. The line numbers, variable names, and default values are as follows:

bootstrap/scss/_variables.scss

```
301 $primary:      $blue !default;
302 $secondary:    $gray-600 !default;
303 $success:      $green !default;
304 $info:         $cyan !default;
305 $warning:      $yellow !default;
306 $danger:       $red !default;
307 $light:        $gray-100 !default;
308 $dark:         $gray-900 !default;
```

These color values represent the following actual colors:

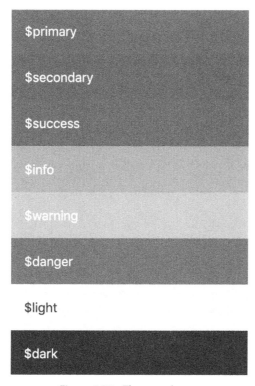

Figure 4.35 – Theme colors

These colors are then grouped into the $theme-colors Sass map:

bootstrap/scss/_variables.scss

```
312 $theme-colors: (
313   "primary":    $primary,
314   "secondary":  $secondary,
315   "success":    $success,
316   "info":       $info,
317   "warning":    $warning,
318   "danger":     $danger,
319   "light":      $light,
320   "dark":       $dark
321 ) !default;
```

Notice that the $theme-colors Sass map contains the specific theme color variables. Nothing more, nothing less. The $grays Sass map didn't contain the $white and $black color variables, while the $colors Sass map did also include the $black, $white, $gray-600, and $gray-800 color variables. This is just to tell you that this difference exists.

We are now finished with the overview of all the available color variables and Sass maps. Let's now see how we can use these for different purposes.

Generating color classes

If you need it, you can easily generate more color classes by using the @each rule built into Sass. You can then iterate over key/value pairs in a Sass map and define which class prefix to use.

Here's the syntax for the @each rule iterating over a Sass map:

```
@each $key, $value in $map {
  .class-prefix-#{$key} {
    css-property: $value;
  }
}
```

As you can see, the key is assigned to the first variable name in the @each expression, and the value is assigned to the second. $key is then used together with a chosen class prefix, and $value is used to set the value of the CSS property.

We will now see how the @each rule can be used to generate different groups of color classes.

> **Custom Sass code placed after importing the required files**
>
> In most of the remaining code examples, our custom Sass code is placed after importing the required files (including the _variables.scss file) and before importing the optional Bootstrap files. This is necessary when we want to use an existing variable as a value for another variable, which is the case when we want to generate color classes based on existing color variables.

Grays

To generate background color classes from the $grays Sass map, you will need to use the following Sass code:

part-1/chapter-4/colors/grays/scss/style.scss

```
// Required
@import "../../../../../bootstrap/scss/functions";
```

```
@import "../../../../../bootstrap/scss/variables";

// Create background color classes from the "$grays" color map
@each $color, $value in $grays {
  .bg-gray-#{$color} {
    background-color: $value;
  }
}

// Required
@import "../../../../../bootstrap/scss/maps";
@import "../../../../../bootstrap/scss/mixins";
@import "../../../../../bootstrap/scss/root";

// Optional Bootstrap CSS
@import "../../../../../bootstrap/scss/reboot";
@import "../../../../../bootstrap/scss/type";
@import "../../../../../bootstrap/scss/images";
// The long list of imports have been reduced here.

// Helpers
@import "../../../../../bootstrap/scss/helpers";

// Utilities
@import "../../../../../bootstrap/scss/utilities";

// Utilities API
@import "../../../../../bootstrap/scss/utilities/api";
```

When you compile this, you will get the regular Bootstrap CSS as well as the following background color classes:

part-1/chapter-4/colors/grays/css/style.css

```
.bg-gray-100 { background-color: #f8f9fa; }
.bg-gray-200 { background-color: #e9ecef; }
.bg-gray-300 { background-color: #dee2e6; }
```

```
.bg-gray-400 { background-color: #ced4da; }
.bg-gray-500 { background-color: #adb5bd; }
.bg-gray-600 { background-color: #6c757d; }
.bg-gray-700 { background-color: #495057; }
.bg-gray-800 { background-color: #343a40; }
.bg-gray-900 { background-color: #212529; }
```

This code can be tested using the following HTML:

part-1/chapter-4/colors/grays/index.html

```
<div class="bg-gray-100">.bg-gray-100</div>
<div class="bg-gray-200">.bg-gray-200</div>
<div class="bg-gray-300">.bg-gray-300</div>
<div class="bg-gray-400">.bg-gray-400</div>
<div class="bg-gray-500">.bg-gray-500</div>
<div class="bg-gray-600">.bg-gray-600</div>
<div class="bg-gray-700">.bg-gray-700</div>
<div class="bg-gray-800">.bg-gray-800</div>
<div class="bg-gray-900">.bg-gray-900</div>
```

Regular colors

To generate background color classes from the $colors Sass map, you will need to use the following Sass code:

part-1/chapter-4/colors/regular-colors/scss/style.scss

```
// Required
@import "../../../../../bootstrap/scss/functions";
@import "../../../../../bootstrap/scss/variables";

// Create background color classes from the "$grays" color map
@each $color, $value in $colors {
  .bg-#{$color} {
    background-color: $value;
  }
}
```

```scss
// Required
@import "../../../../../bootstrap/scss/maps";
@import "../../../../../bootstrap/scss/mixins";
@import "../../../../../bootstrap/scss/root";

// Optional Bootstrap CSS
@import "../../../../../bootstrap/scss/reboot";
@import "../../../../../bootstrap/scss/type";
@import "../../../../../bootstrap/scss/images";
// The long list of imports have been reduced here.

// Helpers
@import "../../../../../bootstrap/scss/helpers";

// Utilities
@import "../../../../../bootstrap/scss/utilities";

// Utilities API
@import "../../../../../bootstrap/scss/utilities/api";
```

When you compile this, you will get the regular Bootstrap CSS as well as the following background color classes:

part-1/chapter-4/colors/regular-colors/css/style.css

```css
.bg-blue { background-color: #0d6efd; }
.bg-indigo { background-color: #6610f2; }
.bg-purple { background-color: #6f42c1; }
.bg-pink { background-color: #d63384; }
.bg-red { background-color: #dc3545; }
.bg-orange { background-color: #fd7e14; }
.bg-yellow { background-color: #ffc107; }
.bg-green { background-color: #198754; }
.bg-teal { background-color: #20c997; }
.bg-cyan { background-color: #0dcaf0; }
.bg-dark { background-color: #000; }
.bg-white { background-color: #fff; }
```

```
.bg-gray { background-color: #6c757d; }
.bg-gray-dark { background-color: #343a40; }
```

This code can be tested using the following HTML:

part-1/chapter-4/colors/regular-colors/index.html

```html
<div class="bg-blue">.bg-blue</div>
<div class="bg-indigo">.bg-indigo</div>
<div class="bg-purple">.bg-purple</div>
<div class="bg-pink">.bg-pink</div>
<div class="bg-red">.bg-red</div>
<div class="bg-orange">.bg-orange</div>
<div class="bg-yellow">.bg-yellow</div>
<div class="bg-green">.bg-green</div>
<div class="bg-teal">.bg-teal</div>
<div class="bg-cyan">.bg-cyan</div>
<div class="bg-dark">.bg-dark</div>
<div class="bg-white">.bg-white</div>
<div class="bg-gray">.bg-gray</div>
<div class="bg-gray-dark">.bg-gray-dark</div>
```

Tints and shades of blue

To generate background color classes from the $blues Sass map, you will need to use the following Sass code:

part-1/chapter-4/colors/tints-and-shades/scss/style.scss

```scss
// Required
@import "../../../../../bootstrap/scss/functions";
@import "../../../../../bootstrap/scss/variables";

// Create background color classes from the "$grays" color
// map
@each $color, $value in $blues {
  .bg-#{$color} {
    background-color: $value;
  }
}
```

```
}

// Required
@import "../../../../../bootstrap/scss/maps";
@import "../../../../../bootstrap/scss/mixins";
@import "../../../../../bootstrap/scss/root";

// Optional Bootstrap CSS
@import "../../../../../bootstrap/scss/reboot";
@import "../../../../../bootstrap/scss/type";
@import "../../../../../bootstrap/scss/images";
// The long list of imports have been reduced here.

// Helpers
@import "../../../../../bootstrap/scss/helpers";

// Utilities
@import "../../../../../bootstrap/scss/utilities";

// Utilities API
@import "../../../../../bootstrap/scss/utilities/api";
```

When you compile this, you will get the regular Bootstrap CSS as well as the following background color classes:

part-1/chapter-4/colors/tints-and-shades/css/style.css

```
.bg-blue-100 { background-color: #cfe2ff; }
.bg-blue-200 { background-color: #9ec5fe; }
.bg-blue-300 { background-color: #6ea8fe; }
.bg-blue-400 { background-color: #3d8bfd; }
.bg-blue-500 { background-color: #0d6efd; }
.bg-blue-600 { background-color: #0a58ca; }
.bg-blue-700 { background-color: #084298; }
.bg-blue-800 { background-color: #052c65; }
.bg-blue-900 { background-color: #031633; }
```

This code can be tested using the following HTML:

part-1/chapter-4/colors/tints-and-shades/index.html

```
<div class="bg-blue-100">.bg-blue-100</div>
<div class="bg-blue-200">.bg-blue-200</div>
<div class="bg-blue-300">.bg-blue-300</div>
<div class="bg-blue-400">.bg-blue-400</div>
<div class="bg-blue-500">.bg-blue-500</div>
<div class="bg-blue-600">.bg-blue-600</div>
<div class="bg-blue-700">.bg-blue-700</div>
<div class="bg-blue-800">.bg-blue-800</div>
<div class="bg-blue-900">.bg-blue-900</div>
```

Mixed colors

You can also create a new custom Sass map with mixed colors specified as color variables or other valid color values and generate color classes based on this using the following Sass code:

part-1/chapter-4/colors/mixed-colors/scss/style.scss

```scss
// Required
@import "..//..//..//../bootstrap/scss/functions";
@import "..//..//..//../bootstrap/scss/variables";

// Create a new "$mixed-colors" map
$mixed-colors: (
  "blue": $blue,
  "green": green,
  "red": #f00,
  "primary": $primary
);

// Create color classes from the "$mixed-colors" map
@each $color, $value in $mixed-colors {
  .bg-#{$color} {
    background-color: $value;
  }
}
```

```
}

// Required
@import "../../../../../bootstrap/scss/maps";
@import "../../../../../bootstrap/scss/mixins";
@import "../../../../../bootstrap/scss/root";

// Optional Bootstrap CSS
@import "../../../../../bootstrap/scss/reboot";
@import "../../../../../bootstrap/scss/type";
@import "../../../../../bootstrap/scss/images";
// The long list of imports have been reduced here.

// Helpers
@import "../../../../../bootstrap/scss/helpers";

// Utilities
@import "../../../../../bootstrap/scss/utilities";

// Utilities API
@import "../../../../../bootstrap/scss/utilities/api";
```

When you compile this, you will get the regular Bootstrap CSS as well as the following background color classes:

part-1/chapter-4/colors/mixed-colors/css/style.css

```
.bg-blue { background-color: #0d6efd; }
.bg-green { background-color: green; }
.bg-red { background-color: #f00; }
.bg-primary { background-color: #0d6efd; }
```

This code can be tested using the following HTML:

part-1/chapter-4/colors/mixed-colors/index.html

```html
<div class="bg-blue">.bg-blue</div>
<div class="bg-green">.bg-green</div>
<div class="bg-red">.bg-red</div>
<div class="bg-primary">.bg-primary</div>
```

Adding color to theme colors

Bootstrap 5 has eight theme colors, which are used for component variations, helpers, utilities, and more. You can add more colors to the $theme-colors Sass map, which is used to generate these different variations. To do this, we will first create a new Sass map with new names for our keys and corresponding values (which can be existing color variables or any other valid color value):

```scss
// Create your own color map
$custom-colors: (
  "tertiary": $indigo,
  "quaternary": $purple,
  "quinary": $pink,
  "senary": $orange,
  "septenary": $teal
);
```

We will then merge this $custom-colors Sass map with the existing $theme-colors Sass map using the map-merge() function built into the sass:map module of Sass. We pass in the two maps that we want to merge as arguments, and the returned value will be stored in the $theme-colors variable. This will then overwrite the default $theme-colors variable, which contains the default theme colors, and as a result, increase our list of available theme colors. The code to merge these two maps is as follows:

```scss
// Merge "$theme-colors" map and "$custom-colors" map
$theme-colors: map-merge($theme-colors, $custom-colors);
```

The complete Sass code to use for this scenario is as follows:

part-1/chapter-4/colors/add-to-theme-colors/scss/style.scss

```scss
// Required
@import "..//..//..//../bootstrap/scss/functions";
```

```scss
@import "../../../../../bootstrap/scss/variables";

// Create your own color map
$custom-colors: (
  "tertiary": $indigo,
  "quaternary": $purple,
  "quinary": $pink,
  "senary": $orange,
  "septenary": $teal
);

// Merge "$theme-colors" map and "$custom-colors" map
$theme-colors: map-merge($theme-colors, $custom-colors);

// Required
@import "../../../../../bootstrap/scss/maps";
@import "../../../../../bootstrap/scss/mixins";
@import "../../../../../bootstrap/scss/root";

// Optional Bootstrap CSS
@import "../../../../../bootstrap/scss/reboot";
@import "../../../../../bootstrap/scss/type";
@import "../../../../../bootstrap/scss/images";
// The long list of imports have been reduced here.

// Helpers
@import "../../../../../bootstrap/scss/helpers";

// Utilities
@import "../../../../../bootstrap/scss/utilities";

// Utilities API
@import "../../../../../bootstrap/scss/utilities/api";
```

We will now see what all these theme colors look like and some examples of how the new theme colors will come into effect in various components and utilities:

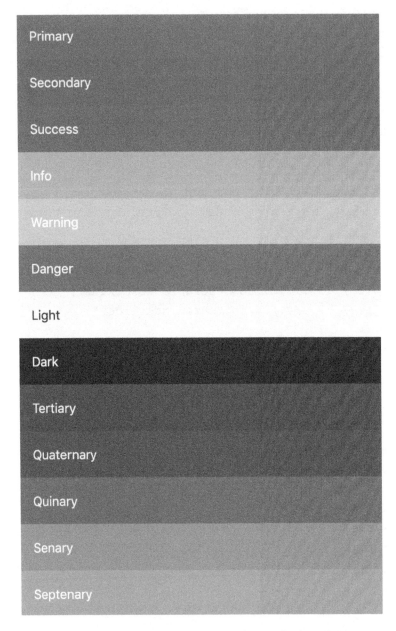

Figure 4.36 – All the colors displayed as background color utilities

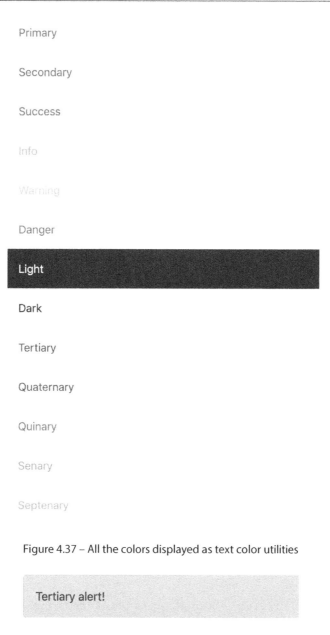

Primary

Secondary

Success

Info

Warning

Danger

Light

Dark

Tertiary

Quaternary

Quinary

Senary

Septenary

Figure 4.37 – All the colors displayed as text color utilities

Tertiary alert!

Figure 4.38 – An alert component with the new tertiary color

Quaternary button

Figure 4.39 – A button component with the new quaternary color

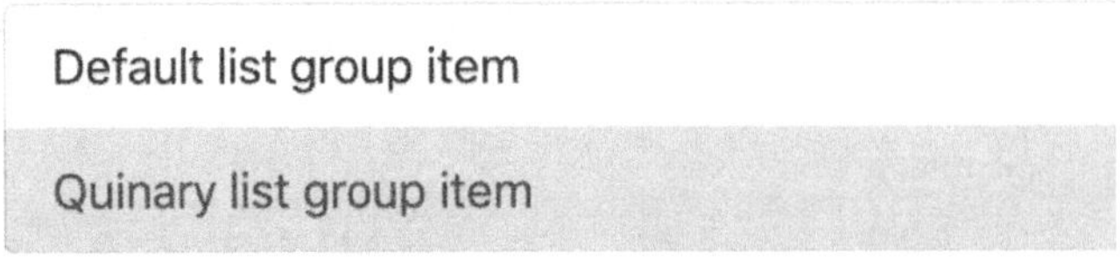

Figure 4.40 – A list group component with the new quinary color

Figure 4.41 – A stretched link helper class with the new senary color

Figure 4.42 – A border utility class with the new septenary color

The full code for this example can be found in the `part-1/chapter-4/colors/add-to-theme-colors` folder.

Removing color from theme colors

To remove a color from the theme colors, we can use the `map-remove()` function built into the `sass:map` module of Sass. As arguments to this function, we pass in the map that we want to remove key/value pairs from, followed by the keys of those key/value pairs we want to remove. The returned value will be stored in the `$theme-colors` variable. This will then overwrite the default `$theme-colors` variable, which contains the default theme colors, and as a result, decrease our list of available theme colors.

The code to remove theme colors from the `$theme-colors` map is as follows:

part-1/chapter-4/colors/remove-from-theme-colors/scss/style.scss

```scss
// Required
@import "../../../../../bootstrap/scss/functions";
@import "../../../../../bootstrap/scss/variables";

// Remove from "$theme-colors" map
$theme-colors: map-remove($theme-colors, "info", "light",
                          "dark");
```

```scss
// Required
@import "../../../../../bootstrap/scss/maps";
@import "../../../../../bootstrap/scss/mixins";
@import "../../../../../bootstrap/scss/root";

// Optional Bootstrap CSS
@import "../../../../../bootstrap/scss/reboot";
@import "../../../../../bootstrap/scss/type";
@import "../../../../../bootstrap/scss/images";
// The long list of imports have been reduced here.

// Helpers
@import "../../../../../bootstrap/scss/helpers";

// Utilities
@import "../../../../../bootstrap/scss/utilities";

// Utilities API
@import "../../../../../bootstrap/scss/utilities/api";
```

After compiling this, we won't be able to use the info, light, and dark colors for any component variations, helpers, or utilities.

The full code for this example can be found in the part-1/chapter-4/colors/remove-from-theme-colors folder.

Defining a custom color palette

To finish this section about colors in Bootstrap 5, we will learn how we can define a custom color palette. This is quite simple. First, we define our custom color values for the theme color variables that we want to change, then we import the Bootstrap 5 required files, and finally, we remove any unneeded theme color from the $theme-colors map. It's important to do it in this order since we first want to define our own color values for the color variables, and then want to modify the $theme-colors map, which is located in the _variables.scss file.

In our example, we want to change the color values for the $primary, $success, $info, $warning, and $danger theme color variables and remove the $secondary theme color.

> **Required theme color keys**
>
> Some theme color keys are required and can't be removed without causing errors, as they are being used by the Sass code of other components. This includes the `primary`, `success`, and `danger` keys. You can replace the values of those keys, but not remove the keys themselves. The `secondary` key is not required and can therefore be removed without causing any errors down the line.

Next, you will see the code needed to achieve this. Notice that we must specify our custom values for the theme color variables before importing the Bootstrap 5 required files:

part-1/chapter-4/colors/custom-color-palette/scss/style.scss

```
// Required
@import "../../../../../bootstrap/scss/functions";


// Define color palette
$primary:       #264653;
$success:       #2A9D8F;
$info:          #E9C46A;
$warning:       #F4A261;
$danger:        #E76F51;


// Required
@import "../../../../bootstrap/scss/variables";


// Remove "secondary" from "$theme-colors" map
$theme-colors: map-remove($theme-colors, "secondary");


// Required
@import "../../../../bootstrap/scss/maps";
@import "../../../../bootstrap/scss/mixins";
@import "../../../../bootstrap/scss/root";


// Optional Bootstrap CSS
@import "../../../../bootstrap/scss/reboot";
@import "../../../../bootstrap/scss/type";
@import "../../../../bootstrap/scss/images";
```

```
// The long list of imports have been reduced here.

// Helpers
@import "../../../../../bootstrap/scss/helpers";

// Utilities
@import "../../../../../bootstrap/scss/utilities";

// Utilities API
@import "../../../../../bootstrap/scss/utilities/api";
```

After compiling this, Bootstrap 5 will now be using the following color palette:

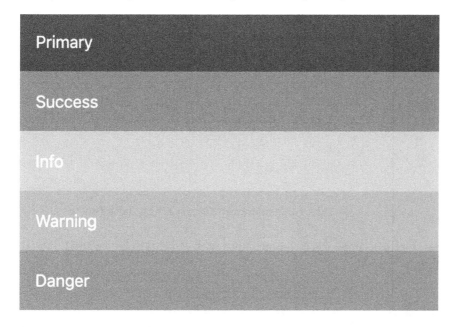

Figure 4.43 – Our custom color palette displayed as background color utilities

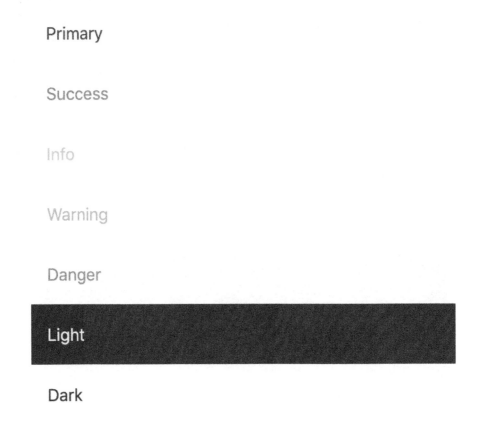

Figure 4.44 – Our custom color palette displayed as text color utilities

The full code for this example can be found in the `part-1/chapter-4/colors/custom-color-palette` folder.

Summary

In this chapter, we have learned all about the global options of Bootstrap 5 and how to change them. We have also learned how to customize the colors of Bootstrap 5, including how to generate color classes and how to add and remove colors used as theme colors.

In the next chapter, we will learn how to customize various elements of Bootstrap 5.

5

Customizing Various Bootstrap 5 Elements

In this chapter, we will learn how to customize the visual style of all the Bootstrap elements that use the Bootstrap 5 variables for styling. We will learn about changes to the layout and content that affects the whole design of your website as well as changes to specific elements that don't have any global effect.

It's useful to know both how to change the general layout and content of your website and how to customize specific elements when you want to change the details of your user interface.

In this chapter, we're going to cover the following topics:

- Customizing the layout
- Customizing content
- Customizing forms
- Customizing components
- Customizing helpers
- Customizing utilities

Technical requirements

- To preview the examples, you will need a code editor and a browser.
- You will need a Sass compiler to compile the Sass files to CSS. Please see *Chapter 2, Using and Compiling Sass*, for different ways to do this.

You can find the code files of the chapter on GitHub at `https://github.com/PacktPublishing/The-Missing-Bootstrap-5-Guide`

Customizing the layout

Here, we will learn how to customize the breakpoints, containers, and grid system to create exactly the responsiveness and general layout that you want for all your content.

Breakpoints

The breakpoints define the minimum widths for when the layout will change and adapt to different screen sizes. These minimum widths are used in media queries.

The line numbers, variable name, and default values for the breakpoints are as follows:

bootstrap/scss/_variables.scss

```
431 $grid-breakpoints: (
432   xs: 0,
433   sm: 576px,
434   md: 768px,
435   lg: 992px,
436   xl: 1200px,
437   xxl: 1400px
438 ) !default;
```

We will now change the minimum widths for all screen sizes using the following Sass code:

part-1/chapter-5/layout/breakpoints/scss/style.scss

```
// Specify the breakpoint sizes
$grid-breakpoints: (
  xs: 0,
  sm: 300px,
  md: 600px,
  lg: 900px,
  xl: 1200px,
  xxl: 1500px
);


@import "..//..//..//../bootstrap/scss/bootstrap.scss";
```

We can now create a simple grid with the following HTML:

part-1/chapter-5/layout/breakpoints/index.html

```
<div class="row">
  <div class="col-12 col-sm-10 col-md-8 col-lg-6 col-xl-4
    col-xxl-2">
  <div class="bg-secondary text-white p-3">Column</div>
  </div>
</div>
```

To see the effect of the changed breakpoints, you should open the example in a browser and resize the window.

Containers

It's possible to define the maximum widths of containers (`.container`) for different screen sizes in the same way as we saw it with breakpoint sizes. These maximum widths are also used in media queries.

The line numbers, variable name, and default values for the maximum widths of containers are as follows:

bootstrap/scss/_variables.scss

```
450 $container-max-widths: (
451   sm: 540px,
452   md: 720px,
453   lg: 960px,
454   xl: 1140px,
455   xxl: 1320px,
456 ) !default;
```

Notice that there's no maximum width for the extra small breakpoint (`xs`).

We will now change the maximum widths of containers for all screen sizes using the following Sass code:

part-1/chapter-5/layout/containers/scss/style.scss

```scss
// Specify the container maximum widths
$container-max-widths: (
  sm: 300px,
  md: 500px,
  lg: 700px,
  xl: 900px,
  xxl: 1100px
);


@import "../../../../../bootstrap/scss/bootstrap.scss";
```

We can now create a simple container with the following HTML:

part-1/chapter-5/layout/containers/index.html

```html
<div class="container">
  <div class="bg-secondary text-white p-3">Content</div>
</div>
```

To see the effect of the changed maximum widths of containers, you should open the example in a browser and resize the window.

Grids

The default number of columns in a grid is 12 and the default gutter width is 1.5rem. This can be changed if you want another number of columns in your grid or another gutter width.

The line numbers, variable name, and default values for the maximum widths of containers are as follows:

bootstrap/scss/_variables.scss

```scss
466 $grid-columns: 12 !default;
467 $grid-gutter-width: 1.5rem !default;
468 $grid-row-columns: 6 !default;
```

We will now change the number of columns in a grid and the default gutter width using the following Sass code:

part-1/chapter-5/layout/grids/scss/style.scss

```scss
// Specify the number of grid columns and the gutter width
$grid-columns: 16;
$grid-gutter-width: 1rem;


@import "..//..//..//../bootstrap/scss/bootstrap.scss";
```

We can now create a simple grid system with the following HTML:

index.html

```html
<div class="row">
  <div class="col-16 col-md-8 col-lg-4">
    <div class="bg-secondary text-white p-3">Content</div>
  </div>
  <div class="col-16 col-md-8 col-lg-4">
    <div class="bg-secondary text-white p-3">Content</div>
  </div>
  <div class="col-8 col-lg-4">
    <div class="bg-secondary text-white p-3">Content</div>
  </div>
  <div class="col-8 col-lg-4">
    <div class="bg-secondary text-white p-3">Content</div>
  </div>
</div>
```

To see the effect of the changed number of columns and gutter width for grids, you should open the example in a browser.

We will now move on to learn how to customize the various content of our website.

Customizing content

The styling of content (typography, images, tables, and figures) can be customized using variables found in the `_variables.scss` file, on lines 543–651 and lines 1500–1513.

We will now see how we can customize different kinds of content.

Typography

There are a lot of variables used to define the overall typography of Bootstrap 5. In fact, there are more than 50 different variables. The variable names are self-explanatory in most cases, so let's take a deep dive and see the full list. The line number, variable name, and default value for all of these elements of typography are as follows:

bootstrap/scss/_variables.scss

```
543 $font-family-sans-serif: system-ui, -apple-system,
    "Segoe UI", Roboto, "Helvetica Neue", Arial,
    "Noto Sans", "Liberation Sans", sans-serif,
    "Apple Color Emoji", "Segoe UI Emoji",
    "Segoe UI Symbol", "Noto Color Emoji" !default;
544 $font-family-monospace: SFMono-Regular, Menlo, Monaco,
    Consolas, "Liberation Mono", "Courier New", monospace
    !default;
545
546 $font-family-base: var(--#{$variable-prefix}
    font-sans-serif) !default;
547 $font-family-code: var(--#{$variable-prefix}
    font-monospace) !default;
548
549
550
551 $font-size-root: null !default;
552 $font-size-base: 1rem !default;
553 $font-size-sm: $font-size-base * .875 !default;
554 $font-size-lg: $font-size-base * 1.25 !default;
555
556 $font-weight-lighter: lighter !default;
557 $font-weight-light: 300 !default;
```

```
558 $font-weight-normal: 400 !default;
559 $font-weight-semibold: 600 !default;
560 $font-weight-bold: 700 !default;
561 $font-weight-bolder: bolder !default;
562
563 $font-weight-base: $font-weight-normal !default;
564
565 $line-height-base: 1.5 !default;
566 $line-height-sm: 1.25 !default;
567 $line-height-lg: 2 !default;
568
569 $h1-font-size: $font-size-base * 2.5 !default;
570 $h2-font-size: $font-size-base * 2 !default;
571 $h3-font-size: $font-size-base * 1.75 !default;
572 $h4-font-size: $font-size-base * 1.5 !default;
573 $h5-font-size: $font-size-base * 1.25 !default;
574 $h6-font-size: $font-size-base !default;
575
576
577
578 $font-sizes: (
579   1: $h1-font-size,
580   2: $h2-font-size,
581   3: $h3-font-size,
582   4: $h4-font-size,
583   5: $h5-font-size,
584   6: $h6-font-size
585 ) !default;
586
587
588
589 $headings-margin-bottom:     $spacer * .5 !default;
590 $headings-font-family:       null !default;
591 $headings-font-style:        null !default;
592 $headings-font-weight:       500 !default;
593 $headings-line-height:       1.2 !default;
```

```
594 $headings-color:              null !default;
595
596
597
598 $display-font-sizes: (
599   1: 5rem,
600   2: 4.5rem,
601   3: 4rem,
602   4: 3.5rem,
603   5: 3rem,
604   6: 2.5rem
605 ) !default;
606
607 $display-font-family: null !default;
608 $display-font-style:  null !default;
609 $display-font-weight: 300 !default;
610 $display-line-height: $headings-line-height !default;
611
612
613
614 $lead-font-size: $font-size-base * 1.25 !default;
615 $lead-font-weight: 300 !default;
616
617 $small-font-size: .875em !default;
618
619 $sub-sup-font-size: .75em !default;
620
621 $text-muted: $gray-600 !default;
622
623 $initialism-font-size: $small-font-size !default;
624
625 $blockquote-margin-y: $spacer !default;
626 $blockquote-font-size: $font-size-base * 1.25 !default;
627 $blockquote-footer-color: $gray-600 !default;
628 $blockquote-footer-font-size: $small-font-size !default;
629
```

```
630 $hr-margin-y: $spacer !default;
631 $hr-color: inherit !default;
632
633
634 $hr-bg-color: null !default;
635 $hr-height: $border-width !default;
636
637
638 $hr-border-color: null !default;
639 $hr-border-width: $border-width !default;
640 $hr-opacity: .25 !default;
641
642 $legend-margin-bottom: .5rem !default;
643 $legend-font-size: 1.5rem !default;
644 $legend-font-weight: null !default;
645
646 $dt-font-weight: $font-weight-bold !default;
647
648 $list-inline-padding: .5rem !default;
649
650 $mark-padding: .2em !default;
651 $mark-bg: $yellow-100 !default;
```

We will now see an example of how we can change some global styles for text color, background color, font family, font size, line height, and links, as well as more specific styles for regular headings, display headings, and lead paragraphs.

Here's the HTML with these typographic elements:

part-1/chapter-5/content/typography/index.html

```
<h2 class="text-muted my-3">Headings</h2>
<h1>&lt;h1&gt; heading</h1>
<h2>&lt;h2&gt; heading</h2>
<h3>&lt;h3&gt; heading</h3>
<h4>&lt;h4&gt; heading</h4>
<h5>&lt;h5&gt; heading</h5>
<h6>&lt;h6&gt; heading</h6>
```

```html
<h2 class="text-muted my-3">Display headings</h2>
<h1 class="display-1">Display heading 1</h1>
<h1 class="display-2">Display heading 2</h1>
<h1 class="display-3">Display heading 3</h1>
<h1 class="display-4">Display heading 4</h1>
<h1 class="display-5">Display heading 5</h1>
<h1 class="display-6">Display heading 6</h1>

<h2 class="text-muted my-3">Lead paragraph</h2>
<p class="lead">Lorem ipsum dolor sit amet,
    consectetur adipiscing elit. In laoreet pellentesque
    lorem sed elementum. Suspendisse maximus convallis ex.
    <a href="#">Etiam eleifend velit leo</a>.
</p>

<h2 class="text-muted my-3">Paragraph</h2>
<p>Lorem ipsum dolor sit amet, consectetur adipiscing elit.
    In laoreet pellentesque lorem sed elementum. Suspendisse
    maximus convallis ex. <a href="#">Etiam eleifend velit
    leo</a>.
</p>
```

And this is what it looks like when using the default Bootstrap 5 styles:

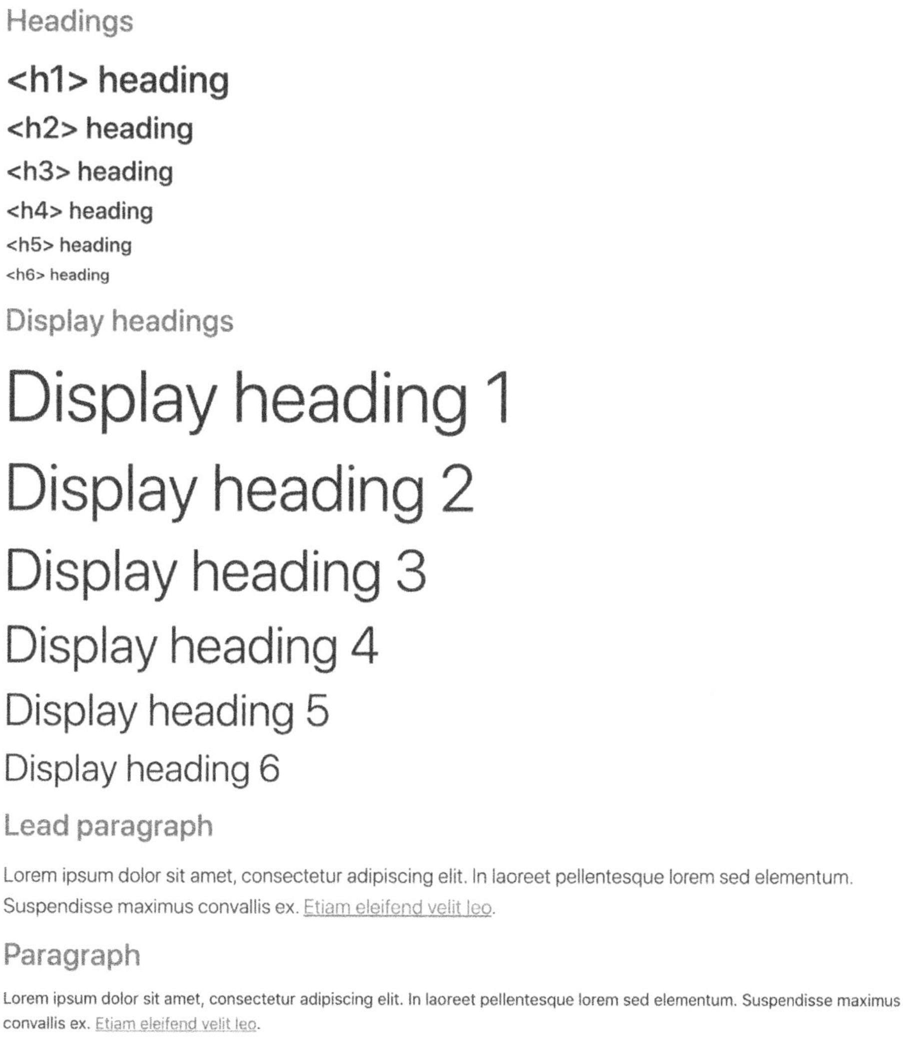

Headings

\<h1\> heading
\<h2\> heading
\<h3\> heading
\<h4\> heading
\<h5\> heading
\<h6\> heading

Display headings

Display heading 1
Display heading 2
Display heading 3
Display heading 4
Display heading 5
Display heading 6

Lead paragraph

Lorem ipsum dolor sit amet, consectetur adipiscing elit. In laoreet pellentesque lorem sed elementum. Suspendisse maximus convallis ex. Etiam eleifend velit leo.

Paragraph

Lorem ipsum dolor sit amet, consectetur adipiscing elit. In laoreet pellentesque lorem sed elementum. Suspendisse maximus convallis ex. Etiam eleifend velit leo.

Figure 5.1 – Typographic elements with default Bootstrap 5 styles

To change the global style for text color and background color, we will use two additional variables. The line number, variable name, and default value for these elements of typography are as follows:

bootstrap/scss/_variables.scss

```
401 $body-bg:              $white !default;
402 $body-color:           $gray-900 !default;
```

And to change the font family from a system font to a custom one, we will be using Google Fonts. We will use the **Roboto** font and import it into our HTML file with just two lines of code. This code should be placed in the <head> tag just after our <link> tag for our Bootstrap 5 CSS file:

part-1/chapter-5/content/typography/index.html

```html
<link rel="preconnect" href="https://fonts.gstatic.com">
<link href="https://fonts.googleapis.com/
css2?family=Roboto:wght@300;400;700&display=swap"
rel="stylesheet">
```

After updating our HTML file, we will now need to define several different variables for typography using the following Sass code:

part-1/chapter-5/content/typography/scss/style.scss

```scss
// Required
@import "../../../../../bootstrap/scss/functions";
@import "../../../../../bootstrap/scss/variables";

// Body styles
$body-bg: $gray-100;
$body-color: $gray-700;

// Basic typography styles
$font-family-base: 'Roboto', sans-serif;
$font-size-base: 1.5rem;
$line-height-base: 1.3;
$line-height-sm: 1;

// Link styles
$link-color: $info;
$link-decoration: none;
$link-hover-color: shift-color($link-color,
                              $link-shade-percentage);
$link-hover-decoration: underline;

// Heading styles
```

```scss
$h1-font-size: $font-size-base * 3.5;
$h2-font-size: $font-size-base * 3;
$h3-font-size: $font-size-base * 2.5;
$h4-font-size: $font-size-base * 2;
$h5-font-size: $font-size-base * 1.5;
$h6-font-size: $font-size-base;
$headings-font-weight: $font-weight-bold;
$headings-line-height: $line-height-sm;
$headings-margin-bottom: $spacer;

// Display styles
$display-font-sizes: (
  1: $h1-font-size * 1.5,
  2: $h2-font-size * 1.5,
  3: $h3-font-size * 1.5,
  4: $h4-font-size * 1.5,
  5: $h5-font-size * 1.5,
  6: $h6-font-size * 1.5
);
$display-font-weight: $font-weight-light;
$display-line-height: $headings-line-height;

// Lead styles
$lead-font-size: $font-size-base * 1.25;
$lead-font-weight: $font-weight-light;

// Required
@import "../../../../../bootstrap/scss/maps";
@import "../../../../../bootstrap/scss/mixins";
@import "../../../../../bootstrap/scss/root";

// Optional Bootstrap CSS
@import "../../../../../bootstrap/scss/reboot";
@import "../../../../../bootstrap/scss/type";
@import "../../../../../bootstrap/scss/images";
// The long list of imports have been reduced here.
```

```
// Helpers
@import "../../../../../bootstrap/scss/helpers";

// Utilities
@import "../../../../../bootstrap/scss/utilities";

// Utilities API
@import "../../../../../bootstrap/scss/utilities/api";
```

After compiling the Sass code, the typographic elements will now look like this:

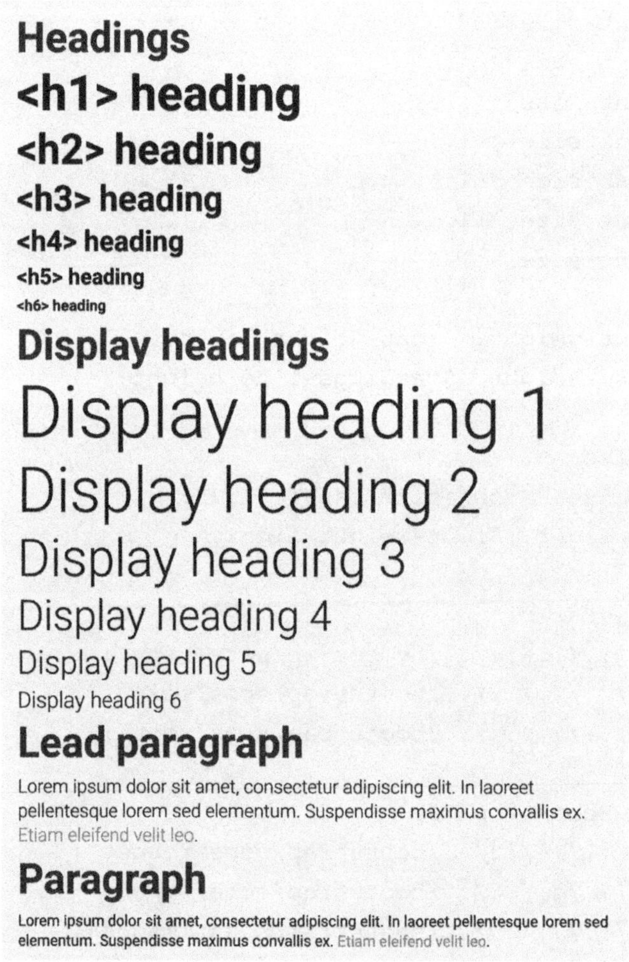

Figure 5.2 – Typographic elements after applying the customizations

Images

You can't customize the look or behavior of images on their own. But you can customize the look of image thumbnails, which will add some styling around an image, but not change the image itself. Here's what a default image thumbnail looks like:

Figure 5.3 – Default image thumbnail

We will now change the padding, background color, border color, and border radius. The line number, variable name, and default value for these properties of an image thumbnail are as follows:

bootstrap/scss/_variables.scss

```
1500: $thumbnail-padding: .25rem;
1501: $thumbnail-bg: $body-bg;
1503: $thumbnail-border-color: $gray-300;
1504: $thumbnail-border-radius: $border-radius;
```

We will change these variables using the following Sass code:

part-1/chapter-5/content/images/scss/style.scss

```
// Required
@import "../../../../../bootstrap/scss/functions";
@import "../../../../../bootstrap/scss/variables";

// Specify variables
$thumbnail-padding: .5rem;
$thumbnail-bg: $gray-200;
$thumbnail-border-color: $gray-500;
$thumbnail-border-radius: 0;
```

```scss
// Required
@import "../../../../../bootstrap/scss/maps";
@import "../../../../../bootstrap/scss/mixins";
@import "../../../../../bootstrap/scss/root";

// Optional Bootstrap CSS
@import "../../../../../bootstrap/scss/reboot";
@import "../../../../../bootstrap/scss/type";
@import "../../../../../bootstrap/scss/images";
// The long list of imports have been reduced here.

// Helpers
@import "../../../../../bootstrap/scss/helpers";

// Utilities
@import "../../../../../bootstrap/scss/utilities";

// Utilities API
@import "../../../../../bootstrap/scss/utilities/api";
```

We can now create a simple image thumbnail with the following HTML:

part-1/chapter-5/content/images/index.html

```html
<img src="img/100x100.png" alt="Image thumbnail"
  class="img-thumbnail">
```

After compiling the Sass code, the image thumbnail will now look like this:

Figure 5.4 – Image thumbnail with padding, background color, border color, and border radius changed

Figures

Here's what a default figure looks like:

Caption for the figure.

Figure 5.5 – Default figure

We will now change the font size and color of the figure caption. The line number, variable name, and default value for these properties of a figure are as follows:

---

bootstrap/scss/_variables.scss

```
1512 $figure-caption-font-size: $small-font-size;
1513 $figure-caption-color: $gray-600;
```

We will change these variables using the following Sass code:

---

part-1/chapter-5/content/figures/scss/style.scss

```
// Required
@import "../../../../../bootstrap/scss/functions";
@import "../../../../../bootstrap/scss/variables";
```

```scss
// Specify variables
$figure-caption-font-size: $font-size-lg;
$figure-caption-color: $body-color;

// Required
@import "../../../../../bootstrap/scss/maps";
@import "../../../../../bootstrap/scss/mixins";
@import "../../../../../bootstrap/scss/root";

// Optional Bootstrap CSS
@import "../../../../../bootstrap/scss/reboot";
@import "../../../../../bootstrap/scss/type";
@import "../../../../../bootstrap/scss/images";
// The long list of imports have been reduced here.

// Helpers
@import "../../../../../bootstrap/scss/helpers";

// Utilities
@import "../../../../../bootstrap/scss/utilities";

// Utilities API
@import "../../../../../bootstrap/scss/utilities/api";
```

We can now create a simple figure with the following HTML:

part-1/chapter-5/content/figures/index.html

```html
<figure class="figure">
  <img src="img/600x400.png" class="figure-img img-fluid"
    alt="Figure image">
  <figcaption class="figure-caption">
    Caption for the figure.</figcaption>
</figure>
```

After compiling the Sass code, a figure will now look like this:

Caption for the figure.

Figure 5.6 – Figure with font size and color for the figure caption changed

Now that we have learned how to customize the various kinds of content, we will now move on to learn about how to customize forms.

Customizing forms

Form elements can be customized using the form variables found in the _variables.scss file on lines 796–1034 and lines 1313–1318. With these variables, you can change things such as form text, form labels, regular inputs, checkboxes and radio buttons, switches, input groups, select elements, range inputs, file inputs, floating labels, and form validation.

As an example, we will customize a range input.

Range

First, let's see what a default range input looks like:

Figure 5.7 – Default range input

We will now change the track height, thumb width, and thumb border radius for the range input. The line number, variable name, and default value for these three properties of the range input are as follows:

bootstrap/scss/_variables.scss

```
972 $form-range-track-height: .5rem;
978 $form-range-thumb-width: 1rem;
982 $form-range-thumb-border-radius: 1rem;
```

We will make the range input *twice as big* by doubling these values. To do this, use the following Sass code:

part-1/chapter-5/forms/range/scss/style.scss

```
// Specify variables
$form-range-track-height: 1rem;
$form-range-thumb-width: 2rem;
$form-range-thumb-border-radius: 2rem;
@import "bootstrap/scss/bootstrap";
```

We can now create a simple range input with the following HTML:

part-1/chapter-5/forms/range/index.html

```
<input type="range" class="form-range">
```

After compiling the Sass code, the range input will now look like this:

Figure 5.8 – Range input with track height, thumb width, and thumb border radius changed

Now that we have seen an example of how to customize a form element, we will continue with how to customize components.

Customizing components

The various components of Bootstrap 5 can be customized using variables found in the _variables. scss file. The variables for each component are grouped together, but the groups are not in alphabetical order. I suggest that you simply search for the component name to find the group of related variables or refer to this list:

- Accordions: lines 1258 – 1288

- Alerts: lines 1439 – 1448

- Badges: lines 1379 – 1384

- Breadcrumbs: lines 1520 – 1530

- Buttons and button groups: lines 747 – 789

- Cards: lines 1236 – 1252

- Carousels: lines 1536 – 1566

- Close buttons: lines 1588 – 1599

- Collapse: no variables or CSS code for this component, only JavaScript

- Dropdowns: lines 1132 – 1179

- List groups: lines 1470 – 1493

- Modals: lines 1391 – 1430

- Navs and tabs: lines 1059 – 1078

- Navbars: lines 1085 – 1123

- Offcanvas: lines 1606 – 1618

- Pagination: lines 1186 – 1222

- Placeholders: lines 1229 – 1230

- Popovers: lines 1325 – 1351

- Progress: lines 1455 – 1463

- Scrollspy: no variables or CSS code for this component, only JavaScript

- Spinners: lines 1573 – 1581

- Toasts: lines 1358 – 1372

- Tooltips: lines 1294 – 1307

We will now see how we can customize some of these components.

Breadcrumbs

Here's what a default breadcrumb component looks like:

Home / Sports / Ball games / Baseball

Figure 5.9 – Default breadcrumb component

This component is composed with the help of 11 different variables. The line numbers, variable names, and default values for these are as follows:

bootstrap/scss/_variables.scss

```
1520 $breadcrumb-font-size: null !default;
1521 $breadcrumb-padding-y: 0 !default;
1522 $breadcrumb-padding-x: 0 !default;
1523 $breadcrumb-item-padding-x: .5rem !default;
1524 $breadcrumb-margin-bottom: 1rem !default;
1525 $breadcrumb-bg: null !default;
1526 $breadcrumb-divider-color: $gray-600 !default;
1527 $breadcrumb-active-color: $gray-600 !default;
1528 $breadcrumb-divider: quote("/") !default;
1529 $breadcrumb-divider-flipped:
        $breadcrumb-divider !default;
1530 $breadcrumb-border-radius: null !default;
```

We will now change the symbol used for the breadcrumb divider from a slash symbol (/) to a greater-than symbol (>). We will change the breadcrumb divider symbol by using the following Sass code:

part-1/chapter-5/components/breadcrumbs/scss/style.scss

```
// Specify variables
$breadcrumb-divider: quote(">");
@import "../../../../bootstrap/scss/bootstrap.scss";
```

We can now create a breadcrumb component with the following HTML:

part-1/chapter-5/components/breadcrumbs/index.html

```
<nav aria-label="Breadcrumb">
  <ol class="breadcrumb">
```

```
    <li class="breadcrumb-item"><a href="#">Home</a></li>
    <li class="breadcrumb-item"><a href="#">Sports</a></li>
    <li class="breadcrumb-item"><a href="#">Ball games</a>
    </li>
    <li class="breadcrumb-item active"
      aria-current="page">Baseball</li>
  </ol>
</nav>
```

After compiling the Sass code, the breadcrumb component will now look like this:

Home > Sports > Ball games > Baseball

Figure 5.10 – Breadcrumb component with the divider symbol changed

Cards

Here's what a grid of card components looks like:

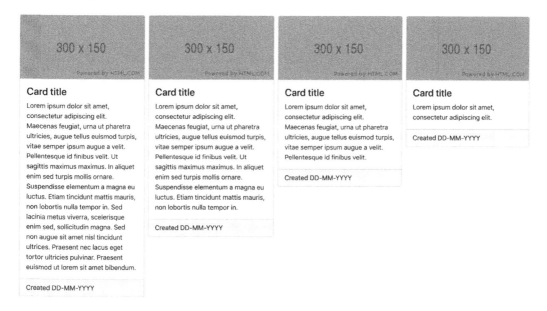

Figure 5.11 – Default grid of card components

The card component is composed with the help of 17 different variables. The line numbers, variable names, and default values for these are as follows:

bootstrap/scss/_variables.scss

```
1236 $card-spacer-y: $spacer !default;
1237 $card-spacer-x: $spacer !default;
1238 $card-title-spacer-y: $spacer * .5 !default;
1239 $card-border-width: $border-width !default;
1240 $card-border-color: rgba($black, .125) !default;
1241 $card-border-radius: $border-radius !default;
1242 $card-box-shadow: null !default;
1243 $card-inner-border-radius: subtract(
        $card-border-radius, $card-border-width) !default;
1244 $card-cap-padding-y: $card-spacer-y * .5 !default;
1245 $card-cap-padding-x: $card-spacer-x !default;
1246 $card-cap-bg: rgba($black, .03) !default;
1247 $card-cap-color: null !default;
1248 $card-height: null !default;
1249 $card-color: null !default;
1250 $card-bg: $white !default;
1251 $card-img-overlay-padding: $spacer !default;
1252 $card-group-margin: $grid-gutter-width * .5 !default;
```

As a default, a card will have its height based on the content inside of it. We can change the card height so the cards in a grid will have equal height by default by using the following Sass code:

part-1/chapter-5/components/cards/scss/style.scss

```
$card-height: 100%;
@import "../../../../../bootstrap/scss/bootstrap.scss";
```

We can now create a grid of card components with the following HTML:

part-1/chapter-5/components/cards/index.html

```
<div class="row row-cols-1 row-cols-md-2 row-cols-xl-3
  row-cols-xxl-4 g-4 mb-4">
  <div class="col">
    <div class="card">
      <img class="card-img-top" src="img/300x150.png"
        alt="Card image">
      <div class="card-body">
        <h4 class="card-title">Card title</h4>
        <p class="card-text">Lorem ipsum dolor sit amet,
          consectetur adipiscing elit. Maecenas feugiat,
          urna ut pharetra ultricies, augue tellus euismod
          turpis, vitae semper ipsum augue a velit.
          Pellentesque id finibus velit. Ut sagittis
          maximus maximus. In aliquet enim sed turpis
          mollis ornare. Suspendisse elementum a magna eu
          luctus. Etiam tincidunt mattis mauris, non
          lobortis nulla tempor in. Sed lacinia metus
          viverra, scelerisque enim sed, sollicitudin
          magna. Sed non augue sit amet nisl tincidunt
          ultrices. Praesent nec lacus eget tortor
          ultricies pulvinar. Praesent euismod ut lorem sit
          amet bibendum.</p>
      </div>
      <div class="card-footer">Created DD-MM-YYYY</div>
    </div>
  </div>
  <!-- Three more card components with different text
    content placed here -->
</div>
```

After compiling the Sass code, a grid of card components will now look like this:

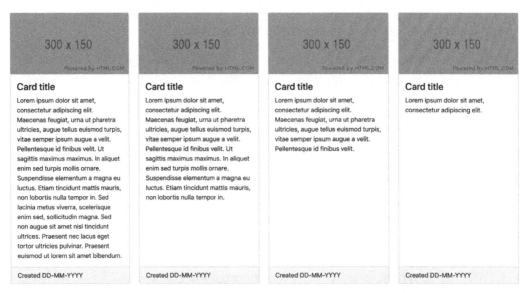

Figure 5.12 – A grid of card components with the card height changed

We have now seen how we can customize components, and next up is a section on how to customize helpers.

Customizing helpers

The only helper that can be customized through the use of variables found in the _variables. scss file is the ratio helper. It has a Sass map with default values that can be modified as you like. Some of the other helpers use theme colors, variables from other elements, or only have non-visual aspects to customize. That's why we're focusing on the ratio helper here.

In this example, we will add more aspect ratios to the map mentioned before, which will then be available to us as additional helper classes. The line numbers, variable name, and default values for the aspect ratios map are as follows:

bootstrap/scss/_variables.scss

```
528 $aspect-ratios: (
529   "1x1": 100%,
530   "4x3": calc(3 / 4 * 100%),
531   "16x9": calc(9 / 16 * 100%),
```

```
532   "21x9": calc(9 / 21 * 100%)
533 ) !default;
```

We will now first create our own Sass ratio map with these new values and then merge it with the existing $aspect-ratios map. You will learn more about working with Sass maps in the next chapter.

To make these changes, we will need to write the following Sass code:

part-1/chapter-5/helpers/ratio/scss/style.scss

```scss
// Required
@import "../../../../../bootstrap/scss/functions";
@import "../../../../../bootstrap/scss/variables";

// Create your own ratio map
$custom-ratios: (
  "1x2": calc(1 / 2 * 100%),
  "2x3": calc(2 / 3 * 100%),
  "3x4": calc(3 / 4 * 100%),
  "4x5": calc(4 / 5 * 100%)
);

// Merge with "$aspect-ratios" map
$aspect-ratios: map-merge($aspect-ratios, $custom-ratios);

// Required
@import "../../../../../bootstrap/scss/maps";
@import "../../../../../bootstrap/scss/mixins";
@import "../../../../../bootstrap/scss/root";

// Optional Bootstrap CSS
@import "../../../../../bootstrap/scss/reboot";
@import "../../../../../bootstrap/scss/type";
@import "../../../../../bootstrap/scss/images";
// The long list of imports have been reduced here.

// Helpers
@import "../../../../../bootstrap/scss/helpers";
```

```scss
// Utilities
@import "../../../../../bootstrap/scss/utilities";

// Utilities API
@import "../../../../../bootstrap/scss/utilities/api";
```

We can now create a simple example with four `<div>` elements with these new different aspect ratios using the following HTML:

---

part-1/chapter-5/helpers/ratio/index.html

```html
<div class="d-flex align-items-start">
  <div class="ratio ratio-1x1">
    <p class="d-flex justify-content-center
      align-items-center border">1x1</p>
  </div>
  <div class="ratio ratio-4x3">
    <p class="d-flex justify-content-center
      align-items-center border">4x3</p>
  </div>
  <div class="ratio ratio-16x9">
    <p class="d-flex justify-content-center
      align-items-center border">16x9</p>
  </div>
  <div class="ratio ratio-21x9">
    <p class="d-flex justify-content-center
      align-items-center border">21x9</p>
  </div>
</div>
```

After compiling the Sass code, we now have the aspect ratios 1x2, 2x3, 3x4, and 4x5 available to use as specific helper classes. These new aspect ratios look like this:

Figure 5.13 – New aspect ratio values for the ratio helper class

We have now seen how we can customize the ratio helper, and in this final section of the chapter, we will see how we can customize utilities.

Customizing utilities

All of the utilities are generated using the utility API and most are declared in the _utilities. scss file, except for the background, borders, colors, position, shadows, and spacing utilities, which have variables and maps defined in the _variables.scss file. We have already learned how to customize text colors and background colors in the previous chapter, and you can learn about the utility API in the next chapter.

Now, we will take a look at some of those utilities that are generated using values from the _variables. scss file.

Borders

The border utilities are generated from variables found in the _variables.scss file on lines 480-500. We will see how we can change the values used to generate the utilities for border width.

The values for border widths are stored in a Sass map, and the line numbers, variable name, and default values are as follows:

bootstrap/scss/_variables.scss

```
481 $border-widths: (
482    1: 1px,
483    2: 2px,
484    3: 3px,
485    4: 4px,
486    5: 5px
487 ) !default;
```

The default border width utilities look like this:

Figure 5.14 – The default sizes for the border width utilities

We will now double the size of the five border width utilities. To change the values for the border width utilities, we will specify the $border-widths Sass map ourselves and thus overwrite the default $border-widths Sass map and its values. To achieve this, we need to write the following Sass code:

part-1/chapter-5/utilities/borders/scss/style.scss

```scss
// Required
@import "..//..//..//../bootstrap/scss/functions";
@import "..//..//..//../bootstrap/scss/variables";

// Specify widths for border utility
$border-widths: (
  1: 2px,
  2: 4px,
  3: 6px,
  4: 8px,
  5: 10px
);
```

```scss
// Required
@import "../../../../../bootstrap/scss/maps";
@import "../../../../../bootstrap/scss/mixins";
@import "../../../../../bootstrap/scss/root";

// Optional Bootstrap CSS
@import "../../../../../bootstrap/scss/reboot";
@import "../../../../../bootstrap/scss/type";
@import "../../../../../bootstrap/scss/images";
// The long list of imports have been reduced here.

// Helpers
@import "../../../../../bootstrap/scss/helpers";

// Utilities
@import "../../../../../bootstrap/scss/utilities";

// Utilities API
@import "../../../../../bootstrap/scss/utilities/api";
```

We can now create a simple example with five `<div>` elements with these new thicker border widths using the following HTML:

---

part-1/chapter-5/utilities/borders/index.html

```html
<div class="border border-1 mb-2">.border-1</div>
<div class="border border-2 mb-2">.border-2</div>
<div class="border border-3 mb-2">.border-3</div>
<div class="border border-4 mb-2">.border-4</div>
<div class="border border-5">.border-5</div>
```

After compiling the Sass code, we now have the new border widths available to use as specific border width utility classes. The new border width utilities look like this:

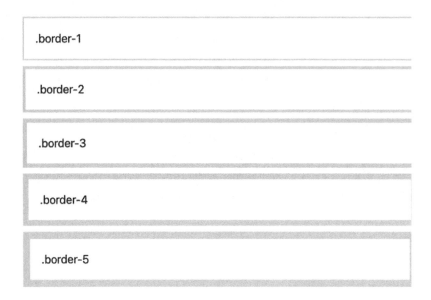

.border-1

.border-2

.border-3

.border-4

.border-5

Figure 5.15 – The new sizes for the border width utilities

Spacing

The spacing utilities are generated from a single variable found in the _variables.scss file. The variable is storing a Sass map, and the values of that map are based on the global $spacer variable. We will see how we can change the values in that Sass map, while still using the $spacer variable.

The line numbers, variable name, and default values are as follows:

bootstrap/scss/_variables.scss

```
375 $spacers: (
376   0: 0,
377   1: $spacer * .25,
378   2: $spacer * .5,
379   3: $spacer,
380   4: $spacer * 1.5,
381   5: $spacer * 3,
382 ) !default;
```

The default spacing utilities for padding look like this:

Figure 5.16 – The default spacing utilities for padding

We will now change the default spacing values and add two more. The new ones will get a letter as their class name suffix instead of a number: q for a *quarter* of the $spacer value and h for *half* of the $spacer value. To achieve this, we will specify the $spacers Sass map ourselves and thus overwrite the default $spacers Sass map and its values. We need to write the following Sass code:

part-1/chapter-5/utilities/spacing/scss/style.scss

```scss
// Required
@import "../../../../../bootstrap/scss/functions";
@import "../../../../../bootstrap/scss/variables";

// Specify spacer sizes
$spacers: (
  0: 0,
  q: $spacer / 4,
  h: $spacer / 2,
  1: $spacer,
  2: $spacer * 2,
  3: $spacer * 3,
  4: $spacer * 4,
```

```
   5: $spacer * 5
);


// Required
@import "../../../../../bootstrap/scss/maps";
@import "../../../../../bootstrap/scss/mixins";
@import "../../../../../bootstrap/scss/root";


// Optional Bootstrap CSS
@import "../../../../../bootstrap/scss/reboot";
@import "../../../../../bootstrap/scss/type";
@import "../../../../../bootstrap/scss/images";
// The long list of imports have been reduced here.


// Helpers
@import "../../../../../bootstrap/scss/helpers";


// Utilities
@import "../../../../../bootstrap/scss/utilities";


// Utilities API
@import "../../../../../bootstrap/scss/utilities/api";
```

After compiling the Sass, we now have the new spacing utilities available to use as specific spacing utility classes. We can then create a simple example with eight `<div>` elements with various padding utilities representing these updated spacing values using the following HTML:

part-1/chapter-5/utilities/spacing/index.html

```
<div class="bg-secondary text-white p-0">p-0</div>
<div class="bg-secondary text-white p-q">p-q - "quarter"
  (1/4) of p-1</div>
<div class="bg-secondary text-white p-h">p-h - "half" (1/2)
  of p-1</div>
<div class="bg-secondary text-white p-1">p-1</div>
<div class="bg-secondary text-white p-2">p-2</div>
<div class="bg-secondary text-white p-3">p-3</div>
```

```
<div class="bg-secondary text-white p-4">p-4</div>
<div class="bg-secondary text-white p-5">p-5</div>
```

The new spacing utilities for padding look like this:

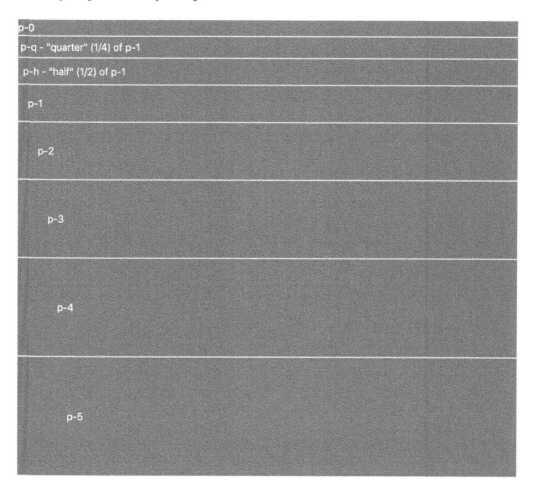

Figure 5.17 – The changed spacing utilities for padding

Summary

In this chapter, we have learned how to customize the various elements of Bootstrap 5, including the layout, content, forms, components, helpers, and utilities. In the next chapter, we will learn all about the utility API.

6

Understanding and Using the Bootstrap 5 Utility API

In this chapter, we will learn how to use the **utility API** to generate and add new simple and complex utilities as well as overwrite, modify, and remove existing utilities.

It's useful to know how to use the utility API when you need to make small adjustments to your components or general layout, for example, to control the spacing or sizing of elements, add contextual color, change the border, or create a layout based on **flexbox**.

In this chapter, we're going to cover the following topics:

- About the utility API
- Understanding the utility API syntax
- Using the utility API

For the two last sections, there will be plenty of code examples to help understand the powerful utility API.

Technical requirements

- To preview the examples, you will need a code editor and a browser. The source code for all code examples can be found here: `https://github.com/PacktPublishing/The-Missing-Bootstrap-5-Guide`.

- You will need a Sass compiler to compile the Sass files to CSS. Please see *Chapter 2, Using and Compiling Sass*, for different ways to do this.

About the utility API

Bootstrap 5 features a so-called utility API, which is used to generate the different utility classes and/
or CSS custom properties (also referred to as CSS variables). It works in the following way:

- The `_utilities.scss` file contains the `$utilities` variable, which is a Sass map containing various settings used by the utility API. It's actually multiple maps that are merged into one single map with nested maps using the `map-merge()` Sass function. There are 83 groups of utility classes, which are grouped by their name. Their settings and values differ in each of them, but some of them share some of the values (such as some of the flex utilities sharing the `flex` class prefix).

- The `$utilities` variable is used in the `utilities/_api.scss` file, which is imported after all the other Bootstrap 5 elements.

- In the `utilities/_api.scss` file, the `$utilities` variable is passed as an argument to a `generate-utility()` mixin, which is located in the `mixins/_utilities.scss` file.

- The `generate-utility()` mixin is the largest and most advanced of Bootstrap 5's various mixins found in the `mixin` subfolder. This is where the real magic happens when a Sass map with the required and optional values is passed to it.

We won't learn how the Sass code in the utility API works in detail, but instead, we will learn its syntax and see different examples of how we can use it to generate and add both simple and complex new utilities as well as overwrite, modify, and remove existing utilities.

Understanding the utility API syntax

Let's now take a look at the syntax of the utility API. First is an overview of the syntax with all the options: one line of comment above each line of code per option. In the comments, you can see the name and, in brackets, whether the option is required or optional, and in the line of code, you can see the name followed by the type of values accepted in square brackets as well as the default value (if any) in brackets:

```
$utilities: (
  // Name (required)
  "[String]": (
    // Property (required)
    property: [name],
    // Values (required)
    values: [space-separated list or map],
    // Class (optional)
```

```
      class: [name (null)],
      // CSS variable utilities (optional)
      css-var: [Boolean (false)],
      // CSS variable name (optional)
      css-variable-name: [name (null)],
      // Local CSS variables (optional)
      local-vars: [map (null)],
      // State (optional)
      state: [space-separated list (null)],
      // Responsive (optional)
      responsive: [Boolean (false)],
      // RFS (optional)
      rfs: [Boolean (false)],
      // Print (optional),
      print: [Boolean (false)],
      // RTL,
      rtl: [Boolean (true)]
    )
  );
```

We will go through each of these options and see what they do together with some examples.

About the code examples

For all code examples in this chapter, the Bootstrap 5 imports have been reduced to include just the necessary ones when working with the utility API. For the examples in this section related to the utility API syntax, the required imports in the top of the SCSS files are as follows:

style.scss

```
// Required
@import "..//..//..//../bootstrap/scss/functions";
@import "..//..//..//../bootstrap/scss/variables";
@import "..//..//..//../bootstrap/scss/maps";
@import "..//..//..//../bootstrap/scss/mixins";
```

For the other examples related to using the utility API, the required imports in the top of the SCSS files are as follows:

style.scss

```
// Required
@import "../../../../../bootstrap/scss/functions";
@import "../../../../../bootstrap/scss/variables";
@import "../../../../../bootstrap/scss/maps";
@import "../../../../../bootstrap/scss/mixins";
@import "../../../../../bootstrap/scss/root";
@import "../../../../../bootstrap/scss/reboot";
```

After the required imports, we import the default utilities, add our own custom code, and finally, import the utilities API. It looks something like this:

style.scss

```
// Utilities
@import "../../../../../bootstrap/scss/utilities";


// Custom code here


// Utilities API
@import "../../../../../bootstrap/scss/utilities/api";
```

Now that we have seen the structure of the SCSS files for this chapter, we can omit the code that's simply importing the Bootstrap 5 partials and focus on the custom code. The HTML examples have also been reduced to show only the necessary code. Remember, for each code example, there are file references to the full example with all the imports in place.

Name

This is the name of the utility, which should be a string in quotes. It's not used in the generated CSS, so it's more a way of organizing the code:

```
$utilities: (
  "Utility name": (
    // Options defined here
  )
);
```

CSS property

The CSS property should be written without any quotes and must be a valid CSS property. It can be one CSS property (most common) or a space-separated list of CSS properties. It's used for the CSS rule and is also the default class name if the `class` key is not defined.

One CSS property

Here's an example with one CSS property:

part-1/chapter-6/api-syntax/css-property-single/scss/style.scss

```scss
// Required imports
// Utilities

$utilities: (
  "Font weight": (
    property: font-weight,
    values: 300 400 700
  )
);


// Utilities API
```

This compiles to the following:

part-1/chapter-6/api-syntax/css-property-single/css/style.css

```css
.font-weight-300 { font-weight: 300 !important }
.font-weight-400 { font-weight: 400 !important }
.font-weight-700 { font-weight: 700 !important }
```

We can now see the effect of this utility by using it with the following HTML:

part-1/chapter-6/api-syntax/css-property-single/index.html

```html
<p class="font-weight-300">Lorem ipsum...</p>
<p class="font-weight-400">Lorem ipsum...</p>
<p class="font-weight-700">Lorem ipsum...</p>
```

To see this in action, open the HTML file in a browser.

Multiple CSS properties

Here's an example with multiple CSS properties:

part-1/chapter-6/api-syntax/css-property-multiple/scss/style.scss

```scss
// Required imports
// Utilities

$utilities: (
  "Spacing": (
    property: margin padding,
    values: $spacers,
    class: spacing
  )
);


// Utilities API
```

This compiles to the following:

part-1/chapter-6/api-syntax/css-property-multiple/css/style.css

```css
.spacing-0 {
  margin: 0 !important;
  padding: 0 !important
}
.spacing-1 {
  margin: .25rem !important;
  padding: .25rem !important
}
.spacing-2 {
  margin: .5rem !important;
  padding: .5rem !important
}
.spacing-3 {
  margin: 1rem !important;
  padding: 1rem !important
```

```
}
.spacing-4 {
  margin: 1.5rem !important;
  padding: 1.5rem !important
}
.spacing-5 {
  margin: 3rem !important;
  padding: 3rem !important
}
```

We can now see the effect of this utility by using it with the following HTML:

part-1/chapter-6/api-syntax/css-property-multiple/index.html

```
<div style="margin: 1rem; padding: 1rem;"
  class="spacing-0">.spacing-0</div>
<div class="spacing-1">.spacing-1</div>
<div class="spacing-2">.spacing-2</div>
<div class="spacing-3">.spacing-3</div>
<div class="spacing-4">.spacing-4</div>
<div class="spacing-5">.spacing-5</div>
```

To see this in action, open the HTML file in a browser.

Values

This specifies the values for the specified CSS property, which are used when generating the class names and CSS rules.

It can be a space-separated list of values to use both in the class name and CSS rule:

```
values: 300 400 700
```

Or, you can use a map if you don't want the class name to be the same as the value:

```
values: (
  light: 300,
  normal: 400,
  bold: 700
)
```

Let's use our first example with one CSS property again and change the values from a list to a map:

part-1/chapter-6/api-syntax/values/scss/style.scss

```scss
// Required imports
// Utilities

$utilities: (
  "Font weight": (
    property: font-weight,
    values: (
      light: 300,
      normal: 400,
      bold: 700
    )
  )
);


// Utilities API
```

This compiles to the following:

part-1/chapter-6/api-syntax/values/css/style.css

```css
.font-weight-light { font-weight: 300 !important }
.font-weight-normal { font-weight: 400 !important }
.font-weight-bold { font-weight: 700 !important }
```

It's also possible to refer to a Sass variable that stores the list or map:

```scss
values: $font-weights
```

We can now see the effect of this utility by using it with the following HTML:

part-1/chapter-6/api-syntax/values/index.html

```html
<p class="font-weight-light">Lorem ipsum...</p>
<p class="font-weight-normal">Lorem ipsum...</p>
<p class="font-weight-bold">Lorem ipsum...</p>
```

To see this in action, open the HTML file in a browser.

Class

This option is used to change the `class` prefix used in the compiled CSS. This is optional, and the prefix should be written without quotes. Consider our first example from before:

part-1/chapter-6/api-syntax/class/scss/style.scss

```scss
// Required imports
// Utilities

$utilities: (
  "Font weight": (
    property: font-weight,
    values: 300 400 700,
    class: fw
  )
);


// Utilities API
```

This compiles to the following:

part-1/chapter-6/api-syntax/class/css/style.css

```css
.fw-300 { font-weight: 300 !important; }
.fw-400 { font-weight: 400 !important; }
.fw-700 { font-weight: 700 !important; }
```

We can now see the effect of this utility by using it with the following HTML:

part-1/chapter-6/api-syntax/class/index.html

```html
<p class="fw-300">Lorem ipsum...</p>
<p class="fw-400">Lorem ipsum...</p>
<p class="fw-700">Lorem ipsum...p>
```

To see this in action, open the HTML file in a browser.

CSS variable utilities

This is a Boolean option that can be used to generate CSS variables for the selector instead of regular CSS rules.

Let's change our first example to generate CSS variables instead of regular CSS rules:

part-1/chapter-6/api-syntax/css-variable-utilities/scss/style.scss

```scss
// Required imports
// Utilities

$utilities: (
  "Font weight": (
    property: font-weight,
    values: 300 400 700,
    css-variable-name: fw,
    css-var: true
  )
);


// Utilities API
```

This compiles to the following:

part-1/chapter-6/api-syntax/css-variable-utilities/css/style.css

```css
.font-weight-300 { --bs-fw: 300 }
.font-weight-400 { --bs-fw: 400 }
.font-weight-700 { --bs-fw: 700 }
```

We can now see the effect of this utility by using it with the following HTML:

part-1/chapter-6/api-syntax/css-variable-utilities/index.html

```html
<p class="font-weight-300">Lorem ipsum...</p>
<p class="font-weight-400">Lorem ipsum...</p>
<p class="font-weight-700">Lorem ipsum...</p>
```

This HTML must be combined with the following CSS, which is located in the `<style>` tag of the HTML file in our example:

part-1/chapter-6/api-syntax/css-variable-utilities/index.html

```
p[class^="font-weight"] { font-weight: var(--bs-fw); }
```

The CSS selector targets all the paragraph elements on the page that have a class starting with `font-weight`, and it then sets the font weight using the `--bs-fw` variable stored together with the various class names.

To see this in action, open the HTML file in a browser.

CSS variable name

This option defines the prefix for the CSS variable utilities coming after the default `--bs-` prefix, which we used together with `css-var: true` in the previous example like this: `css-variable-name: fw`. The full prefix, as we saw, then became `--bs-fw`.

Local CSS variables

Using this Boolean option, the utility API will still generate CSS rules, but also local CSS variables within these rules. You must specify a Sass map as the value, where the keys of the map are the CSS variable names, and the values of the map are the CSS variable values.

Let's change our first example to also generate local CSS variables:

part-1/chapter-6/api-syntax/local-css-variables/scss/style.scss

```scss
// Required imports
// Utilities

$utilities: (
  "Font weight": (
    property: font-weight,
    values: 300 400 700,
    local-vars: (
      font-weight-opacity: 0.5
    )
  )
```

```
);


// Utilities API
```

This compiles to the following:

part-1/chapter-6/api-syntax/local-css-variables/css/style.css

```
.font-weight-300 {
  --bs-font-weight-opacity: .5;
  font-weight: 300 !important
}
.font-weight-400 {
  --bs-font-weight-opacity: .5;
  font-weight: 400 !important
}
.font-weight-700 {
  --bs-font-weight-opacity: .5;
  font-weight: 700 !important
}
```

We can now see the effect of this utility by using it with the following HTML:

part-1/chapter-6/api-syntax/local-css-variables/index.html

```
<p class="font-weight-300">Lorem ipsum...</p>
<p class="font-weight-400">Lorem ipsum...</p>
<p class="font-weight-700">Lorem ipsum...</p>
```

This HTML must be combined with the following CSS, which is located in the `<style>` tag of the HTML file in our example:

part-1/chapter-6/api-syntax/local-css-variables/index.html

```
p[class^="font-weight"] {
  opacity: var(--bs-font-weight-opacity);
}
```

The CSS selector targets all the paragraph elements on the page that have a class starting with `font-weight`, and it then sets the font weight using the `--bs-font-weight-opacity` variable stored together with the various class names.

To see this in action, open the HTML file in a browser.

State

This option is used to generate pseudo-class variations in addition to the normal utility classes. You can specify a single pseudo-class or a space-separated list of pseudo-classes. When using the `state` option, the utility API will generate class names for that pseudo-class, and the name of the pseudo-class will be appended to the class names.

Let's change our first example yet again:

part-1/chapter-6/api-syntax/state/scss/style.scss

```scss
// Required imports
// Utilities

$utilities: (
  "Font weight": (
    property: font-weight,
    values: 300 400 700,
    state: hover
  )
);


// Utilities API
```

This compiles to the following:

part-1/chapter-6/api-syntax/state/css/style.css

```css
.font-weight-300 { font-weight: 300 !important; }
.font-weight-300-hover:hover { font-weight: 300 !important; }
.font-weight-400 { font-weight: 400 !important; }
.font-weight-400-hover:hover { font-weight: 400 !important; }
.font-weight-700 { font-weight: 700 !important; }
.font-weight-700-hover:hover { font-weight: 700 !important; }
```

We can now see the effect of this utility by using it with the following HTML:

part-1/chapter-6/api-syntax/state/index.html

```html
<p class="font-weight-300-hover">Lorem ipsum...</p>
<p class="font-weight-400-hover">Lorem ipsum...</p>
<p class="font-weight-700-hover">Lorem ipsum...</p>
```

To see this in action, open the HTML file in a browser and hover over the paragraphs.

Responsive

This Boolean option is used to generate responsive utilities across all breakpoints. It will insert the device abbreviations as an infix to the class names.

Let's make our example responsive:

part-1/chapter-6/api-syntax/responsive/scss/style.scss

```scss
// Required imports
// Utilities

$utilities: (
  "Font weight": (
    property: font-weight,
    values: 300 400 700,
    responsive: true
  )
);


// Utilities API
```

This compiles to the following:

part-1/chapter-6/api-syntax/responsive/css/style.css

```css
.font-weight-300 { font-weight: 300 !important; }
.font-weight-400 { font-weight: 400 !important; }
.font-weight-700 { font-weight: 700 !important; }
@media (min-width: 576px) {
```

```
  .font-weight-sm-300 { font-weight: 300 !important; }
  .font-weight-sm-400 { font-weight: 400 !important; }
  .font-weight-sm-700 { font-weight: 700 !important; }
}
@media (min-width: 768px) {
  .font-weight-md-300 { font-weight: 300 !important; }
  .font-weight-md-400 { font-weight: 400 !important; }
  .font-weight-md-700 { font-weight: 700 !important; }
}
// and so on...
```

We can now see the effect of this utility by using it with the following HTML:

part-1/chapter-6/api-syntax/responsive/index.html

```
<h3>All breakpoints</h3>
<p class="font-weight-300">Lorem ipsum...</p>
<p class="font-weight-400">Lorem ipsum...</p>
<p class="font-weight-700">Lorem ipsum...</p>

<h3>Breakpoint sm</h3>
<p class="font-weight-sm-300">Lorem ipsum...</p>
<p class="font-weight-sm-400">Lorem ipsum...</p>
<p class="font-weight-sm-700">Lorem ipsum...</p>

// and so on...
```

To see this in action, open the HTML file in a browser and resize the browser window.

RFS

This Boolean option will enable fluid rescaling with the RFS Sass plugin. You will learn more about this plugin in *Chapter 10, Using Bootstrap 5 with Advanced Sass and CSS Features*.

Print

This Boolean option will, in addition to the normal utility classes, generate utility classes for print as well.

Let's use our example one last time:

part-1/chapter-6/api-syntax/print/scss/style.scss

```scss
// Required imports
// Utilities

$utilities: (
  "Font weight": (
    property: font-weight,
    values: 300 400 700,
    print: true
  )
);


// Utilities API
```

This compiles to the following:

part-1/chapter-6/api-syntax/print/css/style.css

```css
.font-weight-300 { font-weight: 300 !important; }
.font-weight-400 { font-weight: 400 !important; }
.font-weight-700 { font-weight: 700 !important; }

@media print {
  .font-weight-print-300 { font-weight: 300 !important; }
  .font-weight-print-400 { font-weight: 400 !important; }
  .font-weight-print-700 { font-weight: 700 !important; }
}
```

We can now see the effect of this utility by using it with the following HTML:

part-1/chapter-6/api-syntax/print/index.html

```html
<p class="font-weight-print-300 ">Lorem ipsum...</p>
<p class="font-weight-print-400 ">Lorem ipsum...</p>
<p class="font-weight-print-700 ">Lorem ipsum...</p>
```

To see this in action, open the HTML file in a browser and then select **Print** in your browser's menu. This will open a **Print** dialog where you can see a preview of the page with the print styles applied.

RTL

This Boolean option specifies whether the utility should be included in the RTL version of the compiled stylesheet. This is a version of Bootstrap 5 with support for right-to-left text across layout, components, and utilities.

!important

All utility classes generated with the utility API have `!important` added to be sure they overwrite styling for components and modifier classes. This can be disabled by setting the `$enable-important-utilities` option to `false`, which we saw earlier in *Chapter 4, Bootstrap 5 Global Options and Colors*.

More examples of the syntax

To see more examples of the syntax for the utility API, you can go through the `_utilities.scss` file in Bootstrap 5. Here, you will see the syntax being used to generate all the default utility classes found in Bootstrap 5.

Using the utility API

We have seen what the syntax of the utility API looks like, and we will now see some examples of how to use it for different purposes. First, we will see examples of how to generate and add both simple and complex new utilities, and then we will see examples of how to overwrite, modify, and remove existing utilities. To do this, we're going to use the following two Sass functions: `map-merge()` (to merge existing maps) and `map-get()` (to get a value associated with a key from a specified Sass map).

Adding a simple utility

First, we will generate and add a simple cursor utility, which can be used to change the cursor when hovering over specific elements. We're specifying the name of the utility (`"cursor"`), the CSS property to use (`cursor`), and the values to use for that CSS property (`auto context-menu copy grab help pointer wait`). These are the minimum required options to specify when using the utility API.

Before using the syntax of the utility API, we're merging the existing utility settings in the `$utilities` variable with this new utility using the `map-merge()` Sass function. This is done to avoid overwriting the `$utilities` variable and losing all the default utilities.

The code looks like this:

part-1/chapter-6/examples/add-simple-utility/scss/style.scss

```scss
// Required imports
// Utilities

// Generate simple cursor utilities
$utilities: map-merge(
  $utilities,
  (
    "cursor": (
      property: cursor,
      values: auto context-menu copy grab help pointer wait
    )
  )
);

// Utilities API
```

This will compile all the default utilities, as well as the following new utilities:

part-1/chapter-6/examples/add-simple-utility/css/style.css

```css
.cursor-auto { cursor: auto !important; }
.cursor-context-menu { cursor: context-menu !important; }
.cursor-copy { cursor: copy !important; }
.cursor-grab { cursor: grab !important; }
.cursor-help { cursor: help !important; }
.cursor-pointer { cursor: pointer !important; }
.cursor-wait{ cursor: wait !important; }
```

We can now see the effect of these utilities by using it with the following HTML:

part-1/chapter-6/examples/add-simple-utility/index.html

```html
<p class="cursor-auto">.cursor-auto</p>
<p class="cursor-context-menu">.cursor-context-menu</p>
```

```
<p class="cursor-copy">.cursor-copy</p>
<p class="cursor-grab">.cursor-grab</p>
<p class="cursor-help">.cursor-help</p>
<p class="cursor-pointer">.cursor-pointer</p>
<p class="cursor-wait">.cursor-wait</p>
```

To see this in action, open the HTML file in a browser and hover with the mouse on the different elements.

Adding a complex utility

Now, here's an example of how to generate and add a complex opacity utility with a lot of the options being used. We're specifying the name of the utility ("opacity"), the CSS property to use (opacity), the values to use for that CSS property as a Sass map (so that the class names can be different from the CSS values), the class prefix to use (o), and the state to make this utility work on hover, and we enable the responsive and print options.

Once again, we're merging the existing utilities with this new one using the map-merge() function.

The code looks like this:

part-1/chapter-6/examples/add-complex-utility/scss/style.scss

```
// Required imports
// Utilities

// Generate complex opacity utilities
$utilities: map-merge(
  $utilities,
  (
    "opacity": (
      property: opacity,
      values: (
        0: 0,
        25: .25,
        50: .5,
        75: .75,
        100: 1,
      ),
      class: o,
```

```
        state: hover,
        responsive: true,
        print: true
      )
    )
);


// Utilities API
```

This will compile all the default utilities, as well as the following new utilities:

part-1/chapter-6/examples/add-complex-utility/css/style.css

```css
.o-0 { opacity: 0 !important }
.o-0-hover:hover { opacity: 0 !important }
.o-25 { opacity: .25 !important }
.o-25-hover:hover { opacity: .25 !important }
.o-50 { opacity: .5 !important }
.o-50-hover:hover { opacity: .5 !important }
.o-75 { opacity: .75 !important }
.o-75-hover:hover { opacity: .75 !important }
.o-100 { opacity: 1 !important }
.o-100-hover:hover { opacity: 1 !important }

@media (min-width: 576px) {
  .o-sm-0 { opacity: 0 !important }
  .o-sm-0-hover:hover { opacity: 0 !important }
  .o-sm-25 { opacity: .25 !important }
  .o-sm-25-hover:hover { opacity: .25 !important }
  .o-sm-50 { opacity: .5 !important }
  .o-sm-50-hover:hover { opacity: .5 !important }
  .o-sm-75 { opacity: .75 !important }
  .o-sm-75-hover:hover { opacity: .75 !important }
  .o-sm-100 { opacity: 1 !important }
  .o-sm-100-hover:hover { opacity: 1 !important }
}


// and so on...
```

We can now see the effect of these utilities by using it with the following HTML:

part-1/chapter-6/examples/add-complex-utility/index.html

```
<h3>All breakpoints</h3>
<p class="o-0">.o-0</p>
<p class="o-0-hover">.o-0-hover</p>
<p class="o-25">.o-25</p>
<p class="o-25-hover">.o-25-hover</p>
<p class="o-50">.o-50</p>
<p class="o-50-hover">.o-50-hover</p>
<p class="o-75">.o-75</p>
<p class="o-75-hover">.o-75-hover</p>
<p style="opacity: 0;" class="o-100">.o-100</p>
<p style="opacity: 0;" class="o-100-hover">.o-100-hover</p>

<h3>Breakpoint sm</h3>
<p class="o-sm-0">.o-sm-0</p>
<p class="o-sm-0-hover">.o-sm-0-hover</p>
<p class="o-sm-25">.o-sm-25</p>
<p class="o-sm-25-hover">.o-sm-25-hover</p>
<p class="o-sm-50">.o-sm-50</p>
<p class="o-sm-50-hover">.o-sm-50-hover</p>
<p class="o-sm-75">.o-sm-75</p>
<p class="o-sm-75-hover">.o-sm-75-hover</p>
<p style="opacity: 0;" class="o-sm-100">.o-sm-100</p>
<p style="opacity: 0;" class="o-sm-100-hover">
  .o-sm-100-hover</p>

// and so on...
```

To see this in action, open the HTML file in a browser and hover with the mouse on the different elements.

Overwriting a utility

You can overwrite an existing utility by using the same name. This method can be used to modify a utility as well, but you must be careful then and use all of the same options.

Here's an example of how to overwrite the sizing utility for `"width"` with a new `"width"` utility that has many more values specified:

Part-1/chapter-6/examples/overwrite-utility/scss/style.scss

```scss
// Required imports
// Utilities

// Overwrite sizing utility for width
$utilities: map-merge(
  $utilities,
  (
    "width": (
      property: width,
      class: w,
      values: (
        10: 10%,
        20: 20%,
        30: 30%,
        40: 40%,
        50: 50%,
        60: 60%,
        70: 70%,
        80: 80%,
        90: 90%,
        100: 100%,
        auto: auto
      )
    )
  )
);

// Utilities API
```

This will compile all the default utilities, as well as the following new utilities:

part-1/chapter-6/examples/overwrite-utility/css/style.css

```
.w-10 { width: 10% !important }
.w-20 { width: 20% !important }
.w-30 { width: 30% !important }
.w-40 { width: 40% !important }
.w-50 { width: 50% !important }
.w-60 { width: 60% !important }
.w-70 { width: 70% !important }
.w-80 { width: 80% !important }
.w-90 { width: 90% !important }
.w-100 { width: 100% !important }
.w-auto { width: auto !important }
```

We can now see the effect of these utilities by using it with the following HTML:

part-1/chapter-6/examples/overwrite-utility/index.html

```
<div class="w-10 bg-secondary text-white p-3 mb-2">.w-10
</div>
<div class="w-20 bg-secondary text-white p-3 mb-2">.w-20
</div>
<div class="w-30 bg-secondary text-white p-3 mb-2">.w-30
</div>
<div class="w-40 bg-secondary text-white p-3 mb-2">.w-40
</div>
<div class="w-50 bg-secondary text-white p-3 mb-2">.w-50
</div>
<div class="w-60 bg-secondary text-white p-3 mb-2">.w-60
</div>
<div class="w-70 bg-secondary text-white p-3 mb-2">.w-70
</div>
<div class="w-80 bg-secondary text-white p-3 mb-2">.w-80
</div>
<div class="w-90 bg-secondary text-white p-3 mb-2">.w-90
</div>
```

```
<div style="width: 50%;" class="w-100 bg-secondary
  text-white p-3 mb-2">.w-100</div>
<div style="width: 50%;" class="w-auto bg-secondary
  text-white p-3">.w-auto</div>
```

To see this in action, open the HTML file in a browser.

Modifying a utility

It's possible to modify an existing utility. In this example, we will rename the `class` prefix for the `"margin-start"` utility from `.ms-*` to `.ml-*`. This will now be identical to the prefix used in Bootstrap 4. This time, we're going to use the `map-get()` function to get the current value of the `"margin-start"` property from the `$utilities` variable to be able to merge it with the `class: ml` property, which will then overwrite the existing `class: ms` property. The code looks like this:

part-1/chapter-6/examples/modify-utility/scss/style.scss

```scss
// Required imports
// Utilities

// Rename class for existing utility
$utilities: map-merge(
  $utilities, (
    "margin-start": map-merge(
      map-get($utilities, "margin-start"),
      ( class: ml ),
    )
  )
);

// Utilities API
```

This will compile all the default utilities, as well as the following new utilities:

part-1/chapter-6/examples/modify-utility/css/style.css

```css
.ml-0 { margin-left: 0 !important }
.ml-1 { margin-left: .25rem !important }
```

```
.ml-2 { margin-left: .5rem !important }
.ml-3 { margin-left: 1rem !important }
.ml-4 { margin-left: 1.5rem !important }
.ml-5 { margin-left: 3rem !important }
.ml-auto { margin-left: auto !important }
```

We can now see the effect of these utilities by using it with the following HTML:

part-1/chapter-6/examples/modify-utility/index.html

```
<div class="ml-1 bg-secondary text-white p-3 mb-2">.ml-1
</div>
<div class="ml-2 bg-secondary text-white p-3 mb-2">.ml-2
</div>
<div class="ml-3 bg-secondary text-white p-3 mb-2">.ml-3
</div>
<div class="ml-4 bg-secondary text-white p-3 mb-2">.ml-4
</div>
<div class="ml-5 bg-secondary text-white p-3 mb-2">.ml-5
</div>
```

To see this in action, open the HTML file in a browser. The renamed class for the `margin-left` utility now works.

Removing a utility

It's possible to remove a utility from the existing set of utilities. Here, you can see how to remove the `"user-select"` and `"pointer-events"` interaction utilities by setting their values to `null`:

part-1/chapter-6/examples/remove-utility/scss/style.scss

```
// Required imports
// Utilities

// Remove interaction utilities
$utilities: map-merge(
  $utilities,
  (
    "user-select": null,
```

```
        "pointer-events": null
    )
);


// Utilities API
```

This will compile all the default utilities except for the `"user-select"` and `"pointer-events"` utilities.

We can now see that these utilities have indeed been removed by trying to use them with the following HTML:

part-1/chapter-6/examples/remove-utility/index.html

```
<h3>User select</h3>
<h4>All</h4>
<p class="user-select-all">Lorem ipsum...</p>
<h4>Auto</h4>
<p style="user-select: none;" class="user-select-auto">
  Lorem ipsum...</p>
<h4>None</h4>
<p class="user-select-none">Lorem ipsum...</p>


<h3>Pointer events</h3>
<h4>None</h4>
<p><a href="#" class="pe-none">Lorem ipsum dolor sit amet,
  consectetur adipiscing elit</a>. In laoreet pellentesque
  lorem sed elementum. Suspendisse maximus convallis ex.
  Etiam eleifend velit leo.</p>
<h4>Auto</h4>
<p><a href="#" style="pointer-events: none;"
  class="pe-auto">Lorem ipsum dolor sit amet, consectetur
    adipiscing elit</a>. In laoreet pellentesque lorem sed
    elementum. Suspendisse maximus convallis ex. Etiam
    eleifend velit leo.</p>
<h4>None for parent, auto for second child</h4>
<p class="pe-none"><a href="#">Lorem ipsum dolor sit amet,
  consectetur adipiscing elit</a>. In laoreet pellentesque
```

```
    lorem sed elementum. Suspendisse maximus convallis ex.
    <a href="#" class="pe-auto">Etiam eleifend velit leo</a>.
  </p>
```

To see this in action, open the HTML file in a browser. The utilities for `"user-select"` and `"pointer-events"` no longer work.

Summary

We have now learned all about the utility API, which is a very powerful tool built into Bootstrap 5. This is also the last chapter about customizing Bootstrap 5 and the last in this first part of the book. In the next part of this book, we will see how all of this can be put into practice as we build a complete website and customize it in many different ways using Sass and some custom JavaScript.

Part Two – Creating a Unique-Looking Website Based on Bootstrap 5 and Customization

In this part of the book, we will learn how to transform a standard-looking Bootstrap 5 website into a unique-looking and custom website by using Bootstrap 5's powerful customization features, as well as some custom styling with Sass. We will also improve the website with various interactive features using custom JavaScript.

This part comprises the following chapters:

- *Chapter 7, Creating the Website Using Default Bootstrap 5 Elements*

- *Chapter 8, Customizing the Website Using Bootstrap 5 Variables, Utility API, and Sass*

- *Chapter 9, Improving the Website with Interactive Features Using JavaScript*

7

Creating the Website Using Default Bootstrap 5 Elements

In this chapter, we will first take a closer look at what kind of website we will create. Then, there's a quick introduction to Bootstrap Icons, which is being used heavily throughout the website to make it more user-friendly and visually appealing. After that follows a description of the page setup, then a description with screenshots of a few global modules that are used across the website, and finally, a description with screenshots of each of the page types being used.

In this chapter, we're going to cover the following main topics:

- About the website
- Bootstrap Icons
- Page setup
- The different global modules of the website
- The different page types of the website

Technical requirements

To preview the examples, you will need a code editor and a browser. There won't be many code examples in this chapter, since the whole website has been created using only default Bootstrap 5 elements. However, the source code for the complete website can be found here:

`https://github.com/PacktPublishing/The-Missing-Bootstrap-5-Guide.`

About the website

The website is an online store with shopping-related pages for a product overview, product details, wishlist, shopping cart, and checkout flow, as well as more content-related pages for various information. It has a total of 12 pages with eight of them being unique in structure and layout, and the remaining four using the same structure and layout.

The website has been designed and developed using only default Bootstrap 5 elements and the content consists of placeholder text and images. Because of this, the website has a wireframe-like appearance. However, if you substitute all text and images, the website will look more real.

As you probably are aware, Bootstrap 5 only contains code for the frontend of a website. Because of this, all the advanced features of the website that require communication with a backend have not been implemented. This includes the search functionality, filters, sorting, form submission, and more. In *Chapter 9, Improving the Website with Interactive Features Using JavaScript*, we will extend the basic functionality with some custom JavaScript to make the website more interactive and user-friendly.

Sitemap

Here's an overview of the pages making up the website and their mutual relationship. A description of all the pages follows later in this chapter:

- Home
- Shop => Product
- About
- Contact
- Wishlist
- Cart
- Frequently Asked Questions
- Shipping
- Returns
- Terms of Service
- Privacy Policy

As you can see, only the Shop and Product pages have a parent-child relationship. All the other pages exist at the top level.

Bootstrap Icons

Bootstrap Icons is a free, high-quality, open source library created by the Bootstrap team. It can be used with or without Bootstrap, and as SVGs, SVG sprites, or web fonts. The first alpha version of this library was released on November 26, 2019. The latest version, v1.8.3, was released on May 25, 2022, and it now contains more than 1,600 icons to choose from.

Bootstrap Icons can be visited at the following URL: `https://icons.getbootstrap.com/`.

From there, you can download and install it in different ways. I have chosen to use the web fonts implementation, which makes it very quick to add icons directly to your HTML code. To add an icon, you simply use the following code:

```
<i class="bi-[Icon name]"></i>
```

Here, `[Icon name]` refers to the name of an icon, for example, `alarm`, so it becomes the following:

```
<i class="bi-alarm"></i>
```

This will show the following icon on the page:

Figure 7.1 – Alarm icon

When using icons as a web font, the color and size can be set in the same way as for text, for example, using Bootstrap 5 utility classes.

In the next section, you can see how the Bootstrap Icons CSS file is linked up in the `<head>` tag of each page.

Page setup

The basic setup of most pages looks like the following code:

```
<!DOCTYPE html>
<html>
  <head>
    <meta charset="utf-8">
    <meta name="viewport" content="width=device-width,
      initial-scale=1">
```

```
    <title>[Page title]</title>
    <link rel="stylesheet" href="../../../
      bootstrap/dist/css/bootstrap.min.css">
    <link rel="stylesheet" href="../../../
      bootstrap-icons/font/bootstrap-icons.css">
  </head>
  <body>
    <header>[Header]</header>
    <div>[Page title]</div>
    <div class="container">
      <!-- Various sections -->
      <section></section>
      <section></section>
      <section></section>
    </div>
    <footer>[Footer]</footer>
    <script src="../../../bootstrap/dist/js/
      bootstrap.bundle.min.js"></script>
  </body>
</html>
```

This is a very basic implementation of Bootstrap 5. Inside the <head> tag, we first see the <meta> tag defining the character set, and then the responsive meta tag:

```
<meta name="viewport" content="width=device-width, initial-
scale=1">
```

Then follows a page title in the <title> tag and links to the minified Bootstrap 5 CSS file, as well as the Bootstrap Icons CSS file.

Inside the <body> tag, we see the basic page structure for most pages with the header module first, then the page title module, various sections inside .container, and then the footer module. Finally, just before the closing </body> tag, we see a <script> tag, with src being the bundled and minified Bootstrap 5 JavaScript file.

Global modules

Before we go through all the different page types, we will see which global modules are used across more than one page type.

In the descriptions that follow, any Bootstrap 5 components being used are highlighted like this: **Component name**. The term *module* refers to a part of a page and has nothing to do with Bootstrap 5.

Header

This global module is used on all page types. It's located at the top of each page and is being used for primary navigation. It's been created using a **Navbar** component and will collapse with most of its content being hidden for breakpoints below `lg`.

Here are three screenshots of the module, as seen on a mobile, tablet, and desktop device:

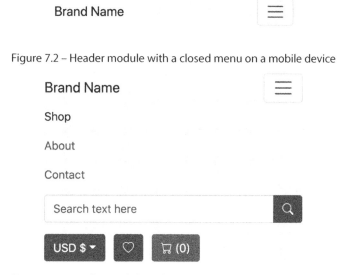

Figure 7.2 – Header module with a closed menu on a mobile device

Figure 7.3 – Header module with a closed menu on a mobile device

Figure 7.4 – Header module on a tablet device

Figure 7.5 – Header module on a desktop device

The left side of the module contains two elements. First, the brand name with a link wrapped around it, and then the main menu with links to the most important pages. The active page will be highlighted in the menu.

The right side of the module contains three elements. First, a search field created as a simple form with an **Input group** component. It's intended to be used as a global search for all the content and products of the website. Then, a currency selector to change the currency used by the shop. It's created with a **Dropdown** component. Finally, a call-to-action section with two links styled as buttons for the wishlist and the cart, respectively.

Footer

This global module is used on all page types. It's located at the bottom of each page and is mainly being used for secondary navigation. It has all the links from the header module as **Quick links**, as well as links for the various information pages, social media networks, and contact information. The module is using a four-column responsive grid, with all columns being stacked initially and then turned into a two-column grid for the sm breakpoint and a four-column grid for the lg breakpoint.

In the following figure, you will see three screenshots of the module as seen on mobile, tablet, and desktop devices:

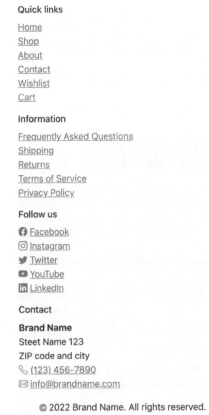

Figure 7.6 – Footer module on a mobile device

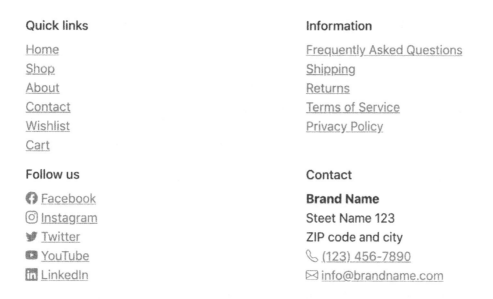

Quick links

Home

Shop

About

Contact

Wishlist

Cart

Information

Frequently Asked Questions

Shipping

Returns

Terms of Service

Privacy Policy

Follow us

Facebook

Instagram

Twitter

YouTube

LinkedIn

Contact

Brand Name

Steet Name 123

ZIP code and city

(123) 456-7890

info@brandname.com

© 2022 Brand Name. All rights reserved.

Figure 7.7 – Footer module on a tablet device

Figure 7.8 – Footer module on a desktop device

The first three columns consist of a heading followed by an unstyled unordered list of links, and in the third column, the link text is prepended with an icon. The last column contains basic contact information inside an `<address>` element. At the very bottom of this module is a centered copyright notice.

Page title

This global module is used on all page types except for the Home page and Product page. It's used right after the header module and is simply a display heading centered on a light gray background.

The only responsive behavior of this module is the responsive font size, which is a default feature of Bootstrap 5.

Here are three screenshots of the module as seen on mobile, tablet, and desktop devices:

Shop

Figure 7.9 – Page title module on a mobile device

Shop

Figure 7.10 – Page title module on a tablet device

Shop

Figure 7.11 – Page title module on a desktop device

We have now seen what the Page title global module looks like, and next up, we will take a look at the Product card global module.

Product card

This global module is being used inside a responsive grid system on the Home page, Shop page, Product page, and Wishlist page. It's a **Card** component containing a product image, a **Badge** component for the tag, product name, brand name, description, stock status, pricing information, and call-to-action buttons.

The only responsive behavior of this module is the responsive font size, which is a default feature of Bootstrap 5.

Here is a screenshot of the module as seen on mobile devices:

Product Name

BRAND NAME

Lorem ipsum dolor sit amet, consectetur adipiscing elit. Duis convallis velit quis sapien sollicitudin ultrices.

⊘ In stock

$199 ~~($299)~~

Figure 7.12 – Product card module on a mobile device

On the Wishlist page, the **Add to wishlist** button is replaced by a **Remove from wishlist** button.

Page types

Here's a description of all the different page types. There are nine different page types used to create the 12 different pages. Eight of them are being used once, and the last one, the Article page, is being used four times.

Home (index.html)

This is the home page for the online store. On this page, the user can see a hero section, learn about the benefits, explore the collections, view popular products, and sign up for the newsletter.

Here is a screenshot of the full page as seen on a desktop device:

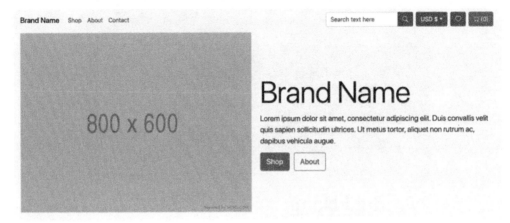

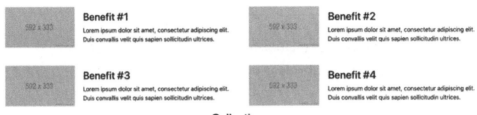

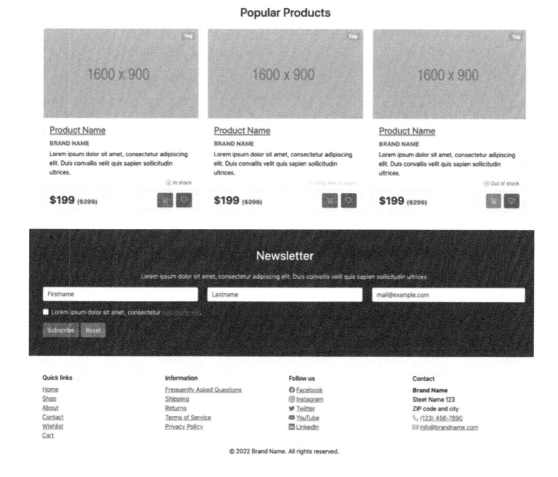

Figure 7.13 – Home page on a desktop device

The overall code structure in the <body> tag for this page can be seen next. The different modules have been replaced with [Name of the module] and they will be further described afterward (except for Header and Footer, which were described in the previous section):

part-2/chapter-7/website/index.html

```
<body>
  [Header]
  [Hero]
  <div class="container">
    [Benefits]
```

```
      [Collections]
      [Popular products]
   </div>
   [Newsletter]
   [Footer]
   [Modal]
   <script src="../../../bootstrap/dist/js/
      bootstrap.bundle.min.js"></script>
</body>
```

Hero

This module is a short introduction to the online store, and it consists of an image, a display heading, a lead paragraph, and two call-to-action buttons. The elements in this layout stack initially and then turn into a two-column grid for the `lg` breakpoint and up.

Benefits

This module consists of an image, a heading, and a paragraph. The layout is created using a responsive nested grid where everything stacks initially. On the `sm` breakpoint, the inner grid changes to two columns, and on the `lg` breakpoint, the outer grid changes to two columns.

Collections

This module displays different collections using a **Carousel** component with a link, image, and caption for each slide.

Popular products

This module shows three products in a responsive three-column grid. Each product is created using the Product card module described in the previous section.

Newsletter

This module consists of a heading, a form in a three-column grid layout, and a link in the label for the checkbox that triggers a modal.

Modal

This module consists of a **Modal** component that is triggered from a link in the Newsletter module as described previously. The content of the modal is for information regarding the newsletter.

Shop (shop.html)

This is the Shop page for the online store. On this page, the user can see a sidebar with filters and the products listed in a responsive grid layout. Above this, we have a breadcrumb, a control for changing the sorting, and buttons for switching the layout of the products from a grid layout to a list layout. For this website, though, only the grid layout of the Shop page has been created. Below the products overview, we have pagination to navigate between the various pages containing the products.

On breakpoints smaller than lg, the filters are contained in an Offcanvas module triggered by a button above the breadcrumb.

Here is a screenshot of the full page as seen on a desktop device:

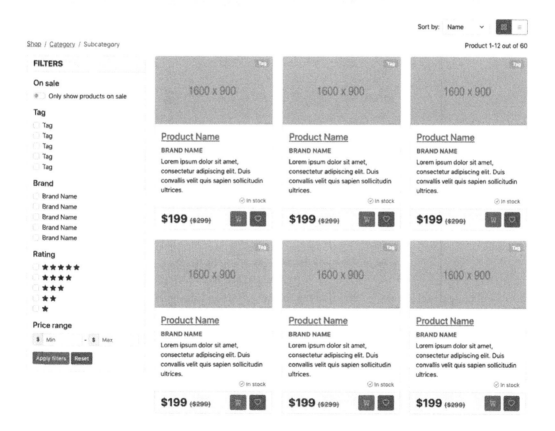

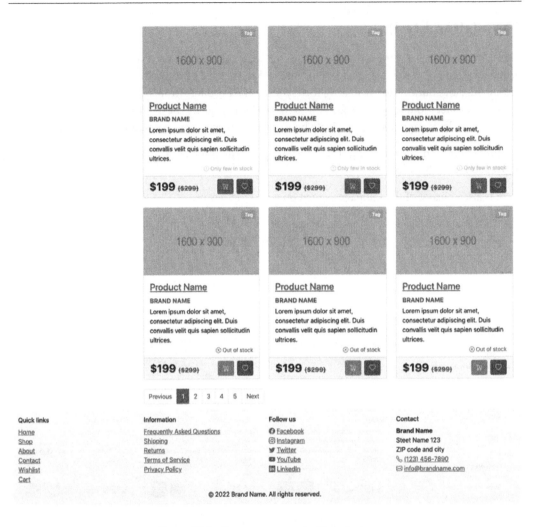

Figure 7.14 – Shop page on a desktop device

The overall code structure in the <body> tag for this page can be seen next. The different modules have been replaced with [Name of the module] and they will be further described afterward (except for Header and Footer, which were described in the previous section):

part-2/chapter-7/website/shop.html

```
<body>
  [Header]
  [Page title]
  <div class="container">
```

```
    [Offcanvas]
    [Sorting and layout]
    [Breadcrumb and search result]
    <div class="row">
      <div class="col-lg-4 col-xxl-3 d-none d-lg-block">
        <aside class="sticky-top pt-lg-3 pb-lg-5">
          [Filters]
        </aside>
      </div>
      <div class="col-lg-8 col-xxl-9 pt-lg-3 mb-5">
        [Products overview]
        [Pagination]
      </div>
    </div>
  </div>
  [Footer]
  <script src="../../../bootstrap/dist/js/
    bootstrap.bundle.min.js"></script>
</body>
```

Offcanvas

This module is created using the **Offcanvas** component and it contains the same filter options as found in the Filter module. It can be opened by a button in the Sorting and layout module. The button is hidden on the lg breakpoint and up.

Sorting and layout

This module is for sorting the product overview and changing the layout. It's created using a <select> element for changing the sorting and a **Button group** component for switching the layout. The module also contains a button to open the Offcanvas module on breakpoints smaller than lg.

Breadcrumb and search result

This module has breadcrumb navigation to the left and search results to the right. The breadcrumb navigation is created using the **Breadcrumb** component.

Filters

This module contains various filter options for the product overview. All the filters are contained inside of a **Card** component, and the individual filters are created using various form elements, such as **Switch**, checkboxes, and **Input groups**.

Product overview

This module shows a responsive grid of products using the Product cart module. Initially, all columns are stacked and then turned into a two-column grid on the `md` breakpoint and a three-column grid on the `xxl` breakpoint.

Pagination

This module uses the **Pagination** component to let the user navigate between multiple pages of a search result.

Product (product.html)

This page shows a breadcrumb for shop navigation, a gallery, details and description of the product, as well as related products and reviews. No Bootstrap 5 components are used for this page, except for the **Breadcrumb** component and the **Badge** component. Instead, lots of utility classes are used together with various typography, form elements, image thumbnails, and blockquotes.

Here is a screenshot of the full page as seen on a desktop device:

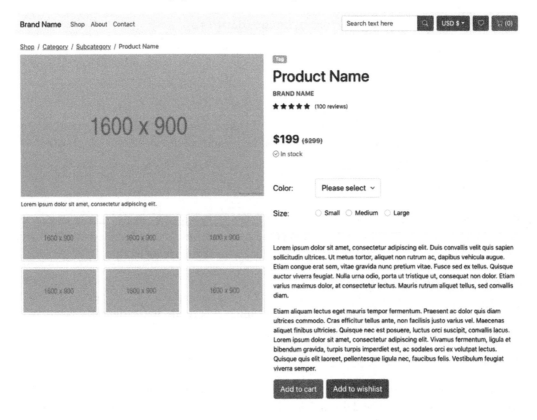

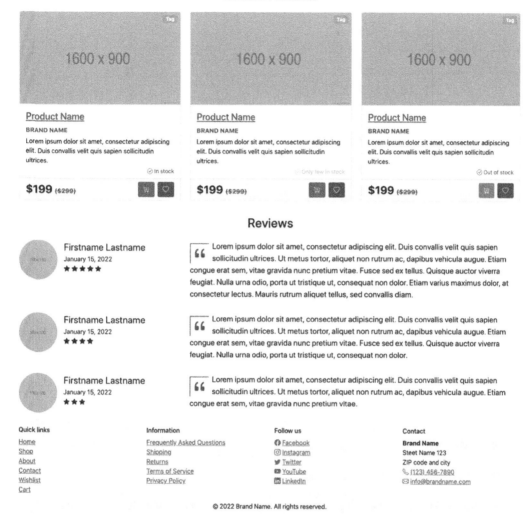

Figure 7.15 – Product page on a desktop device

The overall code structure in the <body> tag for this page can be seen next. The different modules have been replaced with [Name of the module] and they will be further described afterward (except for Header and Footer, which were described in the previous section):

part-2/chapter-7/website/product.html

```
<body>
    [Header]
```

```
<div class="container mt-3 mb-5">
  <section class="border-bottom border-2 border-light
    mb-4 pb-4">
    [Breadcrumb]
    <div class="row">
      <div class="col-lg-6">
        [Gallery]
      </div>
      <div class="col-lg-6">
        [Details and description]
      </div>
    </div>
  </section>
  [Related products]
  [Review]
</div>
[Footer]
<script src="../../../bootstrap/dist/js/
  bootstrap.bundle.min.js"></script>
</body>
```

Breadcrumb

This module contains a breadcrumb navigation used to navigate the shop. It's created with the **Breadcrumb** component.

Gallery

This module contains a large product image with caption structured using the `<figure>` element. Below that is a three-column grid with six image thumbnails.

Details and description

This module consists of various details about the product. It has the same content as in a Product card module, different kinds of form controls for selecting a color and a size, a long description, and two call-to-action buttons.

Related products

This module shows related products. It contains a heading followed by a three-column responsive grid with Product card modules inside the columns.

Reviews

This module shows three blocks of reviews with image, name, date, rating, and the review itself. The default **Blockquote** element of Bootstrap 5 has been enhanced by adding a Bootstrap Icons quote icon in the upper-left corner with the use of 11 utility classes (text, float, spacing, and border utilities).

About (about.html)

This page shows various information about the online store with text and images.

Here is a screenshot of the full page as seen on a desktop device:

Figure 7.16 – About page on a desktop device

The overall code structure in the <body> tag for this page can be seen next. The different modules have been replaced with [Name of the module] and they will be further described afterward (except for Header and Footer, which were described in the previous section):

part-2/chapter-7/website/about.html

```
<body>
  [Header]
  [Page title]
  <div class="container">
    [Story]
    [Office]
    [Brands]
  </div>
  [Footer]
  <script src="../../../bootstrap/dist/js/
    bootstrap.bundle.min.js"></script>
</body>
```

Story

This module contains a heading and three paragraphs about the story of the online store.

Office

This module contains a two-column responsive grid to show images of the office. Each column has `<figure>` wrapping around an image and a figure caption.

Brands

This module shows a responsive grid with brand logos of the products in the online store. Initially, the layout is a two-column grid, which turns into a three-column grid on the `sm` breakpoint and a six-column grid on the `lg` breakpoint.

Contact (contact.html)

This page shows an overview of the team, the location on a map, and a contact form.

Here is a screenshot of the full page as seen on a desktop device:

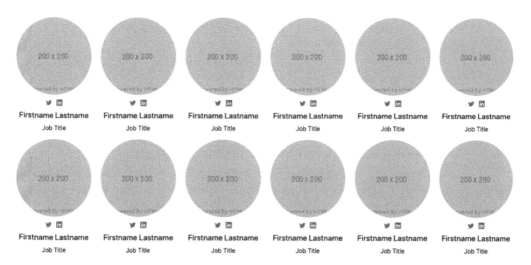

Figure 7.17 – Contact page on a desktop device

The overall code structure in the `<body>` tag for this page can be seen next. The different modules have been replaced with [Name of the module] and they will be further described afterward (except for Header and Footer, which were described in the previous section):

part-2/chapter-7/website/contact.html

```
<body>
  [Header]
  [Page title]
```

```
<div class="container">
  [Team]
  [Location]
  [Contact form]
</div>
[Footer]
<script src="../../../bootstrap/dist/js/
  bootstrap.bundle.min.js"></script>
</body>
```

Team

This module contains a heading, a paragraph, and a responsive grid presenting the team members with images, links to social media networks, names, and job titles. Initially, the layout is a two-column grid, which turns into a three-column grid on the md breakpoint and a six-column grid on the xl breakpoint.

Location

This module contains an embedded map from Google Maps in an <iframe> element. The ratio helper is used to maintain the aspect ratio of the map at 21 by 9.

Contact form

This module contains a heading and a contact form. The layout of the contact form is created using a responsive nested grid where everything stacks initially. On the md breakpoint, the inner grid changes to two columns, and on the xl breakpoint, the outer grid changes to two columns.

Wishlist (wishlist.html)

This page shows the products added to a user's wishlist. In the sidebar to the left, the user can change the wishlist, create a new wishlist, or add all products to the cart at once. In the main area, there's a responsive grid system with Product cards showing all the products on the current wishlist.

Here is a screenshot of the full page as seen on a desktop device:

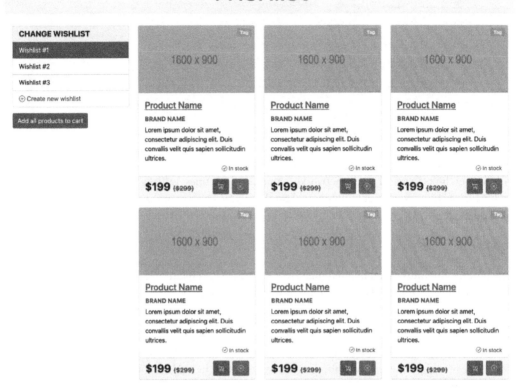

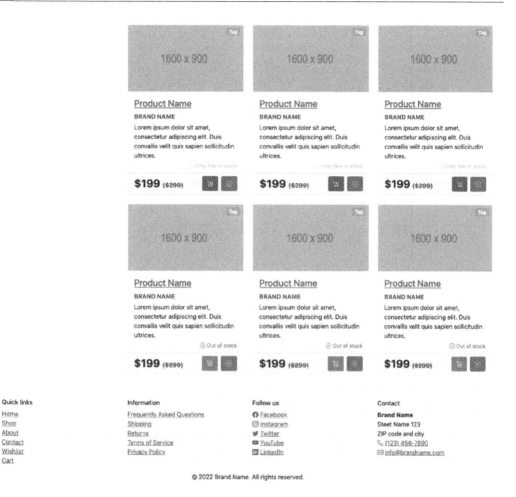

Figure 7.18 – Wishlist page on a desktop device

The overall code structure in the `<body>` tag for this page can be seen next. The different modules have been replaced with [Name of the module] and they will be further described afterward (except for Header and Footer, which were described in the previous section):

part-2/chapter-7/website/wishlist.html

```
<body>
  [Header]
  [Page title]
  <div class="container">
    <div class="row">
```

```
        <div class="col-lg-4 col-xxl-3 mb-3 mb-lg-0">
          [Sidebar]
        </div>
        <div class="col-lg-8 col-xxl-9 pt-lg-3 mb-5">
          [Products overview]
        </div>
      </div>
    </div>
    [Footer]
    [Modal]
    <script src="../../../bootstrap/dist/js/
      bootstrap.bundle.min.js"></script>
  </body>
```

Sidebar

The sidebar module is using the **Card** component to wrap around a **List group** component showing the user's wishlists and a button to create a new wishlist. When clicking that button, a modal module (described shortly) will become visible. Below the card, there's a primary button to add all products to the cart at once.

Products overview

This is a responsive grid system created with the use of the Product card module to show the products on the current wishlist. The user can add a product to the cart, but the **Add to wishlist** action has been replaced by a **Remove from wishlist** button.

Modal

A **Modal** component is triggered when the user clicks the button to create a new wishlist in the sidebar. This modal contains a modal title, a close button, a paragraph, and a simple form with an input group.

Cart (cart.html)

This page shows the cart initially, and the checkout flow hidden behind tab panes. Above the navigation tabs, there's also a progress bar to show the current progress of the checkout flow.

The first tab pane shows the shopping cart, with a list of the products on the left side and a summary showing the total amount on the right side.

The second pane shows the shipping details, with a form for personal details, buttons to select the shipping method, and an info alert. On the right side, there's an expanded summary with a product list and the total amount.

The third pane shows the payment options, with a form for credit card details and a PayPal option on the left side and the expanded summary with a product list and the total amount on the right side.

Here are three screenshots of the full page as seen on a desktop device, with the three tab panes shown one at a time:

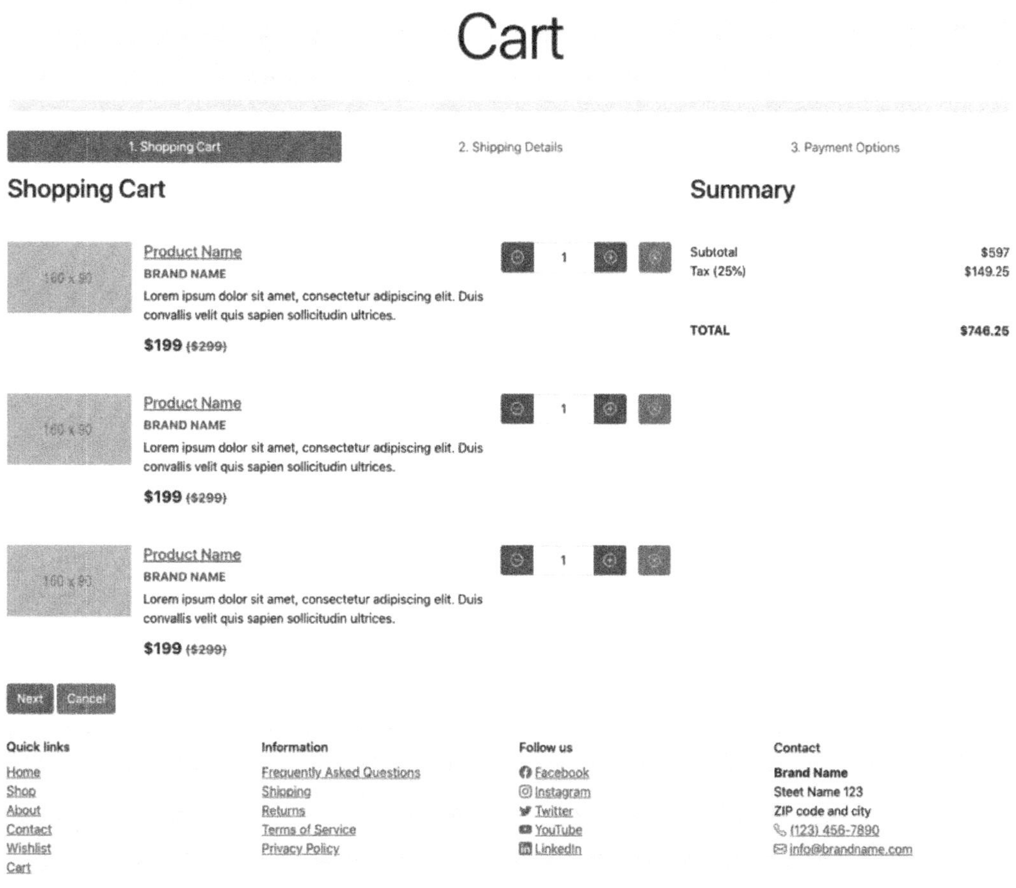

Figure 7.19 – Cart page (tab 1 visible) on a desktop device

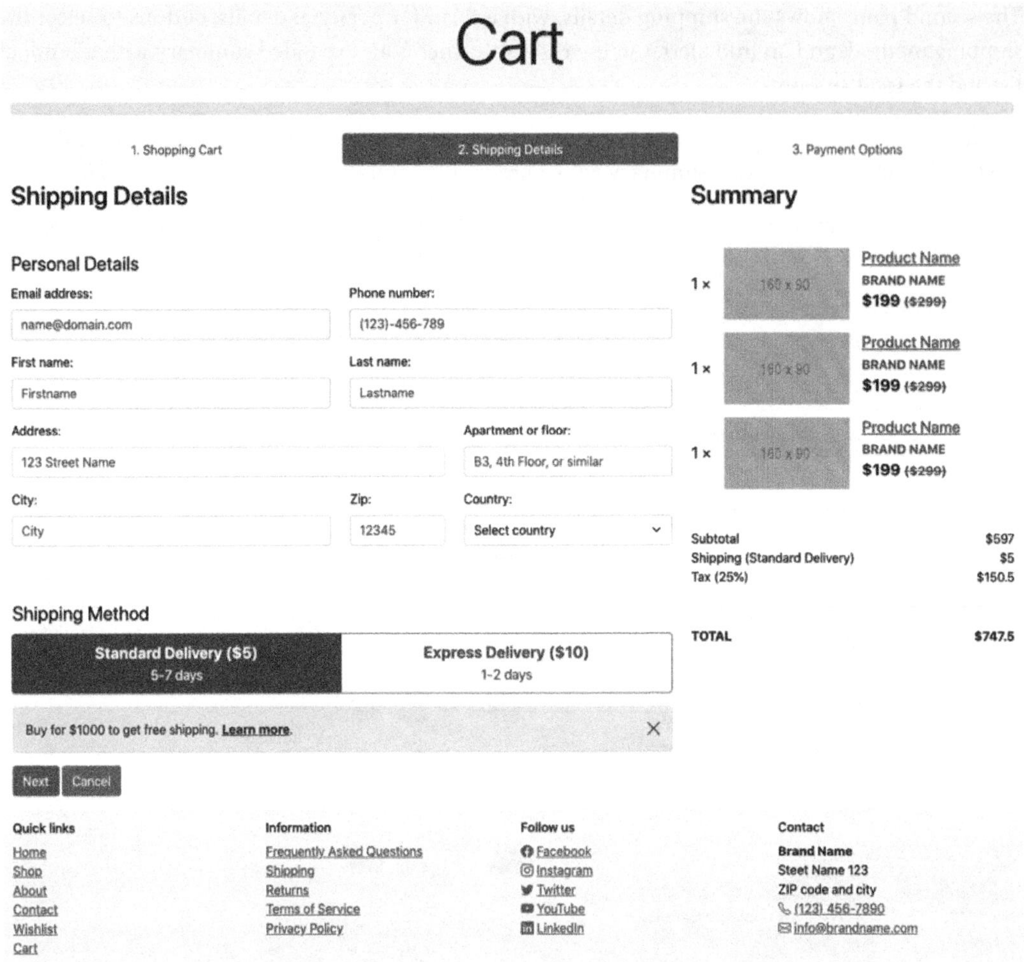

Cart

| 1. Shopping Cart | 2. Shipping Details | 3. Payment Options |

Shipping Details

Personal Details

Email address:
name@domain.com

Phone number:
(123)-456-789

First name:
Firstname

Last name:
Lastname

Address:
123 Street Name

Apartment or floor:
B3, 4th Floor, or similar

City:
City

Zip:
12345

Country:
Select country

Shipping Method

| Standard Delivery ($5) 5-7 days | Express Delivery ($10) 1-2 days |

Buy for $1000 to get free shipping. **Learn more.**   ✕

[Next] [Cancel]

Summary

1 ×	160 x 90	Product Name BRAND NAME **$199** ($299)
1 ×	160 x 90	Product Name BRAND NAME **$199** ($299)
1 ×	160 x 90	Product Name BRAND NAME **$199** ($299)

Subtotal	$597
Shipping (Standard Delivery)	$5
Tax (25%)	$150.5
TOTAL	**$747.5**

Quick links
Home
Shop
About
Contact
Wishlist
Cart

Information
Frequently Asked Questions
Shipping
Returns
Terms of Service
Privacy Policy

Follow us
Facebook
Instagram
Twitter
YouTube
LinkedIn

Contact
Brand Name
Steet Name 123
ZIP code and city
(123) 456-7890
info@brandname.com

Figure 7.20 – Cart page (tab 2 visible) on a desktop device

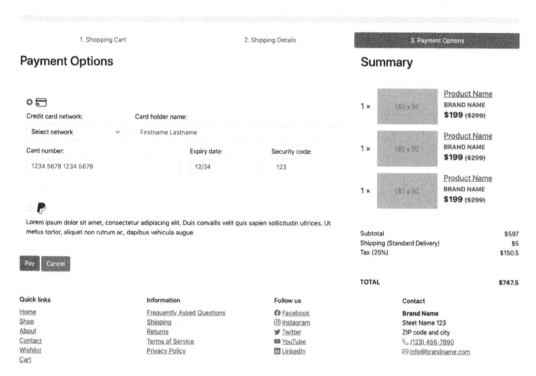

Figure 7.21 – Cart page (tab 3 visible) on a desktop device

The overall code structure in the `<body>` tag for this page can be seen next. The different modules have been replaced with `[Name of the module]` and they will be further described afterward (except for Header and Footer, which were described in the previous section):

part-2/chapter-7/website/cart.html

```
<body>
  [Header]
  [Page title]
  <div class="container">
    [Progress bar]
    [Tab navigation]
    <div class="tab-content">
      <div id="cartTabs-pane-1" class="tab-pane fade show
```

```
active" role="tabpanel" aria-labelledby=
"cartTabs-1">
<div class="row mb-5">
  <div class="col-xl-8 mb-5 mb-xl-0">
    [Shopping cart]
  </div>
  <div class="col-xl-4">
    [Summary]
  </div>
</div>
</div>
<div id="cartTabs-pane-2" class="tab-pane fade"
  role="tabpanel" aria-labelledby="cartTabs-2">
  <div class="row mb-5">
    <div class="col-xl-8 mb-5 mb-xl-0">
      [Shipping details]
    </div>
    <div class="col-xl-4">
      [Summary]
    </div>
  </div>
</div>
<div id="cartTabs-pane-3" class="tab-pane fade"
  role="tabpanel" aria-labelledby="cartTabs-3">
  <div class="row mb-5">
    <div class="col-xl-8 mb-5 mb-xl-0">
      [Payment options]
    </div>
    <div class="col-xl-4">
      [Summary]
    </div>
  </div>
</div>
</div>
</div>
</div>
[Footer]
```

```
<script src="../../../bootstrap/dist/js/
   bootstrap.bundle.min.js"></script>
</body>
```

Progress bar

This module shows the current progress of the checkout flow. It is created with the **Progress** component, and its current value (and width) is set to 0. When that is changed to a positive number from 1-100, the progress bar will become visible with the primary color and be striped and animated.

Tab navigation

This module shows the three steps of the checkout flow with a number and heading in each tab. The tabs can be used to change the visible pane. The module is created using the **Nav** component with the .nav-pills variation to change the navigation tabs from tabs to pills.

Shopping cart

This module is placed on the left side of the first tab pane and shows the shopping cart with a list of the products. The amount of each product can be changed with an **Input group** component and the product can also be removed from the cart. At the very bottom, the user can advance to the next tab or cancel.

Shipping details

This module is placed on the left side of the second pane and shows the shipping details. First, there's a form for personal details laid out with a responsive grid system and then follows a **Button group** component with radio buttons to toggle between two different shipping methods. Below that, there's an info alert about free shipping created with the **Alert** component. At the very bottom, the user can advance to the next tab or cancel.

Payment options

This module is placed on the left side of the third pane and shows the payment options. The user can, with the use of two radio buttons, choose between two payment options. First, there's a form for credit card details laid out with a responsive grid system and below, a PayPal option. At the very bottom, the user can pay or cancel.

Summary

This module is used in all three panes. In the first pane, it only contains information about the total amount, and in the second and third pane, it also contains the list of products in the cart.

Frequently Asked Questions (faq.html)

This page shows three sections, each with a heading followed by an accordion with frequently asked questions and their answers.

Here is a screenshot of the full page as seen on a desktop device:

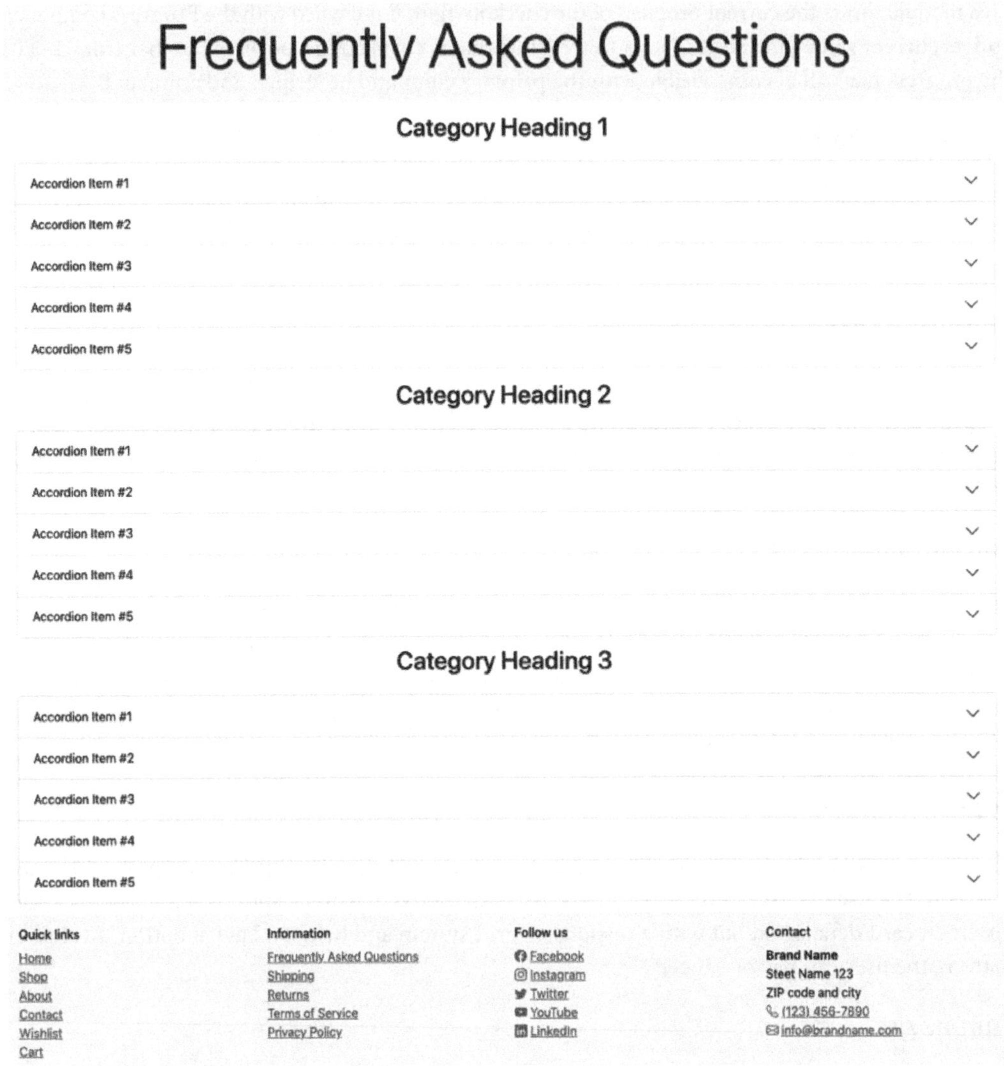

Figure 7.22 – Frequently Asked Questions page on a desktop device

The overall code structure in the <body> tag for this page can be seen next. The different modules have been replaced with [Name of the module] and they will be further described afterward (except for Header and Footer, which were described in the previous section):

part-2/chapter-7/website/faq.html

```
<body>
  [Header]
  [Page title]
  <div class="container">
    [Accordion]
    [Accordion]
    [Accordion]
  </div>
  [Footer]
  <script src="../../../bootstrap/dist/js/
    bootstrap.bundle.min.js"></script>
</body>
```

Accordion

This module consists of a heading and an **Accordion** component. Each accordion item contains a frequently asked question in the accordion header and the corresponding answer in the accordion body. Only one accordion item can be expanded at a time.

Article page (shipping.html, returns.html, terms-of-service.html, and privacy-policy.html)

This page shows general information presented as an article. It has a sticky sidebar with page navigation on the left side, and the main area with an article containing various typography elements, images, and a table.

Here is a screenshot of the full page as seen on a desktop device:

Shipping

PAGE NAVIGATION

Heading #1

Heading #2

Heading #3

Heading #4

Lorem ipsum dolor sit amet, consectetur adipiscing elit. Duis convallis velit quis sapien sollicitudin ultrices. Ut metus tortor, aliquet non rutrum ac, dapibus vehicula augue. Etiam congue erat sem, vitae gravida nunc pretium vitae. Fusce sed ex tellus.

Heading #1

Lorem ipsum dolor sit amet, consectetur adipiscing elit. Duis convallis velit quis sapien sollicitudin ultrices. Ut metus tortor, aliquet non rutrum ac, dapibus vehicula augue. Etiam congue erat sem, vitae gravida nunc pretium vitae. Fusce sed ex tellus. Quisque auctor viverra feugiat. Nulla urna odio, porta ut tristique ut, consequat non dolor. Etiam varius maximus dolor, at consectetur lectus. Mauris rutrum aliquet tellus, sed convallis diam.

Subheading

Lorem ipsum dolor sit amet, consectetur adipiscing elit. Duis convallis velit quis sapien sollicitudin ultrices. Ut metus tortor, aliquet non rutrum ac, dapibus vehicula augue. Etiam congue erat sem, vitae gravida nunc pretium vitae. Fusce sed ex tellus. Quisque auctor viverra feugiat. Nulla urna odio, porta ut tristique ut, consequat non dolor. Etiam varius maximus dolor, at consectetur lectus. Mauris rutrum aliquet tellus, sed convallis diam.

Link to other article

Heading #2

Lorem ipsum dolor sit amet, consectetur adipiscing elit. Duis convallis velit quis sapien sollicitudin ultrices. Ut metus tortor, aliquet non rutrum ac, dapibus vehicula augue. Etiam congue erat sem, vitae gravida nunc pretium vitae. Fusce sed ex tellus. Quisque auctor viverra feugiat. Nulla urna odio, porta ut tristique ut, consequat non dolor. Etiam varius maximus dolor, at consectetur lectus. Mauris rutrum aliquet tellus, sed convallis diam.

- Lorem ipsum dolor sit amet, consectetur adipiscing elit. Duis convallis velit quis sapien sollicitudin ultrices.
- Lorem ipsum dolor sit amet, consectetur adipiscing elit. Duis convallis velit quis sapien sollicitudin ultrices.
- Lorem ipsum dolor sit amet, consectetur adipiscing elit. Duis convallis velit quis sapien sollicitudin ultrices.

Heading #3

Lorem ipsum dolor sit amet, consectetur adipiscing elit. Duis convallis velit quis sapien sollicitudin ultrices. Ut metus tortor, aliquet non rutrum ac, dapibus vehicula augue. Etiam congue erat sem, vitae gravida nunc pretium vitae. Fusce sed ex tellus. Quisque auctor viverra feugiat. Nulla urna odio, porta ut tristique ut, consequat non dolor. Etiam varius maximus dolor, at consectetur lectus. Mauris rutrum aliquet tellus, sed convallis diam.

1. Lorem ipsum dolor sit amet, consectetur adipiscing elit. Duis convallis velit quis sapien sollicitudin ultrices.

2. Lorem ipsum dolor sit amet, consectetur adipiscing elit. Duis convallis velit quis sapien sollicitudin ultrices.

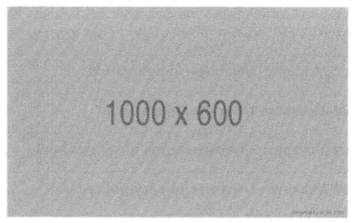

3. Lorem ipsum dolor sit amet, consectetur adipiscing elit. Duis convallis velit quis sapien sollicitudin ultrices.

Heading #4

Lorem ipsum dolor sit amet, consectetur adipiscing elit. Duis convallis velit quis sapien sollicitudin ultrices. Ut metus tortor, aliquet non rutrum ac, dapibus vehicula augue. Etiam congue erat sem, vitae gravida nunc pretium vitae. Fusce sed ex tellus. Quisque auctor viverra feugiat. Nulla urna odio, porta ut tristique ut, consequat non dolor. Etiam varius maximus dolor, at consectetur lectus. Mauris rutrum aliquet tellus, sed convallis diam.

#	First Column	Second Column	Third Column
First Row	Table Cell	Table Cell	Table Cell
Second Row	Table Cell	Table Cell	Table Cell
Third Row	Table Cell	Table Cell	Table Cell

Quick links	Information	Follow us	Contact
Home	Frequently Asked Questions	Facebook	**Brand Name**
Shop	Shipping	Instagram	Steet Name 123
About	Returns	Twitter	ZIP code and city
Contact	Terms of Service	YouTube	(123) 456-7890
Wishlist	Privacy Policy	LinkedIn	info@brandname.com
Cart			

Figure 7.23 – Article page on a desktop device

The overall code structure in the `<body>` tag for this page can be seen next. The different modules have been replaced with [Name of the module] and they will be further described afterward (except for Header and Footer, which were described in the previous section):

part-2/chapter-7/website/shipping.html

part-2/chapter-7/website/returns.html

part-2/chapter-7/website/terms-of-service.html

part-2/chapter-7/website/privacy-policy.html

```
<body>
  [Header]
  [Page title]
  <div class="container">
    <div class="row">
      <div class="col-lg-3 mb-3 mb-lg-0">
        [Page navigation]
      </div>
      <div class="col-lg-9 pt-lg-3">
        [Article]
      </div>
    </div>
  </div>
  [Footer]
  <script src="../../../bootstrap/dist/js/
    bootstrap.bundle.min.js"></script>
</body>
```

Page navigation

The page navigation is created using a **Card** component with a **List group** component inside. It's made sticky using a position helper. It also uses the **Scrollspy** component to highlight the section that's currently being scrolled within.

Article

The article contains various typography elements: a lead paragraph, different headings, regular paragraphs, a link, an unordered list, an ordered list, images, and a table.

Summary

In this chapter, we first got a short introduction to the website project created for this book, including an overview of the sitemap. Then, we learned how Bootstrap Icons are used to make the website more user-friendly and visually appealing.

The rest of this chapter was dedicated to getting an overview of the different global modules and page types being used, including a description of all the different modules being used on each page and how they were created using only default Bootstrap 5 components. This was supplemented with screenshots of all pages as seen on a desktop device.

In the next chapter, we will customize the visual style of our website with Sass.

8

Customizing the Website Using Bootstrap 5 Variables, Utility API, and Sass

In this chapter, we will start customizing the website that was described and previewed in the previous chapter. We will do that primarily by changing some of the Bootstrap 5 variables that are used for styling all the elements of Bootstrap 5. While doing this, we will change some of the gutter and spacing utility classes being used to better match the new style. We will also use the utility API to modify some of the existing utilities and optimize the layout by using these new utility classes. Finally, we will also add our own Sass to customize the website even further.

In this chapter, there will be many code examples and some screenshots, but I recommend that you explore this customized version of the website in a browser on different device sizes to really see the difference from before.

In this chapter, we're going to cover the following main topics:

- Importing Bootstrap 5 files and custom styles
- Default variable overrides
- Variable values using existing variables
- Utilities
- Other custom styling

Technical requirements

- To preview the examples, you will need a code editor and a browser. The source code for all code examples can be found here: `https://github.com/PacktPublishing/The-Missing-Bootstrap-5-Guide`.

- To compile Sass to CSS, you will need any of the following:

    - **Node.js**, if you prefer a **command-line interface (CLI)** using Terminal (macOS) or Command Prompt (Windows)

    - **Scout-App**, if you prefer a **graphical user interface (GUI)**

    - **Visual Studio Code**, if you prefer to use an extension from the Visual Studio Code Marketplace

All these approaches are explained in *Chapter 2, Using and Compiling Sass.*

Importing Bootstrap 5 files and custom styles

In *Chapter 4, Bootstrap 5 Global Options and Colors*, we learned about the bootstrap.scss file and that it contains all the code that will import the individual Sass partial files for the various elements of Bootstrap 5. We will use a slightly different order of these @import statements, which will make customization easier. We will also add @import statements for four of our own SCSS files, which we use to override variables (two files for this), define utilities, and add custom styles, in between the Bootstrap 5 @import statements.

The order of the @import statements is as follows:

- Required import of Bootstrap 5's _functions.scss file

- Import of *our own* _default-variable-overrides.scss file, which is used for default variable overrides

- Required import of Bootstrap 5's _variables.scss file

- Import of *our own* _variable-value-using-variable.scss file, which is used for overriding variable values with existing variables

- Required import of Bootstrap 5's _maps.scss, _mixins.scss, and _root.scss files

- Import of optional Bootstrap 5 partial files for layout, content, forms, and components

- Import of Bootstrap 5's _helpers.scss file

- Import of Bootstrap 5's _utilities.scss file

- Import of *our own* _utilities.scss file, which is used to define the utilities that we want to generate using the utility API

- Import of Bootstrap 5's utilities/_api.scss file used to generate the utility classes

- Import of *our own* _custom-styles.scss file, which is used to add any additional custom SCSS

Next, you will see all the code for the @import statements (the comments plus code for the @import statements regarding our own files have been highlighted):

part-2/chapter-8/website/scss/style.scss

```scss
// Required
@import "../../../../bootstrap/scss/functions";

// Default variable overrides
@import "default-variable-overrides";

// Required
@import "../../../../bootstrap/scss/variables";

// Variable value using existing variable
@import "variable-value-using-variable";

// Required
@import "../../../../bootstrap/scss/maps";
@import "../../../../bootstrap/scss/mixins";
@import "../../../../bootstrap/scss/root";

// Optional Bootstrap CSS
@import "../../../../bootstrap/scss/reboot";
@import "../../../../bootstrap/scss/type";
@import "../../../../bootstrap/scss/images";
@import "../../../../bootstrap/scss/containers";
@import "../../../../bootstrap/scss/grid";
@import "../../../../bootstrap/scss/tables";
@import "../../../../bootstrap/scss/forms";
@import "../../../../bootstrap/scss/buttons";
@import "../../../../bootstrap/scss/transitions";
@import "../../../../bootstrap/scss/dropdown";
@import "../../../../bootstrap/scss/button-group";
@import "../../../../bootstrap/scss/nav";
@import "../../../../bootstrap/scss/navbar";
@import "../../../../bootstrap/scss/card";
@import "../../../../bootstrap/scss/accordion";
@import "../../../../bootstrap/scss/breadcrumb";
@import "../../../../bootstrap/scss/pagination";
```

```scss
@import "../../../../bootstrap/scss/badge";
@import "../../../../bootstrap/scss/alert";
@import "../../../../bootstrap/scss/progress";
@import "../../../../bootstrap/scss/list-group";
@import "../../../../bootstrap/scss/close";
@import "../../../../bootstrap/scss/toasts";
@import "../../../../bootstrap/scss/modal";
@import "../../../../bootstrap/scss/tooltip";
@import "../../../../bootstrap/scss/popover";
@import "../../../../bootstrap/scss/carousel";
@import "../../../../bootstrap/scss/spinners";
@import "../../../../bootstrap/scss/offcanvas";
@import "../../../../bootstrap/scss/placeholders";


// Helpers
@import "../../../../bootstrap/scss/helpers";


// Utilities
@import "../../../../bootstrap/scss/utilities";


// Define utilities
@import "utilities";


// Utilities API
@import "../../../../bootstrap/scss/utilities/api";


// Own custom styles
@import "custom-styles";
```

We are now ready to start customizing our website and adding the customization code into the four different files of our own.

We will start with the code for default variable overrides in the _default-variable-overrides. scss file.

Default variable overrides

Filename: _default-variable-overrides.scss

In this file, we will add *all* customization code regarding colors, global options, global variables, and layout, and *some* of the customization code regarding forms and components. There will also be customization code regarding forms and components (as well as other customization code) in the `_variable-value-using-variable.scss` file, which we will take a closer look at later in this chapter.

Color palette

The first thing we want to do is define our own color palette. Together with typography (which we will customize later in this chapter), this is a very important aspect of a visual design that defines a brand.

We override all contextual color classes by assigning them a new hexadecimal color value, but any other ways to define colors can be used. The `$secondary`, `$light`, and `$dark` variables are assigned a color value from the list of gray colors defined in Bootstrap 5, as noted in the comments. The variables for the gray colors are not imported yet, and therefore, we can't use them as the value for `$secondary`, `$light`, and `$dark`:

part-2/chapter-8/website/scss/_default-variable-overrides.scss line 1-10

```
// Color palette
$primary: #0464a1;
$secondary: #adb5bd; // = $gray-500
$success: #2A9D8F;
$info: #E9C46A;
$warning: #F4A261;
$danger: #E76F51;
$light: #dee2e6; // = $gray-300
$dark: #343a40; // $gray-800
```

After having defined our own color palette, we will now move on to change one of the global options.

Global options

For this website, we only want to change the shadows option of Bootstrap 5. We set it to `true` to have box shadows added to various components:

part-2/chapter-8/website/scss/_default-variable-overrides.scss line 12-14

```
// Shadows
$enable-shadows: true;
```

Global variables

Global variables are variables that are used as values for other variables in many other places. The global variables with the biggest impact are those for spacing and border-radius, which we will change now.

Spacer

We can change the default styling of many Bootstrap 5 elements by modifying the `$spacer` variable, and we can control the values of the spacing utilities by modifying the `$spacers` map.

We will use the new spacing values, as seen in the following code:

part-2/chapter-8/website/scss/_default-variable-overrides.scss line 17-26

```
// Spacer
$spacer: 1.5rem;
$spacers: (
  0: 0,
  1: $spacer / 4,
  2: $spacer / 2,
  3: $spacer,
  4: $spacer * 2,
  5: $spacer * 4,
);
```

Increasing the spacer affects many elements of Bootstrap 5, including the gutter utilities used with the responsive grid system. To get some more consistent spacing between columns when using nested grid systems, we change the `.g-4` class used on the Home page (in the Popular products module), on the Shop page (in the Products overview module), on the Product page (in the Related products module), and on the Wishlist page (in the Products overview module) to `.g-3`.

Another minor adjustment we need to make is to change the `.mt-2` class to `.mt-1` on the three `<div>` elements wrapping the quote icons in the `<blockquote>` elements on the Product page. See the code change here:

part-2/chapter-8/website/product.html

```
// Original code
<div class="text-secondary float-start fs-1 lh-1 mt-2 me-2
border-top border-start border-2 border-secondary p-1"><i
class="bi-quote"></i></div>
// Updated code
```

```
<div class="text-secondary float-start fs-1 lh-1 mt-1 me-2
border-top border-start border-2 border-secondary p-1"><i
class="bi-quote"></i></div>
```

Border radius

We can also change the default styling of many Bootstrap 5 elements by modifying three of the variables related to border radius: $border-radius, $border-radius-sm, and $border-radius-lg. The last border-radius variable, $border-radius-pill, is only used for the border utility, so we won't change that.

The most radical change would be to set all the variables to 0 to remove the border radius from all elements and have straight corners, but we will instead double the default border radius and slightly adjust the other two:

part-2/chapter-8/website/scss/_default-variable-overrides.scss line 28-31

```
// Border radius
$border-radius: .5rem;
$border-radius-sm: .25rem;
$border-radius-lg: .75rem;
```

Layout

It's possible to adjust the styling of the layout regarding breakpoints, containers, and the grid system. If we were to change the number of columns in the grid system, it would require a lot of changes to the markup for our grid systems in our HTML pages, so we will stick to changing the breakpoints and containers for our website.

Breakpoints

The breakpoint settings are used for the grid system and containers as well as for the following elements that have responsive variations: dropdown, list group, modal, navbar, tables, and position helper.

We will increase each breakpoint by 40 pixels to make our grid system differ a bit from the default Bootstrap 5 settings:

part-2/chapter-8/website/scss/_default-variable-overrides.scss line 34-42

```
// Breakpoints
$grid-breakpoints: (
  xs: 0,
  sm: 616px,
```

```
    md: 808px,
    lg: 1032px,
    xl: 1240px,
    xxl: 1440px
);
```

Container

Since we increased the breakpoint sizes by 40 pixels, we will also increase our container max width sizes by 40 pixels. It's not necessary to change both grid breakpoints and container max widths with the same value, but you should make sure to test it when you are making changes to any of those:

part-2/chapter-8/website/scss/_default-variable-overrides.scss 44-51

```
// Container
$container-max-widths: (
    sm: 580px,
    md: 760px,
    lg: 1000px,
    xl: 1180px,
    xxl: 1360px
);
```

We have now made several changes to the layout of Bootstrap 5 and will continue to customize the forms.

Forms

Inputs and buttons are already affected by the global variables for border radius that we changed earlier, but not by the global variables for spacers. Therefore, we will adjust the vertical and horizontal padding of both inputs and buttons here. They share the same variables for padding, typography, focus states, and border width, so we only need to override the padding in one place to affect both inputs and buttons:

part-2/chapter-8/website/scss/_default-variable-overrides.scss line 53-56

```
// Inputs and buttons
$input-btn-padding-y: .5rem;
$input-btn-padding-x: 1em;
```

Components

In the following, we will change various properties of some of the components being used in our website.

Breadcrumb

For the breadcrumb component, we will change the symbol of the breadcrumb divider:

part-2/chapter-8/website/scss/_default-variable-overrides.scss line 59-60

```
// Breadcrumb
$breadcrumb-divider: quote("-");
```

Carousel

For the carousel component, we will increase the width of the control icons on each side and increase the height and spacing of the indicators:

part-2/chapter-8/website/scss/_default-variable-overrides.scss line 62-65

```
// Carousel
$carousel-control-icon-width: 4rem;
$carousel-indicator-height: 10px;
$carousel-indicator-spacer: 10px;
```

Dropdown

For the dropdown component, we will set the minimum width to 0, so it doesn't take up any extra horizontal space when the dropdown items don't contain much text:

part-2/chapter-8/website/scss/_default-variable-overrides.scss line 67-68

```
// Dropdown
$dropdown-min-width: 0;
```

Modal

For the modal component, we will increase the size of the large modal variation, increase the opacity of the backdrop, and change the transition when it's opened and closed:

part-2/chapter-8/website/scss/_default-variable-overrides.scss line 70-73

```
// Modal
$modal-lg: 900px;
$modal-backdrop-opacity: .75;
$modal-fade-transform: rotate(5deg) scale(.9);
```

Navs

For the navs component, we will increase the vertical padding of the nav links to make them larger:

part-2/chapter-8/website/scss/_default-variable-overrides.scss line 75-76

```
// Navs
$nav-link-padding-y: 1rem;
```

Progress

For the progress component, we will increase the height, decrease the animation duration, and decrease the transition duration:

part-2/chapter-8/website/scss/_default-variable-overrides.scss line 78-81

```
// Progress
$progress-height: 2rem;
$progress-bar-animation-timing: .5s linear infinite;
$progress-bar-transition: width .4s ease;
```

Spinner

For the spinner component, we will increase the animation duration to make it spin a little bit slower:

part-2/chapter-8/website/scss/_default-variable-overrides.scss line 83-84

```
// Spinner
$spinner-animation-speed: 1s;
```

We have now made all the customizations regarding default variable overrides, so we will move on to further customization with variable values using existing variables.

Variable values using existing variables

Filename: `_variable-value-using-variable.scss`

In this file, we will add *all* customization code for content, *some* of the customization code for forms and components, and the customization code for one helper class. The reason we import this file after the import of the required Bootstrap 5 `_variables.scss` file is that we want to use existing variables from `_variables.scss` as the new value when overriding the different variables related to content, some variables for forms and components, and a variable for a helper class. This is especially helpful when we want to assign color variables to other variables.

Some of the code in the `_variable-value-using-variable.scss` file doesn't have to be placed there and could as well have been placed in the `_default-variable-overrides.scss` file. But, I have chosen to group related variables together as much as possible, and that's why all variables related to for example content have been grouped together here.

Content

The Content category of Bootstrap 5 contains typography, images, tables, and figures. We will make changes to all of that, except for tables.

Typography

As mentioned earlier, typography is a very important aspect of visual design. Because of this, we will make major changes to the overall typography.

First, we will use these two free fonts from Google Fonts: Roboto and Comfortaa. These can be implemented by adding the following three `<link>` tags to the `<head>` element just before the closing `</head>` tag in all HTML files:

*.html line 9-11

```
<link rel="preconnect" href="https://fonts.googleapis.com">
<link rel="preconnect" href="https://fonts.gstatic.com"
crossorigin>
<link href="https://fonts.googleapis.com/
css2?family=Comfortaa:wght@300;500&family=Roboto:wght@300;400;
700&display=swap" rel="stylesheet">
```

The two Google Fonts are now available to use, and they will be added as a value to the `$font-family-base` and `$headings-font-family` variables in the next code block.

Here's an overview of all the changes we are making to the typography:

- Background color and text color of <body>
- Default font family, font size, and line height
- Styles for links
- Font family, font sizes, font weight, line height, and margin-bottom for regular headings
- Font sizes and line height for display headings
- Font size for the lead paragraph

See how all these changes are made in the following code:

part-2/chapter-8/website/scss/_variable-value-using-variable.scss line 2-37

```scss
// Typograhy
// Body styles
$body-bg: $gray-100;
$body-color: $gray-700;
// Basic typography styles
$font-family-base: 'Roboto', sans-serif;
$font-size-base: 1.125rem;
$line-height-base: 1.4;
$line-height-sm: 1.2;
// Link styles
$link-decoration: none;
$link-hover-color: shift-color($link-color,
$link-shade-percentage);
$link-hover-decoration: underline;
// Heading styles
$headings-font-family: 'Comfortaa', cursive;
$h1-font-size: $font-size-base * 3;
$h2-font-size: $font-size-base * 2.5;
$h3-font-size: $font-size-base * 2;
$h4-font-size: $font-size-base * 1.75;
$h5-font-size: $font-size-base * 1.5;
$h6-font-size: $font-size-base * 1.25;
$headings-font-weight: $font-weight-bold;
```

```scss
$headings-line-height: $line-height-sm;
$headings-margin-bottom: $spacer * 0.25;
// Display styles
$display-font-sizes: (
  1: $h1-font-size * 1.5,
  2: $h2-font-size * 1.5,
  3: $h3-font-size * 1.5,
  4: $h4-font-size * 1.5,
  5: $h5-font-size * 1.5,
  6: $h6-font-size * 1.5
);
$display-line-height: $headings-line-height;
// Lead styles
$lead-font-size: $font-size-base * 1.375;
```

Images

For images, we will make some changes to the image thumbnail. We will increase the padding, change the background color, change the border color, and decrease the border radius:

---

part-2/chapter-8/website/scss/_variable-value-using-variable.scss line 39-43

```scss
// Images
$thumbnail-padding: .5rem;
$thumbnail-bg: $body-bg;
$thumbnail-border-color: $gray-500;
$thumbnail-border-radius: $border-radius-sm;
```

Notice that we just set the background color of image thumbnails to the background color of <body>, which we just changed in the preceding typography code block. We will use that variable ($body-bg) or the related variable for the text color of <body> ($body-color) for all the remaining customizations in this file.

Figures

For figures, we will increase the font size and change the text color for the figure caption:

part-2/chapter-8/website/scss/_variable-value-using-variable.scss line 45-47

```
// Figures
$figure-caption-font-size: $font-size-lg;
$figure-caption-color: $body-color;
```

Forms

We will set the background color of input elements, checkboxes, radio buttons, and select elements. We do this by first assigning the $body-bg value to $input-bg, and then using that variable ($input-bg) as the value for the $form-check-input-bg and $form-select-bg variables:

part-2/chapter-8/website/scss/_variable-value-using-variable.scss line 49-53

```
// Form controls
$input-bg: $body-bg;
$form-check-input-bg: $input-bg;
$form-select-bg: $input-bg;
```

Components

As you can see next, we will place those component variables that need the $body-bg variable as the value for their background color here (in this file and after the customization for content).

Card

For the card component, we will change the background color:

part-2/chapter-8/website/scss/_variable-value-using-variable.scss line 56-57

```
// Card
$card-bg: $body-bg;
```

List group

For the list group component, we will change the background color:

part-2/chapter-8/website/scss/_variable-value-using-variable.scss line 59-60

```
// List group
$list-group-bg: $body-bg;
```

Helpers

Helpers can't be customized using variables in the `_variables.scss` file, since they don't have the same visual properties as the rest of the Bootstrap 5 elements. The exception to this is the ratio helper, which we will see next.

Ratio

The ratio helper classes are generated from the `$aspect-ratios` Sass map. We can add more values to this map by merging it with a custom map:

part-2/chapter-8/website/scss/_variable-value-using-variable.scss line 62-69

```
// Ratio
// Create custom ratio map
$custom-ratio: (
  "5x3": calc(3 / 5 * 100%)
);
// Merge "$aspect-ratios" and "$custom-ratio"
$aspect-ratios: map-merge($aspect-ratios, $custom-ratio);
```

In the preceding code, the new `$custom-ratio` Sass map is created with the new property and aspect ratio 5 by 3. The value is based on the same calculation as the existing values in the `$aspect-ratios` Sass map. When these maps are merged, we now get the new `.ratio-5x3` helper class. After this change, we need to update the ratio helper class already being used on our Contact page like so:

part-2/chapter-8/website/contact.html

```
// Original code
<div class="ratio ratio-21x9">
```

```
    <iframe src="[URL for Google Maps embed]"
      allowfullscreen></iframe>
</div>
// Updated code
<div class="ratio ratio-5x3">
    <iframe src="[URL for Google Maps embed]"
      allowfullscreen></iframe>
</div>
```

We have now made all the customization for helpers, so we will move on to customizing utilities.

Utilities

Filename: _utilities.scss

In this file, we will add all customization code that uses the utility API. Some utilities have already been customized because their values are based on variables from the _variables.scss file, which we have already been overriding earlier in this chapter. This includes the spacing utilities and various text utilities. Additional customization requires code using the utility API.

Before modifying any utilities with the utility API, we should consider which utilities, of those we are already using, are not adequate or flexible enough in their current form, and then modify them.

For our website, we will improve two things on the Cart page. First, we want to improve the responsive layout of the elements in the Products overview in the **Shopping Cart** tab pane by using more flexible sizing utilities. Second, we want to adjust our existing use of borders on the <div> element that wraps around our Products overview in the **Summary** section of the **Shipping Details** tab pane and **Payment Options** tab pane by using more flexible border utilities.

Since we're not just modifying the values of some utilities but are making them more flexible and thus generating more utility classes we can use, we will also have to update the HTML accordingly.

Sizing

We want to change the sizing utility for width, so we can better control the layout of some of the elements across breakpoints. We will make the utilities for width responsive and add the extra properties and values 33: 33% and 67: 67% using the following code:

part-2/chapter-8/website/scss/_utilities.scss line 1-20

```
// Make sizing utilities for width responsive and add extra
// values
$utilities: map-merge(
```

```
$utilities,
(
  "width": (
    property: width,
    responsive: true,
    class: w,
    values: (
      25: 25%,
      33: 33%,
      50: 50%,
      67: 67%,
      75: 75%,
      100: 100%,
      auto: auto
    )
  )
)
);
```

This will generate a lot of new responsive width utility classes as well as new classes for the new properties and values we added, so we will now update our HTML in the following way:

part-2/chapter-8/website/cart.html

```
// Original code
<div class="d-flex align-items-start me-3 mb-3 mb-md-0">[code
for product]</div>
<div class="d-flex">
  <div class="input-group w-auto me-3">[code for input
    group]</div>
  [code for remove button]
</div>
// Updated code
<div class="d-flex align-items-start me-3 mb-3 mb-md-0 w-md-67
w-lg-75 w-xl-67 w-xxl-75">[code for product]</div>
<div class="d-flex w-75 w-sm-50 w-md-33 w-lg-25 w-xl-33
w-xxl-25">
  <div class="input-group w-auto me-3">[code for input
```

```
      group]</div>
    [code for remove button]
  </div>
```

In the preceding code, we are now using 4 and 6 width utility classes, respectively, for two different parts of our layout. If we take the second part, we can see that we are adjusting the width for every existing breakpoint. This is sometimes necessary to get the best possible layout when working with responsive design.

Border

We want to improve the use of borders on the `<div>` element that wraps around our Products overview in the **Summary** section of the **Shipping Details** tab pane and **Payment Options** tab pane. Currently, there's a border at the bottom across all breakpoints, and that doesn't align with the responsive grid layout being used in the **Summary** section. The elements in the **Summary** section are stacked on the `xs`, `sm`, `xl`, and `xxl` breakpoints and turned into a two-column grid on the breakpoints in between (`md` and `lg`). We want the border to be placed on the right side for the `md` and `lg` breakpoints, and at the bottom for all other breakpoints.

To accomplish this, we need to make the border utilities for `border-width`, `border-bottom`, and `border-end` responsive, and we can do that with the following code:

part-2/chapter-8/website/scss/_utilities.scss line 22-38

```
// Make border utilities for border-width, border-bottom
// and border-end responsive
$utilities: map-merge(
  $utilities, (
    "border-width": map-merge(
      map-get($utilities, "border-width"),
      ( responsive: true ),
    ),
    "border-bottom": map-merge(
      map-get($utilities, "border-bottom"),
      ( responsive: true ),
    ),
    "border-end": map-merge(
      map-get($utilities, "border-end"),
      ( responsive: true ),
    ),
```

```
    )
);
```

This will generate a lot of new responsive border utility classes, so we will now need to update our HTML. We will also use spacing utilities for padding and margins to optimize the layout of this part of the page, and the result can be seen in the following:

part-2/chapter-8/website/cart.html

```
// Original code
<div class="border-bottom border-2 border-light mb-4 pb-
4">[code for products]</div>
// Updated code
<div class="border-bottom border-2 border-light mb-4 pb-4
border-bottom-md-0 border-end-md border-md-2 pb-md-0 mb-md-0
border-bottom-xl border-end-xl-0 border-xl-2 pb-xl-4 mb-xl-
4">[code for products]</div>
```

We have now made all customization for utilities, so we will move on to other custom styling.

Other custom styling

Filename: _custom-styles.scss

In this file, we will add all customization code for components that can't be done by overriding existing variables from the _variables.scss file. Instead, we will target the components using CSS class selectors and modify the styles using a mix of regular CSS and Sass code. Even though we can't override existing variables, we can still use them as values for our CSS properties, which we will do for the two components in this section.

Alert

We want to add a thick border on the left side of the alert component with the border color inheriting the text color and the thickness being half the value of the $spacer variable:

part-2/chapter-8/website/scss/_custom-styles.scss line 1-4

```
// Customize the left border of the alert component
.alert {
  border-left: ($spacer * .5) solid;
}
```

The shorthand for `border-left` used in the preceding code is equal to the following:

```
border-left-width: $spacer * .5;
border-left-style: solid;
border-left-color: currentColor;
```

Because of the default `currentColor` border-color value, the color of the left border will inherit the color of the text color of the alert, which depends on the type of alert being used. On our website, we currently use the info alert on the **Cart** page in the **Shipping Method** section, so the color of the left border will be the `$info` color.

Offcanvas

We want to give the header of the **offcanvas** component the same background color and bottom border as the header of the **card** component. We will use card-related variables from the `_variables.scss` file as values for our CSS properties. This results in the following code:

part-2/chapter-8/website/scss/_custom-styles.scss line 6-10

```
// Customize the background color and bottom border of the
// header of the offcanvas component
.offcanvas-header {
  background-color: $card-cap-bg;
  border-bottom: $card-border-width solid $card-border-color;
}
```

Summary

In this chapter, we have learned how customization of Bootstrap 5 works in practice in relation to a real website. First, we learned how to mix and order the `@import` statements for Bootstrap 5 Sass partials and our own Sass partials to achieve maximum customizability. Then, we learned how to customize various elements of layout, content, forms, components, and helpers using Bootstrap 5 variables. After that, we learned how to modify existing utilities using the utility API to make them more flexible and improve the layout of our website. Finally, we learned how we can customize components in other ways than the default ways using our own Sass code.

In the next chapter, we will see how we can improve and extend our website even further, including how to add a custom component and adding interactive features.

9

Improving the Website with Interactive Features Using JavaScript

In this chapter, we will learn how to improve our website with different interactive features. These features will be created using JavaScript and, in most cases, the JavaScript-based components of Bootstrap 5. In the previous chapter, we customized the *look* of our website – in this chapter, we will customize the *feel* of our website.

Bootstrap 5 has several interactive components that use JavaScript. Some of them are initialized automatically via the use of data attributes, for example, the **accordion**, **carousel**, **dropdown**, **offcanvas**, **navbar**, **modal**, and **tab** components, which we are currently using on the website. Other components require custom initialization using JavaScript, which is the case for popover, toast, and tooltip components. Form validation requires custom JavaScript to be executed at the correct time, and the spinner component should only be visible when the browser is in a loading state. As you can tell, JavaScript is used in different ways and for different purposes with Bootstrap 5.

In this chapter, we will see how we can use JavaScript to improve our website with interactive features for the following scenarios:

- Adding a tooltip component to a form label
- Adding toast components to product-related actions
- Changing the product quantity in the Shopping Cart form
- Adding form validation
- Adding form submission loading indicators
- Adding form success messages
- Creating programmatic tabs navigation

- Updating the progress status in the checkout flow

- Creating a lightbox for the product gallery

All of these scenarios will influence the *feel* and *behavior* of various parts or components of our website, and that's why they're included in this chapter.

Technical requirements

- To preview the examples, you will need a code editor and a browser. The source code for all code examples can be found here: `https://github.com/PacktPublishing/The-Missing-Bootstrap-5-Guide`

- To compile Sass to CSS, you will need one of the following:

  - **Node.js**, if you prefer a **command-line interface (CLI)** using Terminal (Mac) or Command Prompt (Windows)

  - **Scout-App**, if you prefer a **graphical user interface (GUI)**

  - **Visual Studio Code**, if you prefer to use an extension from the Visual Studio Code Marketplace

All these approaches are explained in *Chapter 2, Using and Compiling Sass*.

About the code examples

Before we take a closer look at each example in the coming sections, here are a few notes about the code examples that are good to know in advance. I encourage you to look at the various files mentioned for each code example in this chapter in your own editor so that you can see the changes yourself. Also, I encourage you to view the project in the browser so that you can experience the improvements being made. This chapter is about interactive features, so to see the real difference it makes, it has to be viewed in a browser.

Simple and clean JavaScript code

The custom JavaScript code for the website is written with simple and clean JavaScript. The focus has been to make it easy to understand, and not necessarily best practice. All code is placed in the same `script.js` file after the `bootstrap.bundle.min.js` Bootstrap 5 JavaScript file.

Page IDs

Page IDs have been added to the <body> tag on the **Index**, **Shop**, **Product**, **Contact**, **Wishlist**, and **Cart** pages. They have been added to better control when certain JavaScript code should be executed by the browser. As a result of this, the JavaScript code in script.js is generally grouped according to which page or pages the code should be executed on, and it also appears in roughly the same order as presented in this chapter.

The updated code on the <body> tag looks like this:

part-2/chapter-9/website/index.html line 13

```
<body id="homePage">
```

part-2/chapter-9/website/shop.html line 13

```
<body id="shopPage">
```

part-2/chapter-9/website/product.html line 13

```
<body id="productPage">
```

part-2/chapter-9/website/contact.html line 13

```
<body id="contactPage">
```

part-2/chapter-9/website/wishlist.html line 13

```
<body id="wishlistPage">
```

part-2/chapter-9/website/cart.html line 13

```
<body id="cartPage">
```

And here's an illustration of what the conditional `if` statements using these IDs look like:

part-2/chapter-9/website/js/script.js

```
// Variables for individual pages
const homePage = document.querySelector('#homePage'); // index.
html
// Used like this for one page only
if (homePage) {
  [code added here]
}
// Used like this for multiple pages
if (homePage || shopPage || productPage) {
  [code added here]
}
```

The conditional `if` statements for the page variables will not be shown in the code examples, since I want those to be as simple as possible. In fact, the `if` statements in the source code can be ignored. They are not essential for understanding how to implement the various interactive features but are "just" used to handle when the different parts of the code are executed to not "break" the code.

Partial and complete code

In this chapter, some of the code examples won't look like the complete and finished source code. This is because, for some of the interactive features, as a starting point, I will show you the minimum required code. Then, later on, I will add new code to the existing code examples when we add additional features. This approach has been chosen to guide you, step by step, on how the code works.

When a code example is updated with new code for another feature, the new code will be highlighted. Here's an illustration of what that means:

script.js

```
this is the minimum required code
  for an interactive feature
  this is new code
    for another feature that we add to
  the existing code example
that we can think of as partial code
```

Original and updated code

Some of the code examples show both the original code (from *Chapter 8, Customizing the Website Using Bootstrap 5 Variables, Utility API and Sass*) and the new updated code. The code will be presented in the same code block above each other and with code highlighting for the updated code, as follows:

script.js

```
// Original code
<label for="securityCode">Lorem ipsum</label>
// Updated code
<label class="form-label d-flex justify-content-between"
for="securityCode">Lorem ipsum</label>
```

Line numbers

To make the navigation of the source code easier, line numbers have been added to most of the code examples in addition to the file path. This is especially true for the JavaScript and Sass code examples but also some of the HTML code examples.

Adding a tooltip component to a form label

Now we will add a tooltip component to a form label in the checkout flow on the **Cart** page to provide the user with some helpful contextual information triggered on mouse hover (or tap on a touch device). We will add this tooltip component to an icon placed next to the label for the input of the security code for a credit card found in the form in the **Payment Options** tab pane.

The first thing we need to do is to add the proper markup. After the label text, we will add a `.bi-question-circle` icon colored with `.text-info`, and then put the required attributes for our tooltip component into that icon. Our markup will be updated in the following way:

part-2/chapter-9/website/cart.html

```
// Original code
<label class="form-label d-flex justify-content-between"
for="securityCode">Security code:</label>
// Updated code
<label class="form-label d-flex justify-content-between"
for="securityCode">Security code: <i class="bi-question-circle
text-info" data-bs-toggle="tooltip" title="Lorem ipsum dolor
sit amet, consectetur adipiscing elit. Duis convallis velit
quis sapien sollicitudin ultrices."></i></label>
```

Tooltip components are not initialized automatically through the use of `data-bs-toggle="tooltip"`, which we might expect. Instead, for performance reasons, tooltip components must be initialized by ourselves. Therefore, we will add the following JavaScript, which will initialize all the tooltip components on the page using the `Tooltip()` constructor:

part-2/chapter-9/website/js/script.js line 3-7

```
// Initialize all tooltips
const tooltipTriggerElements = document.
querySelectorAll('[data-bs-toggle="tooltip"]');
for (let i = 0; i < tooltipTriggerElements.length; i++) {
  new bootstrap.Tooltip(tooltipTriggerElements[i])
}
```

With these changes, you will be able to see the new icon and tooltip component in action in the browser. Currently, we only have one tooltip on our website, so we could have chosen another implementation, but I like this way since it will accommodate any extra tooltip that we might choose to add later.

Adding toast components to product-related actions

Now we will add toast components that are triggered by different product-related actions, for example, when clicking on the action buttons in the footer of the product cards on the **Home**, **Shop**, **Cart**, **Product**, and **Wishlist** pages.

Before creating the individual toast components, we will add a toast container to each of the previously mentioned pages, located just after the opening `<body>` tag and before the `<header>` tag. We will use the following code:

```
<div class="toast-container position-fixed end-0 mt-3 me-3"></div>
```

Now, we have a problem the toast container won't be properly positioned along the z axis of our layout. Other components on the page will be placed on top, which we don't want. This is the case for the navbar, button group, and dropdown components. We will fix this issue by using one of the following Bootstrap 5 `z-index` variables in our custom style sheet:

bootstrap/scss/_variables.scss

```
1068 $zindex-dropdown:              1000 !default;
1069 $zindex-sticky:               1020 !default;
1070 $zindex-fixed:                1030 !default;
1071 $zindex-offcanvas-backdrop:   1040 !default;
```

```
1072 $zindex-offcanvas:              1045 !default;
1073 $zindex-modal-backdrop:         1050 !default;
1074 $zindex-modal:                  1055 !default;
1075 $zindex-popover:                1070 !default;
1076 $zindex-tooltip:                1080 !default;
```

From the preceding list, we can see that the $zindex-fixed variable will be a good fit. That's because our toast container is already using the .position-fixed class, and we want it to appear on top of the currency dropdown in our header and below the offcanvas backdrop. Then, we can add the following Sass code to our custom style sheet:

part-2/chapter-9/website/scss/_custom-styles.scss line 12-15

```scss
// Add z-index to get the right position along the z-axis
.toast-container {
  z-index: $zindex-fixed;
}
```

We'll use the toast component in the following scenarios:

- Adding a product to the cart
- Adding a product to the wishlist
- Adding all products to the cart
- Removing a product from the wishlist
- Removing a product from the cart

We will now go through all of them one by one.

Adding a product to the cart

We want to show a toast component when the user clicks on the **Add to cart** button, which is located in the footer of the product cards on the **Home**, **Shop**, **Product**, and **Wishlist** pages.

First, we will add the following markup to our toast container on all the aforementioned pages:

part-2/chapter-9/website/index.html

```html
<div class="toast js-cartToast" role="status" aria-live="polite" aria-atomic="true">
  <div class="toast-header fw-bold">Added to cart</div>
```

```
<div class="toast-body">Product Name was added to the
  cart.</div>
</div>
```

Notice in the preceding code that we have added the `.js-cartToast` class to the Bootstrap 5 code for a default toast component. We will use that as a hook for the JavaScript that we use to initialize the toast component.

Before we do that, we will also need to update our **Add to cart** buttons by adding the `.js-addToCart` class as a hook for our JavaScript, too:

part-2/chapter-9/website/index.html

```
<button type="button" class="btn btn-primary me-2 js-
addToCart">
  <i class="bi-cart-plus"></i><span class=
    "visually-hidden">Add to cart</span>
</button>
```

Now we can show the toast component using the `Toast()` constructor and the `show()` method when any of the **Add to cart** buttons are clicked on with the following JavaScript code:

part-2/chapter-9/website/js/script.js line 20-27

```
// Handle button click and show toast when adding product
// to cart
const addToCartButtons = document.querySelectorAll('.js-
addToCart');
const addToCartToast = document.querySelector('.js-cartToast');
for (let i = 0; i < addToCartButtons.length; i++) {
  addToCartButtons[i].addEventListener('click', function() {
    new bootstrap.Toast(addToCartToast).show();
  })
}
```

Using JavaScript Methods with Interactive Bootstrap 5 Components

The `show()` method will be used many times for the interactive features in this chapter. We will learn more about how to use JavaScript methods with the interactive Bootstrap 5 components in *Chapter 11, Using Bootstrap 5 with Advanced JavaScript Features*.

Adding a product to the wishlist

We want to show a toast component when the user clicks on a button in the **Add to wishlist** dropdown located in the footer of the product cards on the **Home**, **Shop**, and **Product** pages.

First, we will add the following markup to our toast container on all of the aforementioned pages:

part-2/chapter-9/website/index.html

```
<div class="toast js-wishlistToast" role="status" aria-
live="polite" aria-atomic="true">
  <div class="toast-header fw-bold">Added to wishlist</div>
  <div class="toast-body">Product Name was added to the
    wishlist.</div>
</div>
```

Notice in the preceding code that we have added the `.js-wishlistToast` class to the Bootstrap 5 code for a default toast component. We will use that as a hook for the JavaScript that we use to initialize the toast component.

Before we do that, we will also need to update the buttons in our **Add to wishlist** dropdown by adding the `.js-addToWishlist` class as a hook for our JavaScript, too:

part-2/chapter-9/website/index.html

```
<div class="dropdown">
  <button type="button" class="btn btn-secondary"
    id="addToWishlistDropdown1" data-bs-toggle="dropdown"
    aria-expanded="false"><i class="bi-heart"></i><span
    class="visually-hidden">Add to wishlist</span></button>
  <div class="dropdown-menu" aria-
    labelledby="addToWishlistDropdown1">
    <h6 class="dropdown-header">Select wishlist</h6>
    <button type="button" class="dropdown-item js-
      addToWishlist">Wishlist #1</button>
    <button type="button" class="dropdown-item js-
      addToWishlist">Wishlist #2</button>
    <button type="button" class="dropdown-item js-
      addToWishlist">Wishlist #3</button>
  </div>
</div>
```

Now we can initialize the toast component when any of the buttons in any of the **Add to wishlist** dropdowns are clicked on using the following JavaScript code:

part-2/chapter-9/website/js/script.js line 34-41

```javascript
// Handle button click and show toast when adding product
// to wishlist
const addToWishlistButtons = document.querySelectorAll('.js-
addToWishlist');
const addToWishlistToast = document.querySelector('.js-
wishlistToast');
for (let i = 0; i < addToWishlistButtons.length; i++) {
  addToWishlistButtons[i].addEventListener('click',
    function() {
    new bootstrap.Toast(addToWishlistToast).show();
  })
}
```

Adding all products to the cart

We want to show a toast component when the user clicks on the **Add all products to cart** button located in the `<aside>` element on the Wishlist page.

First, we will add the following markup to our toast container on that page:

part-2/chapter-9/website/wishlist.html

```html
<div class="toast js-addAllToast" role="status" aria-
live="polite" aria-atomic="true">
  <div class="toast-header fw-bold">All added to cart</div>
  <div class="toast-body">All products from wishlist were
    added to the cart.</div>
</div>
```

Notice in the preceding code that we have added the `.js-addAllToast` class to the Bootstrap 5 code for a default toast component. We will use that as a hook for the JavaScript that we use to initialize the toast component.

Before we do that, we will also need to update the **Add all products to cart** button by adding the `.js-addAllToCart` class as a hook for our JavaScript, too:

part-2/chapter-9/website/wishlist.html

```html
<button type="button" class="btn btn-primary mt-3 js-addAllToCart">Add all products to cart</button>
```

Now we can initialize the toast component when the **Add all products to cart** button is clicked on using the following JavaScript code:

part-2/chapter-9/website/js/script.js line 48-53

```js
// Handle button click and show toast when adding all
// products to cart
const addAllToCartButton = document.querySelector('.js-addAllToCart');
const addAllToCartToast = document.querySelector('.js-addAllToast');
addAllToCartButton.addEventListener('click', function() {
  new bootstrap.Toast(addAllToCartToast).show();
})
```

Removing a product from the wishlist

We want to show a toast component when the user clicks on the **Remove from wishlist** button located in the footer of the product cards on the **Wishlist** page. At the same time, we also want to remove the product card from the page and the related markup from the DOM.

First, we will add the following markup to our toast container on that page:

part-2/chapter-9/website/wishlist.html

```html
<div class="toast js-wishlistToast" role="status" aria-live="polite" aria-atomic="true">
  <div class="toast-header fw-bold">Removed from wishlist</div>
  <div class="toast-body">Product Name was removed from the wishlist.</div>
</div>
```

Notice in the preceding code that we have added the `.js-wishlistToast` class to the Bootstrap 5 code for a default toast component. We will use that as a hook for the JavaScript that we use to initialize the toast component.

Before we do that, we will also need to update our **Remove from wishlist** buttons by adding the `.js-removeFromWishlist` class as a hook for our JavaScript, too:

part-2/chapter-9/website/wishlist.html

```html
<button type="button" class="btn btn-danger js-removeFromWishlist">
  <i class="bi-x-circle"></i><span class="visually-hidden">Remove from wishlist</span>
</button>
```

Now we can initialize the toast component when any of the **Remove from wishlist** buttons are clicked on, plus remove the element from the DOM using the following JavaScript code:

part-2/chapter-9/website/js/script.js line 55-63

```javascript
// Handle button click and show toast + remove element from
// DOM when removing product from wishlist
const removeFromWishlistButtons = document.querySelectorAll('.js-removeFromWishlist');
const removeFromWishlistToast = document.querySelector('.js-wishlistToast');
for (let i = 0; i < removeFromWishlistButtons.length; i++) {
  removeFromWishlistButtons[i].addEventListener('click',
    function() {
    new bootstrap.Toast(removeFromWishlistToast).show();
    removeFromWishlistButtons[i].closest(
      '.card').parentElement.remove();
  })
}
```

Removing a product from the cart

Here, we want to show a toast component when the user clicks on the remove button in the products overview in the **Shopping Cart** tab pane of the **Cart** page. At the same time, we also want to remove a product from the page and the related markup from the DOM.

First, we will add the following markup to our toast container on that page:

part-2/chapter-9/website/cart.html

```
<div class="toast js-cartToast" role="status" aria-
live="polite" aria-atomic="true">
  <div class="toast-header fw-bold">Removed from cart</div>
  <div class="toast-body">Product Name was removed from the
    cart.</div>
</div>
```

Notice in the preceding code that we have added the `.js-cartToast` class to the Bootstrap 5 code for a default toast component. We will use that as a hook for the JavaScript that we use to initialize the toast component.

Before we do that, we will also need to update our remove buttons by adding the `.js-removeFromCart` class as a hook for our JavaScript, too:

part-2/chapter-9/website/cart.html

```
<button type="button" class="btn btn-danger js-
removeFromCart"><i class="bi-x-circle"></i></button>
```

Now we can initialize the toast component when any of the remove buttons are clicked on, plus remove the element from the DOM using the following JavaScript code:

part-2/chapter-9/website/js/script.js line 71-78

```
// Handle button click and show toast + remove element from DOM
when removing product from cart
const removeFromCartButtons = document.querySelectorAll('.js-
removeFromCart');
const removeFromCartToast = document.querySelector('.js-
cartToast');
for (let i = 0; i < removeFromCartButtons.length; i++) {
  removeFromCartButtons[i].addEventListener('click',
    function() {
    new bootstrap.Toast(removeFromCartToast).show();
    removeFromCartButtons[i].parentElement.
      parentElement.remove();
  })
}
```

Now we are finished adding toast components to the different product-related actions. Next, we will move on with a feature to change the quantity of the individual products in the shopping cart.

Changing the product quantity in the shopping cart

In the products overview in the shopping cart tab of the **Cart** page, the user can adjust the product quantity of each product using an input group with buttons next to the current value. To implement the functionality of decreasing and increasing the value when clicking on these buttons, we will add the `.js-productQuantity` class to the input group component for each product and use it as a hook to our JavaScript. The markup for our input group component will be updated in the following way:

part-2/chapter-9/website/cart.html

```html
<div class="input-group me-3 js-productQuantity">
  <button type="button" class="btn btn-secondary"><i
    class="bi-dash-circle"></i></button>
  <input type="text" class="form-control text-center"
    value="1" aria-label="Product quantity">
  <button type="button" class="btn btn-secondary"><i
    class="bi-plus-circle"></i></button>
</div>
```

Now we can use the following JavaScript to either decrease the quantity (if it's larger than 1, so it never goes to 0 or below) or increase it:

part-2/chapter-9/website/js/script.js line 81-94

```javascript
// Handle button click on input group buttons and adjust
// value of input
const productQuantityInputGroup = document.querySelectorAll('.
js-productQuantity');
for (let i = 0; i < productQuantityInputGroup.length; i++) {
  let productQuantityInput =
    productQuantityInputGroup[i].querySelector(
    '.form-control');
  const productQuantitySubtractButton =
    productQuantityInputGroup[i].querySelectorAll(
    '.btn')[0];
  const productQuantityAddButton =
```

```
      productQuantityInputGroup[i].querySelectorAll(
      '.btn')[1];
    productQuantitySubtractButton.addEventListener('click',
      function() {
      if (productQuantityInput.value > 1) {
        productQuantityInput.value--;
      }
    })
    productQuantityAddButton.addEventListener('click',
      function() {
      productQuantityInput.value++;
    })
  }
```

After adding this feature, we will continue with adding form validation to all our forms.

Adding form validation

Bootstrap 5 has form validation as one of its features, so we want to take advantage of that for some of our forms: the newsletter form on the **Home** page, the contact form on the **Contact** page, and the two forms in the **Shipping Details** and **Payment Options** tabs on the **Cart** page.

The first thing we need to do is to add an id attribute to all of our form elements, so we can use that to target them from our JavaScript code. Additionally, we need to add the novalidate attribute to the form elements, which is used to disable the browser default feedback tooltips, while still providing access to form validation through JavaScript. So, we need to make the following updates to our markup:

part-2/chapter-9/website/index.html line 306

```
<form class="text-white" id="newsletterForm" novalidate>
```

part-2/chapter-9/website/contact.html line 185

```
<form id="contactForm" novalidate>
```

part-2/chapter-9/website/cart.html line 172

```
<form id="shippingForm" novalidate>
```

part-2/chapter-9/website/cart.html line 336

```
<form id="paymentForm" novalidate>
```

Now we need to add feedback messages for both the valid and invalid states. This will be added right after each form control that has the required attribute and where we want a feedback message. The only place we don't want such a feedback message is for the checkbox in the newsletter form. That's because the styles for the valid and invalid states are enough for the user to understand this kind of form control.

Here's how the markup for the first form field of the newsletter form on the Home page should be updated to accommodate feedback messages:

part-2/chapter-9/website/index.html

```
<div class="mb-3">
  <label for="firstName" class="visually-hidden">First
    name:</label>
  <input type="text" class="form-control"
    placeholder="Firstname" id="firstName" required>
  <p class="valid-feedback">Valid feedback text</p>
  <p class="invalid-feedback">Invalid feedback text</p>
</div>
```

After these feedback messages have been added to all the form fields where we want them to be in all of the forms mentioned earlier, we can now implement the form validation in JavaScript.

First, we will store the form in a variable and listen for the submit event of the form, which is triggered when clicking on the submit button. If the form is invalid, we will prevent the form from submitting, and outside this condition, the .was-validated class is added to the form to show the correct styles and feedback messages for the valid and invalid states.

Here's the JavaScript for the form validation of the newsletter form:

part-2/chapter-9/website/js/script.js line 104-123

```
// Newsletter form
const newsletterForm = document.
querySelector('#newsletterForm');
newsletterForm.addEventListener('submit', function (event) {
  if (!newsletterForm.checkValidity()) {
    event.preventDefault();
```

```
    event.stopPropagation();
  }
  newsletterForm.classList.add('was-validated');
}, false)
```

After trying to submit an invalid form, the validation will be run again whenever the user updates any of the form fields in the form. It's only the first validation that isn't run until the user tries to submit the form.

Adding form submission loading indicators

We want to add a loading indicator for the form submission of the newsletter form, contact form, and payment form, so the user can see that the browser is waiting for a response from the server. For our website, we won't submit any forms to a server or wait for any response, so we will emulate this behavior.

Our loading indicator will simply be the spinner component of Bootstrap 5 (to be precise, the border spinner variation) replacing the text of the submit button.

The first thing we need to do is to add an `id` attribute to all of the submit buttons, where we want a loading indicator to be. Then, we can use those `id` attributes later to target the submit buttons from our JavaScript code.

This is what the updated markup for our submit buttons will look like:

part-2/chapter-9/website/index.html

```
<button type="submit" class="btn btn-primary"
id="newsletterButton">Subscribe</button>
```

part-2/chapter-9/website/contact.html

```
<button type="submit" class="btn btn-primary"
id="contactButton">Submit</button>
```

part-2/chapter-9/website/cart.html

```
<button type="submit" class="btn btn-primary"
id="paymentButton">Pay</button>
```

We will add the markup for the spinner component to a variable in our JavaScript using the following code:

part-2/chapter-9/website/js/script.js line 98-100

```
// Markup for spinner component used on various forms
const spinnerMarkup = '<span class="spinner-border spinner-
border-sm me-2" role="status" aria-hidden="true"></span>Please
wait...';
```

Now this variable can be used to insert the spinner component into our submit button when we need it.

We will add the code for our loading indicator inside the script used to handle form validation. If the form is valid, first, we will prevent the form from submitting (so that we can emulate the loading behavior). Then, we will replace the text of the submit button with the spinner component and disable the submit button too. After that, we will use the `setTimeout()` method to emulate a loading time of 2000 milliseconds, after which the spinner component inside the submit button will be replaced with some new text.

The updated code for form submission with a loading indicator, again using the newsletter form as an example, will now look like this:

part-2/chapter-9/website/js/script.js line 104-123

```
// Newsletter form
const newsletterForm = document.
querySelector('#newsletterForm');
newsletterForm.addEventListener('submit', function (event) {
  if (!newsletterForm.checkValidity()) {
    event.preventDefault();
    event.stopPropagation();
  } else {
    event.preventDefault();
    const newsletterButton =
      document.querySelector('#newsletterButton');
    newsletterButton.innerHTML = spinnerMarkup;
    newsletterButton.disabled = true;
    setTimeout(function() {
      const newsletterConfirmationText = 'Subscribed';
      newsletterButton.innerHTML =
```

```
        newsletterConfirmationText;
    }, 2000)
  }
  newsletterForm.classList.add('was-validated');
}, false)
```

Now we have added the form submission loading indicators, but we have one more interactive feature for our forms. This is a form success message, which we will create next.

Adding form success messages

In the previous example, when the loading had finished after form submission, the text of the submit button was replaced. Now we want to also add form success messages below our forms when loading has finished.

We will use the alert component with the $success color for our success message, and we will place it inside the collapse component, so it can be displayed with a vertical transition. To achieve this, first, we will add the following markup to our forms after the submit and reset buttons and just before the closing </form> tag, again using the newsletter form as an example:

part-2/chapter-9/website/index.html

```html
<div class="collapse mt-3" id="newsletterConfirmation">
  <div class="alert alert-success">
    <h3 class="alert-heading h4">Subscribed!</h3>
    <p class="mb-0">Lorem ipsum dolor sit amet, consectetur
      adipiscing elit. Donec mattis posuere consequat.
      Nulla fermentum sodales augue, vitae ornare eros
      ornare quis. Donec lectus est, congue eu risus quis,
      tempus sagittis nunc.</p>
  </div>
</div>
```

In our JavaScript, we will now update the code used inside the `setTimeout()` method. We will store the collapse component from the previous code block inside a variable and use that to show the collapse component by using the `Collapse()` constructor and the `show()` method. The alert component will then be displayed using a vertical transition. Using the newsletter form as an example, the updated JavaScript code looks like this:

part-2/chapter-9/website/js/script.js line 104-123

```javascript
// Newsletter form
const newsletterForm = document.
querySelector('#newsletterForm');
newsletterForm.addEventListener('submit', function (event) {
  if (!newsletterForm.checkValidity()) {
    event.preventDefault();
    event.stopPropagation();
  } else {
    event.preventDefault();
    const newsletterButton =
      document.querySelector('#newsletterButton');
    newsletterButton.innerHTML = spinnerMarkup;
    newsletterButton.disabled = true;
    setTimeout(function() {
      const newsletterConfirmationText = 'Subscribed';
      newsletterButton.innerHTML =
        newsletterConfirmationText;
      const newsletterConfirmationElement =
        document.querySelector('#newsletterConfirmation');
      new bootstrap.Collapse(
        newsletterConfirmationElement).show();
    }, 2000)
  }
  newsletterForm.classList.add('was-validated');
}, false)
```

The last two code blocks use the newsletter form as an example. The code for the contact form and payment form is similar.

Creating programmatic tabs navigation

Currently, the user can use the tabs navigation on the **Cart** page to navigate between the three tabs. We want to disable the buttons used for tabs navigation and instead make use of programmatic tabs navigation. This means that the active tab pane will change automatically when the user goes through the checkout flow by using the submit button in each form, labeled **Next**, **Next**, and **Pay**, respectively.

First, we need to update our markup to disable the buttons used for tabs navigation. For each button, we will add the `.disabled` class to get the correct styling and remove the `data-bs-toggle="tab"` attribute to disable the functionality to change the tab on click. The updated markup looks like this:

part-2/chapter-9/website/cart.html

```
<ul class="nav nav-pills nav-justified mb-5" role="tablist">
  <li class="nav-item" role="presentation">
    <button type="button" id="cartTabs-1" class="nav-link
    active disabled" data-bs-toggle="tab" data-bs-
    target="#cartTabs-pane-1" role="tab" aria-
    controls="cartTabs-pane-1" aria-selected="true">1.
    Shopping Cart</button>
  </li>
  <li class="nav-item" role="presentation">
    <button type="button" id="cartTabs-2" class="nav-link
    disabled" data-bs-toggle="tab" data-bs-
    target="#cartTabs-pane-2" role="tab" aria-
    controls="cartTabs-pane-2" aria-selected="false">2.
    Shipping Details</button>
  </li>
  <li class="nav-item" role="presentation">
    <button type="button" id="cartTabs-3" class="nav-link
    disabled" data-bs-toggle="tab" data-bs-
    target="#cartTabs-pane-3" role="tab" aria-
    controls="cartTabs-pane-3" aria-selected="false">3.
    Payment Options</button>
  </li>
</ul>
```

Before adding the JavaScript for changing the tabs programmatically, we will create a little helper function that is used to scroll the page to the top with a smooth transition. The helper function consists of the following code:

part-2/chapter-9/website/js/script.js line 154-160

```
// Scroll effect for forms
function scrollToTop() {
  scroll({
    top: 0,
    behavior: "smooth"
  });
}
```

Now we will look at how to create the JavaScript for the programmatic tabs navigation. We want to navigate from the **Shopping Cart** tab pane to the **Shipping Details** tab pane and again from the **Shipping Details** tab pane to the **Payment Options** tab pane. Since each tab needs to be activated individually, and we also need different behavior for each form in the **Shopping Cart** and **Shipping Details** tab panes, we will go through them one by one.

> **Storing Form Values Through the Checkout Flow**
>
> We're not storing the input values in each form through the checkout flow when we switch to the tab pane. This must be done in a way that will make it work for a real project.

Shopping Cart tab pane

In our JavaScript, we will wait for the `submit` event of the form and then prevent the default form submission. After that, we will call our helper function, `scrollToTop()`, and add a `setTimeout()` method with a delay of `600` milliseconds. This is so that the browser has enough time to scroll the page to the top before executing the following code.

Inside the `setTimeout()` method, we will store the button for the second tab in a variable and use that to show the corresponding tab pane using the `Tab()` constructor and the `show()` method. The button for the tab is connected to the related tab pane through the `data-bs-target` attribute:

part-2/chapter-9/website/js/script.js line 165-177

```
// Shopping Cart form
const shoppingCartForm = document.
querySelector('#shoppingCartForm');
```

```
shoppingCartForm.addEventListener('submit', function (event) {
  event.preventDefault();
  // Go to cart tab 2
  scrollToTop();
  setTimeout(function() {
    const cartTabs2Element =
      document.querySelector('#cartTabs-2');
    new bootstrap.Tab(cartTabs2Element).show();
  }, 600)
}, false)
```

Shipping Details tab pane

The difference with this form compared to the **Shopping Cart** form is that it also has form validation, which we implemented earlier in this chapter. So for this form, a similar code that was used for the **Shopping Cart** form is placed inside the `else` part of the conditional statement, as follows:

part-2/chapter-9/website/js/script.js line 179-198

```
// Shipping Details form
const shippingForm = document.querySelector('#shippingForm');
shippingForm.addEventListener('submit', function (event) {
  if (!shippingForm.checkValidity()) {
    event.preventDefault();
    event.stopPropagation();
  } else {
    event.preventDefault();
    // Go to cart tab 3
    scrollToTop();
    setTimeout(function() {
      const cartTabs3Element =
        document.querySelector('#cartTabs-3');
      new bootstrap.Tab(cartTabs3Element).show();
    }, 600)
  }
  shippingForm.classList.add('was-validated');
}, false)
```

Now we have created the programmatic tabs navigation and can continue with a feature to update the progress status in the checkout flow.

Updating the progress status in the checkout flow

The last thing we want to improve for the checkout flow on the **Cart** page is to update the progress component as the tab panes are switched. In the **Shopping Cart** tab pane, initially, the progress should be 0 percent, and when the switch to the **Shipping Details** tab pane happens, the progress should be updated to 33 percent. When the form on the **Shipping Details** tab pane is submitted and the switch to the **Payment Options** tab pane happens, the progress should be updated to 67 percent. Finally, when the form on the **Payment Options** tab pane has been submitted and the success message has been displayed, the progress should be updated to 100 percent.

To update the progress component, we need to change the width property and the aria-valuenow attribute of the .progress-bar element (a child element of the progress component). The value of the aria-valuenow attribute will be updated directly with JavaScript, and the value of the width property can be updated either directly with inline styling or indirectly with classes. We will look at both approaches.

Updating the progress using inline styling

For this approach, first, we will update our markup with inline styling for the width of the element. We will set it to the initial value of 0, and this is necessary when we want to have the transition effect from one value to another. Not setting the width to 0 in advance will make the width of the .progress-bar element "jump" from one value to the other. Here's the updated code:

part-2/chapter-9/website/cart.html

```
<div class="progress mb-4" id="cartProgress">
  <div class="progress-bar progress-bar-striped progress-
    bar-animated" style="width: 0;" role="progressbar"
    aria-valuenow="00" aria-valuemin="0" aria-
    valuemax="100"></div>
</div>
```

In our JavaScript, first, we will store the `.progress-bar` element of our progress component in a variable like so:

part-2/chapter-9/website/js/script.js line 162-163

```
// Progress component which is animated by the tabs
// navigation below
const cartProgressBar = document.querySelector('#cartProgress
.progress-bar');
```

Then, we will add two more lines of JavaScript at the end of the `setTimeout()` method for each form on the Cart page. This will update the value of the inline styling and the `aria-valuenow` attribute. The updated code will look like this, using the **Shopping Cart** form as an example:

part-2/chapter-9/website/js/script.js line 165-177

```
// Shopping Cart form
const shoppingCartForm = document.
querySelector('#shoppingCartForm');
shoppingCartForm.addEventListener('submit', function (event) {
  event.preventDefault();
  // Go to cart tab 2
  scrollToTop();
  setTimeout(function() {
    const cartTabs2Element =
      document.querySelector('#cartTabs-2');
    new bootstrap.Tab(cartTabs2Element).show();
    cartProgressBar.style.width = "33%";
    cartProgressBar.ariaValueNow = 33;
  }, 600)
}, false)
```

We won't use this approach with inline styling. That's because we want to make use of the width utility classes, `.w-33` and `.w-67`, which we generated using the utility API when we customized the styling of our website.

Updating the progress using classes

For this approach to work, we also need to specify the width of `.progress-element` explicitly to be able to get the transition effect when adding width utility classes. We could keep the inline styling in our markup, but since we want to avoid inline styling for this approach, instead, we will specify the width in our custom style sheet as follows:

part-2/chapter-9/website/scss/_custom-styles.scss line 17-20

```scss
// Set the width of the .progress-bar so we can use the
// transition effect when adding width utility classes
.progress-bar {
  width: 0;
}
```

Now, in our JavaScript, we will add and remove the width utility classes, `.w-33`, `.w-67`, and `.w-100`, to achieve the same result as before. The code to update the `aria-valuenow` attribute will remain the same, and the code will still be placed at the end of the `setTimeout()` method. It will look like this in the three different forms:

part-2/chapter-9/website/js/script.js line 174-175, line 192-194, line 216-218

```js
// Shopping Cart form
cartProgressBar.classList.add("w-33");
cartProgressBar.ariaValueNow = 33;

// Shipping Details form
cartProgressBar.classList.remove("w-33");
cartProgressBar.classList.add("w-67");
cartProgressBar.ariaValueNow = 67;

// Payment Options form
cartProgressBar.classList.remove("w-67");
cartProgressBar.classList.add("w-100");
cartProgressBar.ariaValueNow = 100;
```

The last thing we want to do is to stop the animation for the progress component when it reaches 100 percent. To stop this, we simply need to remove the `.progress-bar-animated` class from the `.progress-bar` element when the transition from 67 percent to 100 percent has finished. In the previous chapter, when we customized the website using Bootstrap 5 variables, we set the animation duration of the `.progress-bar` element to 0.5 seconds using the `$progress-bar-animation-timing` variable in the `_default-variable-overrides.scss` file. Therefore, we will put the code to remove the `.progress-bar-animated` class inside a `setTimeout()` method with a delay of `500` milliseconds like so:

part-2/chapter-9/website/js/script.js line 219-221

```
setTimeout(function() {
  cartProgressBar.classList.remove("progress-bar-
    animated");
}, 500)
```

Now we are done adding interactive features to our Cart page, and we only have one more interactive feature to create.

Creating a lightbox for the product gallery

The last interactive feature we want to make for the website is a lightbox for the product gallery on the **Product** page. We will simply use the modal component to display a large image when clicking on one of the thumbnail images.

First, we will insert the minimum code for a modal at the bottom of our `product.html` file, after the closing `</footer>` tag and before the two `<script>` tags. We will make the modal large and vertically centered by using the `.modal-xl` and `.modal-dialog-centered` modifier classes. We won't have any modal header, modal body, or modal footer since we don't want any padding or other UI elements in the modal. We only want our large image and the backdrop of the modal surrounding it. It will still be possible to close the modal using the *Escape* key or by clicking outside of it somewhere on the backdrop. The class on the `<img>` tag will be used as a hook for our JavaScript:

part-2/chapter-9/website/product.html line 408-414

```
<div class="modal fade" id="productGallery" tabindex="-1" aria-
hidden="true">
  <div class="modal-dialog modal-xl modal-dialog-centered">
    <div class="modal-content">
      <img class="js-productGalleryImage">
    </div>
```

```
    </div>
  </div>
```

Now, we need to update the markup for the links surrounding the thumbnail images. A class will be used as a hook for our JavaScript, two data attributes will be used to initialize the modal component, and one data attribute will be used to store the URL for the large image that we want to show in the modal. The updated code for the first thumbnail image will look like this:

part-2/chapter-9/website/product.html line 85

```
<a href="#" class="js-productGalleryThumbnail" data-bs-
toggle="modal" data-bs-target="#productGallery" data-
src="img/1600x900.png"><img src="img/185x104.png" class="img-
thumbnail" alt="Product image"></a>
```

In our JavaScript, first, we will store all the image thumbnails in our product gallery in a variable using the class we just added as a hook and store the empty image in the modal in a variable using the class we provided as a hook earlier. Then, we will loop through the image thumbnails and listen for the `click` event. In that click event, we will set the empty `src` attribute of the `<img>` tag to the value of the `data-src` attribute defined on the image thumbnail. Since this code will be executed at the same time the modal is triggered, a large image will now be displayed inside of the modal. The next time an image thumbnail is clicked on, the `src` attribute will be replaced by a new value from the `data-src` attribute. The JavaScript for this is as follows:

part-2/chapter-9/website/js/script.js line 231-238

```
// Handle button click and open product gallery with
// specific "src" value
const productGalleryThumbnails = document.querySelectorAll('.
js-productGalleryThumbnail');
const productGalleryImage = document.querySelector('.js-
productGalleryImage');
for (let i = 0; i < productGalleryThumbnails.length; i++) {
  productGalleryThumbnails[i].addEventListener('click',
    function() {
    productGalleryImage.src =
      productGalleryThumbnails[i].dataset.src;
  })
}
```

Now we have created our own lightbox for the product gallery and have finished adding interactive features to our website.

Summary

In this chapter, we learned how we can improve our website with interactive features using JavaScript. Some of these features were based on Bootstrap 5 components that require custom JavaScript to work, while other features were created without the use of Bootstrap 5 components.

When going through all the scenarios in this chapter, we saw how it makes the website more appealing and engaging with these new interactive features being added.

This chapter concludes Part 2 of this book, which was centered around how to create a website using only Bootstrap 5 and then customizing and improving it with Sass and JavaScript. In Part 3, we will uncover more ways to work with Bootstrap 5 using the Sass and CSS features and learn how to optimize the usage of the Bootstrap 5 code and files.

Part Three – Advanced Topics Related to Bootstrap 5

In the final part of the book, we will learn about advanced topics related to Bootstrap 5 that have not been covered in the previous parts about customization. First, we will learn about advanced Sass and CSS features that can be used for various purposes, then we will learn about advanced JavaScript features, and finally, we will learn how to optimize the compiled Bootstrap 5 CSS and JavaScript code (including using a module bundler).

This part comprises the following chapters:

- *Chapter 10, Using Bootstrap 5 with Advanced Sass and CSS Features*
- *Chapter 11, Using Bootstrap 5 with Advanced JavaScript Features*
- *Chapter 12, Optimizing Bootstrap 5 CSS and JavaScript Code*

10
Using Bootstrap 5 with Advanced Sass and CSS Features

In this chapter, we will look at advanced Sass and CSS features related to Bootstrap 5. In the previous chapters, we customized the look and feel of the website, but this time we will primarily change the way we write our code without any effect on the look and feel. And in addition to that, we will look at various other features through some isolated examples.

We will first see how we can use various Bootstrap 5 Sass mixins to write our code in different ways, and after that, we will see some examples of the Bootstrap 5 Sass functions.

Then we will see how we can use the extend feature of Sass for semantic HTML and to create custom components.

After that, we will learn about the best – and recommended – approach to creating custom components using the Bootstrap 5 variables, mixins, and functions.

Towards the end of the chapter, we will see how we can take advantage of the CSS custom properties that come with Bootstrap 5 to create a dark color theme and customize a component and a helper.

Finally, we will look at Bootstrap's side project, RFS, and learn how to use it for calculating automated responsive CSS values.

In this chapter, we're going to cover the following main topics:

- Using Bootstrap 5 Sass mixins
- Using Bootstrap 5 Sass functions
- Extending Bootstrap 5 classes for semantic HTML
- Extending Bootstrap 5 classes to create custom components

- Creating a custom component using Bootstrap 5 variables, mixins, and functions
- Using Bootstrap 5 CSS custom properties
- Using the RFS Sass plugin

As mentioned previously, for some of these topics we will update parts of our code for the website, while for other topics we will only see isolated examples related to that topic.

Technical requirements

- To preview the examples, you will need a code editor and a browser. The source code for all code examples can be found here: `https://github.com/PacktPublishing/The-Missing-Bootstrap-5-Guide`

- To compile Sass to CSS, you will need one of the following:

  - **Node.js**, if you prefer a **command-line interface (CLI)** using Terminal (Mac) or Command Prompt (Windows)

  - **Scout-App**, if you prefer a **graphical user interface (GUI)**

  - **Visual Studio Code**, if you prefer to use an extension from the Visual Studio Code Marketplace

All these approaches are explained in *Chapter 2, Using and Compiling Sass*.

Using Bootstrap 5 Sass mixins

Bootstrap 5 contains many Sass mixins. Some of them are used by other parts of Bootstrap 5, while a few of them are not. All of them can be used in your own Sass code as well. In this section, we will first get an overview of the various mixins contained in Bootstrap 5, what they are used for, and how they relate to other Bootstrap 5 code. Then we will see different examples of how to use some of these mixins.

Mixin overview

In the `mixins` folder, we have a total of 25 files, which are all Sass partials. Here's an overview of the files with comments about which elements (components, helpers, or other) of Bootstrap 5 are using these mixins, if any:

bootstrap/scss/mixins

```
_alert.scss // Alerts
_backdrop.scss // Modal, Offcanvas
_border-radius.scss // Used by many
_box-shadow.scss // Used by many
```

```
_breakpoints.scss // Used by many
_buttons.scss // Buttons
_caret.scss // Dropdowns
_clearfix.scss // Carousel, Clearfix
_color-scheme.scss // Not used
_container.scss // Container
_deprecate.scss // Not used
_forms.scss // Validation
_gradients.scss // 1 used by many, 7 not being used
_grid.scss // Grid
_image.scss // Images
_list-group.scss // List group
_lists.scss // Typography, Pagination
_pagination.scss // Pagination
_reset-text.scss // Popovers, Tooltips
_resize.scss // Not used
_table-variants.scss // Tables
_text-truncate.scss // Text truncation
_transition.scss // Used by many
_utilities.scss // Utility API
_visually-hidden.scss // Visually hidden
```

We will now see how we can group some of these mixins in three different ways depending on their usage.

Mixins depending on global options

Some mixins depend on the global options that we learned about in *Chapter 4, Bootstrap 5 Global Options and Colors*. So, these mixins will only return code if the specific option is enabled:

```
_border-radius.scss: @mixin border-radius
_box-shadow.scss: @mixin box-shadow
_caret.scss: @mixin caret
_deprecate.scss: @mixin deprecate
_forms.scss: @mixin form-validation-state
_gradients.scss: @mixin gradient-bg
_transition.scss: @mixin transition
```

Mixins that are not used

Some mixins are actually not used by other Bootstrap 5 code. We will see what some of these mixins can be used for later in this section:

```
_color-scheme.scss: @mixin color-scheme
_gradients.scss: @mixin gradient-x, @mixin gradient-y, @mixin
gradient-directional, @mixin gradient-x-three-colors, @mixin
gradient-y-three-colors, and @mixin gradient-radial
_resize.scss: @mixin resizable
```

Mixins used for variants

Some mixins are used to create different variations of primarily Bootstrap 5 components. This could be variations for contextual color, size, and breakpoint-specific behavior:

```
_alert.scss: @mixin alert-variant
_buttons.scss: @mixin button-variant, @mixin button-outline-
variant, and @mixin button-size
_list-group.scss: @mixin list-group-item-variant
_pagination.scss: @mixin pagination-size
_table-variants.scss: @mixin table-variant
```

Examples

We will now see a few examples of how we can use some of the mixins in our own code. We will not update our website with these mixins but instead, see some standalone examples.

Responsive grid system

In this example, we will create a responsive grid system, including a container, using various mixins.

For this example, we have the following semantic HTML using only default HTML elements and no classes:

part-3/chapter-10/examples/mixins/responsive-grid-system/index.html

```
<!DOCTYPE html>
<html>
  <head>
    <meta charset="utf-8">
    <meta name="viewport" content="width=device-width,
```

```
      initial-scale=1">
    <title>Container and Grid Mixins</title>
    <link rel="stylesheet" href="css/style.css">
  </head>
  <body>
    <header>Header</header>
    <main>
      <nav>Nav</nav>
      <article>Article</article>
      <aside>Aside</aside>
    </main>
    <footer>Footer</footer>
  </body>
</html>
```

We will now first add a container to the <body> element. When using a mixin for this, it will create a fluid container, and this is what we will use in our example. It requires some more custom code to create the same behavior as the default .container class with different max-width instances across breakpoints.

After adding the container, we will create a simple responsive grid using the <main> element as the row and the <nav>, <article>, and <aside> elements as columns. We won't add any mixins to the <header> and <footer>.

The necessary Sass code for this example is the following:

part-3/chapter-10/examples/mixins/responsive-grid-system/scss/style. scss

```
// Bootstrap 5
@import "../../../../../../bootstrap/scss/bootstrap.scss";

body {
  @include make-container();
}
main {
  @include make-row();
}
nav {
```

```
    @include make-col-ready();
    @include media-breakpoint-up(lg) {
     @include make-col(3);
    }
  }
  article {
    @include make-col-ready();
    @include media-breakpoint-up(lg) {
      @include make-col(6);
    }
  }
  aside {
    @include make-col-ready();
    @include media-breakpoint-up(lg) {
      @include make-col(3);
    }
  }
```

When this example is viewed in a browser, we will see that the layout of the page is now using a container and a responsive grid system.

Media queries for breakpoints

In this example, we will take a closer look at mixins for media queries for breakpoints. In the _breakpoints.scss file, we will find four mixins and four functions, where three of the functions are primarily used by those mixins and one, breakpoint-infix(), is used by various components in other files. For now, we will focus on the mixins.

Here's an overview of the various mixins for media queries for breakpoints together with a short description of what they do:

```
media-breakpoint-up($name, $breakpoints: $grid-breakpoints)
```

- For viewport sizes with the minimum breakpoint width
- Breakpoint specified by the $name argument
- The content block passed to the mixin will be applied to the specified breakpoint width and wider
- No media query for the smallest breakpoint

```
media-breakpoint-down($name, $breakpoints: $grid-breakpoints)
```

- For viewport sizes with the maximum breakpoint width

- Breakpoint specified by the $name argument

- The content block passed to the mixin will be applied to the specified breakpoint width and narrower

```
media-breakpoint-between($lower, $upper, $breakpoints: $grid-
breakpoints)
```

- For viewport sizes that span multiple breakpoint widths

- Breakpoints specified by the $lower and $upper arguments

- The content block passed to the mixin will be applied between the specified lower and upper breakpoint widths

```
media-breakpoint-only($name, $breakpoints: $grid-breakpoints)
```

- For viewport sizes between the minimum and maximum breakpoint widths

- Breakpoint specified by the $name argument

- The content block passed to the mixin will be applied between the specified breakpoint's minimum and maximum widths only

The $breakpoints argument is an optional argument with the default value $grid-breakpoints. This means that it will use the breakpoint widths defined in the $grid-breakpoints map.

To see these mixins in action, here's an example that initially hides some elements and then displays them with the use of the different mixins. First, here's the HTML for the example, where we use the classes .up, .down, .between, and .only, which will be used as selectors in our Sass:

---

part-3/chapter-10/examples/mixins/media-queries-for-breakpoints/index.html

```
<!DOCTYPE html>
<html>
  <head>
    <meta charset="utf-8">
    <meta name="viewport" content="width=device-width,
      initial-scale=1">
    <title>Media queries for breakpoints</title>
    <link rel="stylesheet" href="css/style.css">
  </head>
```

```html
<body class="p-4">
  <div class="up">@include media-breakpoint-up(lg):
    Visible on breakpoint sizes lg, xl and xxl</div>
  <div class="down">@include media-breakpoint-down(md):
    Visible on breakpoint sizes xs and sm</div>
  <div class="between">@include media-breakpoint-
    between(md, xl): Visible on breakpoint size md and
    lg</div>
  <div class="only">@include media-breakpoint-only(sm):
    Visible on breakpoint size sm</div>
</body>
</html>
```

And here's the Sass code, where we initially hide all elements and then display them using the various mixins:

part-3/chapter-10/examples/mixins/media-queries-for-breakpoints/scss/style.scss

```scss
// Bootstrap 5
@import "../../../../../../bootstrap/scss/bootstrap.scss";

.up {
  display: none;
  @include media-breakpoint-up(lg) {
    display: block;
  };
}
.down {
  display: none;
  @include media-breakpoint-down(md) {
    display: block;
  };
}
.between {
  display: none;
  @include media-breakpoint-between(md, xl) {
```

```
      display: block;
    };
  }
  .only {
    display: none;
    @include media-breakpoint-only(sm) {
      display: block;
    };
  }
```

If you look at this example in a browser and resize the window, you will then see that the `<div>` elements are only visible at certain breakpoints.

Helpers

In this example, we will use two of the helper mixins. We will use the visually hidden mixin for a heading element and the text truncation mixin for a paragraph element. The HTML code for this example is as follows:

part-3/chapter-10/examples/mixins/helpers/index.html

```
<!DOCTYPE html>
<html>
  <head>
    <meta charset="utf-8">
    <meta name="viewport" content="width=device-width,
      initial-scale=1">
    <title>Helper Mixins</title>
    <link rel="stylesheet" href="css/style.css">
  </head>
  <body>
    <h1>Title for screen readers</h1>
    <p>Lorem ipsum dolor sit amet, consectetur adipiscing
        elit. Duis convallis velit quis sapien sollicitudin
        ultrices. Ut metus tortor, aliquet non rutrum ac,
        dapibus vehicula augue. Etiam congue erat sem, vitae
        gravida nunc pretium vitae. Fusce sed ex tellus.
        Quisque auctor viverra feugiat. Nulla urna odio,
```

```
       porta ut tristique ut, consequat non dolor. Etiam
       varius maximus dolor, at consectetur lectus. Mauris
       rutrum aliquet tellus, sed convallis diam.</p>
    </body>
</html>
```

The Sass code used for this example is as follows:

part-3/chapter-10/examples/mixins/helpers/scss/style.scss

```
// Bootstrap 5
@import "../../../../../../bootstrap/scss/bootstrap.scss";

h1 {
   @include visually-hidden();
}
p {
   @include text-truncate();
}
```

When this example is viewed in a browser, the heading element will now be hidden from the screen, but visible to screen readers, while the paragraph will have its text on one line only with the text being truncated at the end followed by an ellipsis.

Dark color theme

In this example, we will see how we can define a dark color theme (also known as dark mode) using the color scheme mixin. The mixin is effective when the user is browsing with *dark mode* turned on in their browser or operating system. The color scheme mixin is currently not used by Bootstrap 5, but is still made available for us to use if we want to. In the next minor version of Bootstrap 5, v5.3.0, Bootstrap will have support for *dark mode*, and then the mixin will probably be used across various elements of the Sass code. Until then, we will create our own dark color theme for *dark mode*.

The source code for the mixin looks like this:

bootstrap/scss/mixins/_color-scheme.scss

```scss
@mixin color-scheme($name) {
  @media (prefers-color-scheme: #{$name}) {
    @content;
  }
}
```

As you can see, we pass the name of the color theme (which in this case is *dark*) to the mixin and then all the CSS rules inside of it. Those rules are then placed inside a media query, and the name is used as the value for the media feature `prefers-color-scheme: #{$name}`.

We will now use the mixin to create a dark color theme for our website. Inside of the mixin, we will add various CSS rules to target the elements where we want the color to change. Basically, we want the light colors to be dark and the dark colors to be light. Our code looks like this:

part-3/chapter-10/website/scss/_custom-styles.scss line 22-51

```scss
// Dark color theme
@include color-scheme(dark) {
  // Body color
  body {
    background-color: $dark;
    color: $light;
  }
  // Color utilities
  .bg-light {
    background-color: $dark !important;
  }
  .bg-dark {
    background-color: $gray-700 !important;
  }
}
```

```scss
// Components
.accordion-button,
.accordion-item,
.card,
.list-group-item {
  background-color: $dark;
}
.accordion-button,
.breadcrumb-item.active,
.figure-caption,
.list-group-item,
.navbar-light .navbar-brand,
.navbar-light .navbar-nav .nav-link {
  color: $light;
}
}
```

As you can see in the preceding code, we are first defining some base colors for the `<body>` element. Then we're overwriting the background color utilities for light and dark colors using the `!important` rule since utility classes by default have the `!important` rule. Finally, we're overwriting those components that have a light background color or dark text color.

The dark color theme can be seen in all detail when viewing our updated website (the `website` folder in the code for this chapter) in a browser, and here's a screenshot of the Home page:

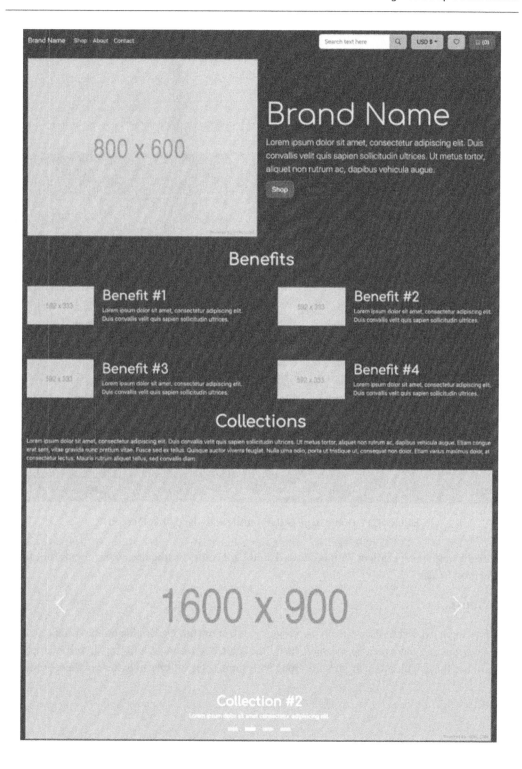

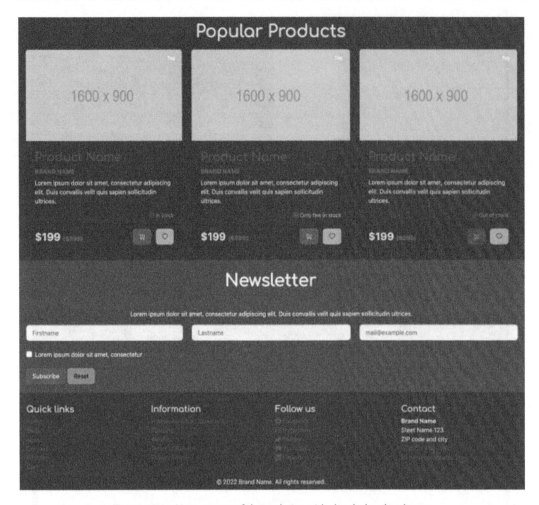

Figure 10.1 – Home page of the website with the dark color theme

You might want to experiment with other dark and light colors for the dark color theme, but this is the method to use.

Gradients

In this example, we will see how we can use various gradient mixins. Depending on the specific gradient mixin, various arguments can be specified, including color, degree, angle, and stop. In our example, we will just use the default mixin arguments along with some color utilities to better see these gradients.

In the HTML for this example, we have a number of `<div>` elements with some sizing and color utilities added. Notice that we have added a background color to the first and last example since those gradients are white by default. We also add the name of the mixin as a class and as the text of the `<div>` element, and that class will be used in our Sass code. First, here's the HTML code:

part-3/chapter-10/examples/mixins/gradients/index.html

```
<!DOCTYPE html>
<html>
  <head>
    <meta charset="utf-8">
    <meta name="viewport" content="width=device-width,
      initial-scale=1">
    <title>Gradient Mixins</title>
    <link rel="stylesheet" href="css/style.css">
  </head>
  <body>
    <div class="p-5 text-light bg-dark gradient-
      bg">gradient-bg</div>
    <div class="p-5 text-light gradient-x">gradient-x</div>
    <div class="p-5 text-light gradient-y">gradient-y</div>
    <div class="p-5 text-light gradient-
      directional">gradient-directional</div>
    <div class="p-5 text-light gradient-x-three-
      colors">gradient-x-three-colors</div>
    <div class="p-5 text-light gradient-y-three-
      colors">gradient-y-three-colors</div>
    <div class="p-5 text-light gradient-radial">gradient-
      radial</div>
    <div class="p-5 text-light bg-dark gradient-
      striped">gradient-striped</div>
  </body>
</html>
```

In our Sass code, we will first set the global option `$enable-gradients` to `true`, which is required to be able to use the `gradient-bg` mixin. Instead, it's also possible to use the `.bg-gradient` class on an element without the need to enable the global option for gradients. But since this section is about using mixins, we will use the mixin version of this gradient.

After enabling the global option for gradients, we will use the before-mentioned classes as CSS selectors in our Sass code and include the various gradient mixins:

part-3/chapter-10/examples/mixins/gradients/scss/style.scss

```scss
// Bootstrap 5
$enable-gradients: true;
@import "../../../../../../bootstrap/scss/bootstrap.scss";

.gradient-bg {
  @include gradient-bg();
}
.gradient-x {
  @include gradient-x();
}
.gradient-y {
  @include gradient-y();
}
.gradient-directional {
  @include gradient-directional();
}
.gradient-x-three-colors {
  @include gradient-x-three-colors();
}
.gradient-y-three-colors {
  @include gradient-y-three-colors();
}
.gradient-radial {
  @include gradient-radial();
}
.gradient-striped {
  @include gradient-striped();
}
```

The various gradients look like this:

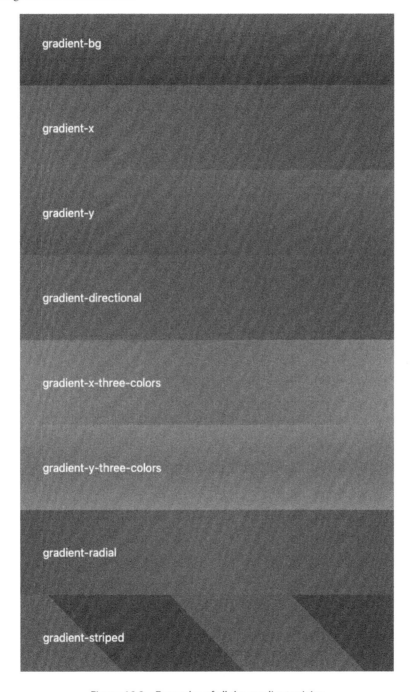

Figure 10.2 – Examples of all the gradient mixins

Using Bootstrap 5 Sass functions

Bootstrap 5 contains various Sass functions, and most of them are placed in the `_functions.scss` file. Some of these functions are used to evaluate the source code or manipulate Sass maps, but in this section, we will focus on the more useful color functions. There are a number of different color functions in Bootstrap 5, and we will now see examples of how we can use some of those in our own Sass code. We won't use any of these functions for our website but instead, look at some isolated examples.

Tint color

The `tint-color()` function increases the lightness of a color by mixing it with white using the color mix function of Sass. You specify the `$color` and how much you want it to lighten, defined as the `$weight`.

The code for the function looks like this:

bootstrap/scss/_functions.scss line 205-208

```
@function tint-color($color, $weight) {
  @return mix(white, $color, $weight);
}
```

Here's an example of how to tint the `$primary` color by `25%`:

part-3/chapter-10/examples/functions/scss/style.scss line 4-6

```
.bg-primary-tinted {
  background-color: tint-color($primary, 25%);
}
```

The resulting CSS will be as follows:

part-3/chapter-10/examples/functions/css/style.css

```
.bg-primary-tinted {
  background-color: #4a92fe;
}
```

Here, you can see what this looks like in the browser, shown together with the `$primary` color:

Figure 10.3 – Example of the tint-color function used with the primary color

Shade color

The shade-color() function increases the darkness of a color by mixing it with black using the color mix function of Sass. You specify the $color and how much you want it to darken, defined as the $weight.

The code for the function looks like this:

bootstrap/scss/_functions.scss line 210-213

```
@function shade-color($color, $weight) {
  @return mix(black, $color, $weight);
}
```

Here's an example of how to shade the $primary color by 25%:

part-3/chapter-10/examples/functions/scss/style.scss line 7-9

```
.bg-primary-shaded {
  background-color: shade-color($primary, 25%);
}
```

The resulting CSS will be as follows:

part-3/chapter-10/examples/functions/css/style.css

```
.bg-primary-shaded {
  background-color: #0a53be;
}
```

Here, you can see what this looks like in the browser, shown together with the `$primary` color:

Figure 10.4 – Example of the shade-color function used with the primary color

Shift color

The `shift-color()` function is a combination of the tint and shade color functions. If the `$weight` is positive, the `$color` will be shaded, else it will be tinted.

The code for the function looks like this:

bootstrap/scss/_functions.scss line 215-218

```
@function shift-color($color, $weight) {
  @return if($weight > 0, shade-color($color, $weight),
    tint-color($color, -$weight));
}
```

Here's an example of how to shift the `$primary` color by `25%` and `-25%` respectively:

part-3/chapter-10/examples/functions/scss/style.scss line 10-15

```
.bg-primary-shifted-positive {
  background-color: shift-color($primary, 25%);
}
.bg-primary-shifted-negative {
  background-color: shift-color($primary, -25%);
}
```

The resulting CSS will be as follows:

part-3/chapter-10/examples/functions/css/style.css

```css
.bg-primary-shifted-positive {
  background-color: #0a53be;
}
.bg-primary-shifted-negative {
  background-color: #4a92fe;
}
```

Here, you can see what this looks like in the browser, shown together with the $primary color:

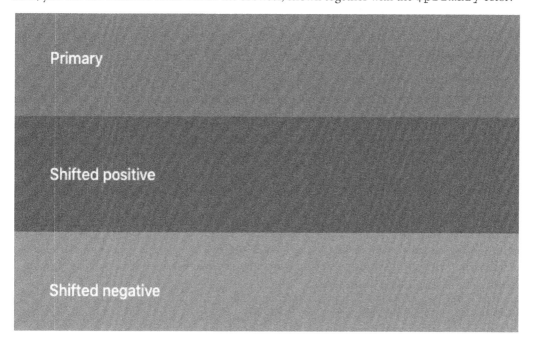

Figure 10.5 – Example of the shift-color function used with the primary color

Color contrast

The color-contrast() function returns a contrast color (by default, either the $black or $white color) based on a specified base color with regards to accessibility standards. This is useful when looping through a map of colors, where you want to assure that, for example, the text color has the right color contrast ratio in relation to the background color specified in the map. We now want to see how we can do just that: generate a contrast color for each color in the $theme-colors map. Here's the Sass code we will use to generate classes using the names of the colors in the map prefixed with .contrast-color-:

part-3/chapter-10/examples/functions/scss/style.scss line 17-21

```scss
@each $color, $value in $theme-colors {
  .contrast-color-#{$color} {
    color: color-contrast($value);
  }
}
```

This will then generate the following CSS:

part-3/chapter-10/examples/functions/css/style.css

```css
.contrast-color-primary { color: #fff; }
.contrast-color-secondary { color: #fff; }
.contrast-color-success { color: #fff; }
.contrast-color-info { color: #000; }
.contrast-color-warning { color: #000; }
.contrast-color-danger { color: #fff; }
.contrast-color-light { color: #000; }
.contrast-color-dark { color: #fff; }
```

In the CSS, we can see that either the contrast color #fff (white) or #000 (black) has been selected for each color in the $theme-colors map when using the color-contrast() function to ensure a high-enough color contrast ratio.

Here, you can see what this looks like in the browser:

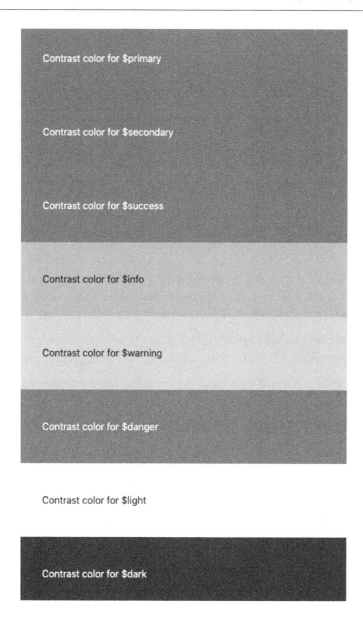

Figure 10.6 – Example of the color-contrast function used with the theme colors

We have now seen how to use some of Bootstrap 5's color functions with Sass. Next up, we will take a look at how to extend Bootstrap 5 classes for semantic HTML.

Extending Bootstrap 5 classes for semantic HTML

When using Bootstrap 5, you can end up adding a lot of classes to your markup, which will make it hard to swap out the Bootstrap 5 styles with your own set of styles, should you wish to do that sometime in the future. Instead, you can choose to only use semantic HTML elements, while still using the Bootstrap 5 styling. Your HTML can have no classes at all or only the classes you choose (and the naming of these classes as well). So, the structure of the HTML and the (optional) classes can be anything you want.

To understand why this might be desirable, we will consider the Bootstrap 5 CSS rulesets as two different things:

- A set of styling rules (the CSS declaration blocks)
- A vocabulary for these styling rules (the selectors)

We want the benefits of the styling rules, but we don't want to rely on its vocabulary, which is the specific Bootstrap 5 classes. We can achieve this by using semantic HTML on our page and extending the Bootstrap 5 classes with Sass instead of using them directly in the markup.

It's a big task to apply this method to all the HTML in our website, so instead, we will simply see an example of how this works.

Consider this simple layout created the normal way using Bootstrap 5 classes:

part-3/chapter-10/examples/semantic-extend/default/index.html

```
<!DOCTYPE html>
<html>
  <head>
    <meta charset="utf-8">
    <meta name="viewport" content="width=device-width,
      initial-scale=1">
    <title>Semantic Extending</title>
    <link rel="stylesheet" href="../../../../../
      bootstrap/dist/css/bootstrap.min.css">
  </head>
  <body>
    <div class="container">
      <h1 class="display-1 text-center">Heading</h1>
      <p class="lead">Lorem ipsum dolor sit amet,
        consectetur adipiscing elit. Duis convallis velit
```

```
    quis sapien sollicitudin ultrices.</p>
<div class="row">
  <nav class="col-lg-3">
    <div class="list-group">
      <a href="#" class="list-group-item list-group-
        item-action">List group item one</a>
      <a href="#" class="list-group-item list-group-
        item-action">List group item two</a>
      <a href="#" class="list-group-item list-group-
        item-action">List group item three</a>
    </div>
  </nav>
  <article class="col-lg-6">
    <h2 class="display-6">Article Heading</h2>
    <p>Lorem ipsum dolor sit amet, consectetur
      adipiscing elit. Duis convallis velit quis
      sapien sollicitudin ultrices. Ut metus tortor,
      aliquet non rutrum ac, dapibus vehicula augue.
      Etiam congue erat sem, vitae gravida nunc
      pretium vitae. Fusce sed ex tellus. Quisque
      auctor viverra feugiat. Nulla urna odio,
      porta ut tristique ut, consequat non dolor.
      Etiam varius maximus dolor, at consectetur
      lectus. Mauris rutrum aliquet tellus, sed
      convallis diam.</p>
  </article>
  <aside class="col-lg-3">
    <div class="card">
      <div class="card-body">
        <a href="#" class="btn btn-primary">Contact
          support</a>
      </div>
    </div>
  </aside>
</div>
<footer>
```

```html
          <ul class="list-inline text-center">
            <li class="list-inline-item"><a href="#">Footer
              link one</a></li>
            <li class="list-inline-item"><a href="#">Footer
              link two</a></li>
            <li class="list-inline-item"><a href="#">Footer
              link three</a></li>
          </ul>
        </footer>
      </div>
    </body>
  </html>
```

Now, we will remove all the Bootstrap 5 classes and only rely on semantic HTML elements:

part-3/chapter-10/examples/semantic-extend/extended-classes/index. html

```html
<!DOCTYPE html>
<html>
  <head>
    <meta charset="utf-8">
    <meta name="viewport" content="width=device-width,
      initial-scale=1">
    <title>Semantic Extending</title>
    <link rel="stylesheet" href="css/style.css">
  </head>
  <body>
    <header>
      <h1>Heading</h1>
      <p>Lorem ipsum dolor sit amet, consectetur adipiscing
         elit. Duis convallis velit quis sapien
         sollicitudin ultrices.</p>
    </header>
    <main>
      <nav>
        <div>
```

```html
          <a href="#">List group item one</a>
          <a href="#">List group item two</a>
          <a href="#">List group item three</a>
        </div>
      </nav>
      <article>
        <h2>Article Heading</h2>
        <p>Lorem ipsum dolor sit amet, consectetur
          adipiscing elit. Duis convallis velit quis
          sapien sollicitudin ultrices. Ut metus tortor,
          aliquet non rutrum ac, dapibus vehicula augue.
          Etiam congue erat sem, vitae gravida nunc
          pretium vitae. Fusce sed ex tellus. Quisque
          auctor viverra feugiat. Nulla urna odio, porta
          ut tristique ut, consequat non dolor. Etiam
          varius maximus dolor, at consectetur lectus.
          Mauris rutrum aliquet tellus, sed convallis
          diam.</p>
      </article>
      <aside>
        <div>
          <div>
            <a href="#">Contact support</a>
          </div>
        </div>
      </aside>
    </main>
    <footer>
      <ul>
        <li><a href="#">Footer link one</a></li>
        <li><a href="#">Footer link two</a></li>
        <li><a href="#">Footer link three</a></li>
      </ul>
    </footer>
  </body>
</html>
```

Now there's no evidence of Bootstrap 5 in our markup. To still benefit from the Bootstrap 5 styling, we need to extend the Bootstrap 5 classes using the @extend rule of Sass, like so:

part-3/chapter-10/examples/semantic-extend/extended-classes/scss/style.scss

```scss
// Bootstrap 5
@import "../../../../../../bootstrap/scss/bootstrap.scss";

body {
  @extend .container;
}
header {
  h1 {
    @extend .display-1, .text-center;
  }
  p {
    @extend .lead;
  }
}
main {
  @extend .row;
  > nav {
    @extend .col-lg-3;
    > div {
      @extend .list-group;
      a {
        @extend .list-group-item, .list-group-item-action;
      }
    }
  }
  > article {
    @extend .col-lg-6;
    h2 {
      @extend .display-6;
    }
  }
```

```
  > aside {
    @extend .col-lg-3;
    > div {
      @extend .card;
      > div {
        @extend .card-body;
        > a {
          @extend .btn, .btn-primary;
        }
      }
    }
  }
}
footer {
  > ul {
    @extend .list-inline, .text-center;
    > li {
      @extend .list-inline-item;
    }
  }
}
```

We will now see the same visual result in the browser. The markup has been changed, but the visual style remains the same.

> **Semantic HTML with Bootstrap 5**
>
> It should be noted that it is completely possible to use semantic HTML elements together with the Bootstrap 5 classes since these classes can be used for any HTML element you want. The method described in this section is intended for use with semantic HTML without any classes or only with the classes (and the naming of these classes) we want.

Extending Bootstrap 5 classes to create custom components

In this section, we will see how we can extend existing Bootstrap 5 classes using the @extend rule of Sass. With this method, it will be possible to create the same UI elements, but with less HTML code, which is better for readability.

We will use this method for three of our UI elements in our website: the **Page** title global module, the blockquote in the **Reviews** section of the **Product** page, and the bottom border of the **Summary** section of the **Cart** page.

The Page title global module

The Page title global module is used on all pages except for the **Home** page and **Product** page. The visual style of this module looks like the jumbotron component found in previous versions of Bootstrap. We will now extend the Bootstrap 5 classes being used by the Page title global module to make the markup simpler. We will use the name *jumbotron* for this custom component.

In our HTML for the new custom component, we have to keep a parent element (`.jumbotron`), so that we can give the component a background color spanning the full width, and then restrain the actual content within a child element (`.jumbotron-heading`) by extending the `.container` class there:

part-3/chapter-10/website/shop.html line 67-69

```
// Original code
<div class="bg-light py-5 mb-5">
  <div class="container">
    <h1 class="display-1 text-center mb-0">Shop</h1>
  </div>
</div>
// Updated code
<div class="jumbotron">
  <h1 class="jumbotron-heading">Shop</h1>
</div>
```

In our style sheet, we can now extend all the classes like so:

part-3/chapter-10/website/scss/_custom-styles.scss line 53-59

```
// Create a custom jumbotron component that extends various
// Bootstrap 5 classes
.jumbotron {
  @extend .bg-light, .py-5, .mb-5;
}
```

```
.jumbotron-heading {
  @extend .container, .display-1, .text-center, .mb-0;
}
```

Blockquote in the Reviews section

In the **Reviews** section of the **Product** page, we have three reviews with a blockquote being used in each of them. This blockquote contains a quote icon that's using a lot of utility classes to give it a custom look. We will now extend the Bootstrap 5 classes being used by and within the blockquote to make the markup simpler. We will use the name quote for this custom component.

In our HTML for the new custom component, we could have just extended the classes being used by the icon, and then kept the parent .blockquote class. But we want to make this an alternative component to the default blockquote element, and that's why we will also extend the .blockquote class on the parent, so that we can give it a new name:

part-3/chapter-10/website/product.html line 307-310

```
// Original code
<blockquote class="blockquote">
  <div class="text-secondary float-start fs-1 lh-1 mt-1
    me-2 border-top border-start border-2 border-secondary
    p-1"><i class="bi-quote"></i></div>
  <p>[Text]</p>
</blockquote>
// Updated code
<blockquote class="quote">
  <div class="quote-icon"><i class="bi-quote"></i></div>
  <p>[Text]</p>
</blockquote>
```

In our style sheet, we can now extend all the classes like so:

part-3/chapter-10/website/scss/_custom-styles.scss line 61-67

```
// Create a custom quote component that extends various
Bootstrap 5 classes
.quote {
  @extend .blockquote;
}
```

```
.quote-icon {
  @extend .text-secondary, .float-start, .fs-1, .lh-1,
    .mt-1, .me-2, .border-top, .border-start, .border-2,
    .border-secondary, .p-1;
}
```

Border in the Summary section

In the **Summary** section in the **Shipping Details** tab pane and **Payment Options** tab pane of the **Cart** page, there is a bottom border created with extensive use of responsive border and spacing utilities to achieve the desired design (currently a total of 30 utility classes are used). We will now extend the Bootstrap 5 utility classes being used to create the bottom border to make the markup simpler. We will use the name `summary-border` for this custom component.

The updated HTML code looks like this:

part-3/chapter-10/website/cart.html line 271

```
// Original code
<div class="border-bottom border-2 border-light mb-4 pb-4
border-bottom-md-0 border-end-md border-md-2 pb-md-0 mb-md-0
border-bottom-xl border-end-xl-0 border-xl-2 pb-xl-4 mb-xl-4">
</blockquote>
// Updated code
<div class="summary-border">[Summary section code]</div>
```

In our style sheet, we can now extend all the classes like so:

part-3/chapter-10/website/scss/_custom-styles.scss line 69-72

```
// Create a custom summary border component that extends border
and spacing utilities
.summary-border {
  @extend .border-bottom, .border-2, .border-light, .mb-4,
    .pb-4, .border-bottom-md-0, .border-end-md, .border-md-
    2, .pb-md-0, .mb-md-0, .border-bottom-xl, .border-end-
    xl-0, .border-xl-2, .pb-xl-4, .mb-xl-4, .border-bottom,
    .border-2, .border-light, .mb-4, .pb-4, .border-
```

```
    bottom-md-0, .border-end-md, .border-md-2, .pb-md-0,
    .mb-md-0, .border-bottom-xl, .border-end-xl-0, .border-
    xl-2, .pb-xl-4, .mb-xl-4;
}
```

Important rote about the @extend rule

The @extend rule of Sass is becoming less popular and many recommend not using it. The reason is that it will alter the source order and create unwanted groupings of the CSS. Even though it might reduce the CSS file size, it might end up being bad for network performance. This discussion will quickly become technical and lengthy, so if you want to learn more, I encourage you to google "Sass extend performance" or similar. The @placeholder and @mixin rules of Sass might be better to achieve the same things, but when you don't want to alter the source code (which we don't want when using Bootstrap 5, as explained earlier in this book), then the method described here is viable.

We have now learned how to extend Bootstrap 5 classes to create custom components. Next up, we will see how we can create a custom component in another way using Bootstrap 5 variables, mixins, and functions.

Creating a custom component using Bootstrap 5 variables, mixins, and functions

In the previous section, we saw how we could extend existing Bootstrap 5 classes using the @extend rule of Sass to create a custom component. In this section, we will see how we can create a custom component with Sass using the approach recommended by the team behind Bootstrap. This approach first of all entails reusing as many Bootstrap variables, mixins, and functions as possible, so that the custom component will be affected by any customization of the global options and Bootstrap variables. Secondly, the component will be based on a base class that groups as many shared properties as possible, and then a range of modifier classes that group individual styles together.

The custom component that we're going to create is a timeline component, and it looks like this:

2022

Lorem ipsum dolor sit amet, consectetur adipiscing elit. Duis convallis velit quis sapien sollicitudin ultrices.

2021

Lorem ipsum dolor sit amet, consectetur adipiscing elit. Duis convallis velit quis sapien sollicitudin ultrices...

2020

Lorem ipsum dolor sit amet, consectetur adipiscing elit. Duis convallis velit quis sapien sollicitudin ultrices.

2019

Lorem ipsum dolor sit amet, consectetur adipiscing elit. Duis convallis velit quis sapien sollicitudin ultrices.

2018

Lorem ipsum dolor sit amet, consectetur adipiscing elit. Duis convallis velit quis sapien sollicitudin ultrices.

Figure 10.7 – The custom timeline component

In the screenshot, we see the base class being used, but we will also create modifier classes for contextual color variants and responsive horizontal variants. For the timeline component, we're using an unordered list with a number of list items inside. We're using the class `.timeline` for the parent element and the class `.timeline-item` for the list items inside. Inside each list item, we then have an element with the class `.timeline-time` for the time of each event and a paragraph with the class `.timeline-text` for the description of each event.

The HTML for this custom component looks like this:

part-3/chapter-10/examples/custom-component/index.html

```
<ul class="timeline">
  <li class="timeline-item">
    <div class="timeline-time">2022</div>
    <p class="timeline-text">Lorem ipsum dolor sit amet,
      consectetur adipiscing elit. Duis convallis velit
      quis sapien sollicitudin ultrices.</p>
  </li>
```

```
  [More timeline items here]
</ul>
```

In our Sass code, we first import the Bootstrap 5 files, and then we define the CSS rules using as many Bootstrap 5 variables and mixins as possible, so our component will be affected by any customization we might use elsewhere in our Sass code. We're using Bootstrap 5 variables for spacing, borders, colors, and font weight, and we're using mixins to create an unstyled list and to add a shadow if the global option for shadows ($enable-shadows) is enabled.

The Sass code for our custom component is as follows:

part-3/chapter-10/examples/custom-component/scss/style.scss line 1-40

```scss
// Bootstrap 5
@import "../../../../../bootstrap/scss/bootstrap.scss";

.timeline {
  @include list-unstyled;
  margin: $spacer 0;
}
.timeline-item {
  padding-bottom: $spacer;
  border-left: $border-width solid $border-color;
  position: relative;
  padding-left: $spacer;
  margin-left: .625rem;

  &:last-child{
    border: 0;
    padding-bottom: 0;
  }

  &::before {
    content: '';
    width: 1.2rem;
    height: 1.2rem;
    background: $white;
    border: $border-width solid $border-color;
```

```scss
      @include box-shadow($box-shadow-inset);
      border-radius: 50%;
      position: absolute;
      left: -.6rem;
      top: 0;
    }
  }
  .timeline-time {
    font-weight: $font-weight-bold;
    top: -0.1875rem;
    position: relative;
  }
  .timeline-text {
    margin-bottom: 0;
  }
```

Creating contextual color variants

Now, we will create contextual color variants for our component. We want the component to have a range of modifier classes that can be added to individual timeline items, which will then set the color of the following three items:

- The text color of the `.timeline-time` element

- The border color of the `.timeline-item` element

- The border color of the `::before` pseudo-element of the `.timeline-item` element

To generate the various modifier classes for the contextual color variants, we will use a Sass loop to loop through the `$theme-colors` map. In that loop, the key is assigned to the `$state` variable and the value is assigned to the `$value` variable. The `$state` variable is then used to generate the various classes, while the `$value` variable is used to add the color to the different elements.

The Sass code looks like this:

part-3/chapter-10/examples/custom-component/scss/style.scss line 42-54

```scss
@each $state, $value in $theme-colors {
  .timeline-item-#{$state} {
    border-color: $value;
```

```scss
    &::before {
      border-color: $value;
    }

    .timeline-time {
      color: $value;
    }
  }
}
```

Using this method, we will generate modifier classes for each theme color, such as, for example, the .timeline-item-primary modifier class for the $primary color. These modifier classes will then be added to our HTML in the following way:

part-3/chapter-10/examples/custom-component/index.html

```html
<ul class="timeline">
  <li class="timeline-item timeline-item-primary
">
    <div class="timeline-time">2022</div>
    <p class="timeline-text">Lorem ipsum dolor sit amet,
      consectetur adipiscing elit. Duis convallis velit
      quis sapien sollicitudin ultrices.</p>
  </li>
  [More timeline items here]
</ul>
```

Here's a screenshot of what the different contextual color variants look like:

2022

Lorem ipsum dolor sit amet, consectetur adipiscing elit. Duis convallis velit quis sapien sollicitudin ultrices.

2021

Lorem ipsum dolor sit amet, consectetur adipiscing elit. Duis convallis velit quis sapien sollicitudin ultrices...

2020

Lorem ipsum dolor sit amet, consectetur adipiscing elit. Duis convallis velit quis sapien sollicitudin ultrices.

2019

Lorem ipsum dolor sit amet, consectetur adipiscing elit. Duis convallis velit quis sapien sollicitudin ultrices.

2018

Lorem ipsum dolor sit amet, consectetur adipiscing elit. Duis convallis velit quis sapien sollicitudin ultrices.

2018

Lorem ipsum dolor sit amet, consectetur adipiscing elit. Duis convallis velit quis sapien sollicitudin ultrices.

Lorem ipsum dolor sit amet, consectetur adipiscing elit. Duis convallis velit quis sapien sollicitudin ultrices.

2018

Lorem ipsum dolor sit amet, consectetur adipiscing elit. Duis convallis velit quis sapien sollicitudin ultrices.

Figure 10.8 – The custom timeline component with the contextual color variants

Creating responsive horizontal variants

Now, we will create responsive horizontal variants for our component. We want the component to have a range of modifier classes that can be added to the parent element, which will then define at what breakpoint the component will be displayed in the horizontal version.

Here's a screenshot of what the horizontal version looks like:

2022	**2021**	**2020**	**2019**	**2018**
Lorem ipsum dolor sit amet, consectetur adipiscing elit. Duis convallis velit quis sapien sollicitudin ultrices.	Lorem ipsum dolor sit amet, consectetur adipiscing elit. Duis convallis velit quis sapien sollicitudin ultrices...	Lorem ipsum dolor sit amet, consectetur adipiscing elit. Duis convallis velit quis sapien sollicitudin ultrices.	Lorem ipsum dolor sit amet, consectetur adipiscing elit. Duis convallis velit quis sapien sollicitudin ultrices.	Lorem ipsum dolor sit amet, consectetur adipiscing elit. Duis convallis velit quis sapien sollicitudin ultrices.

Figure 10.9 – The custom timeline component in the horizontal version

To generate the various modifier classes for the responsive horizontal variants, we will use a Sass loop to loop through the $grid-breakpoints map. In that loop, the key is assigned to the $breakpoint variable and is then first used as an argument for the media-breakpoint-up() mixin. Inside the media query, the $breakpoint variable is used as an argument for the breakpoint-infix() function to generate a value for the $infix variable, which is then used to generate the various class names with the correct breakpoint infix (-sm, -md, -lg, -xl, or -xxl).

The Sass code looks like this:

part-3/chapter-10/examples/custom-component/scss/style.scss line 56-75

```
@each $breakpoint in map-keys($grid-breakpoints) {
  @include media-breakpoint-up($breakpoint) {
    $infix: breakpoint-infix($breakpoint, $grid-
      breakpoints);

    .timeline-horizontal#{$infix} {
      display: flex;
      padding-top: 0.6rem;
      overflow-y: scroll;

      .timeline-item {
        border-left: none;
```

```
        border-top: $border-width solid $border-color;


        &::before {
          top: -0.6rem;
        }
      }
    }
  }
}
```

Using this method, we will generate modifier classes for each breakpoint, such as, for example, the `.timeline-horizontal-sm` modifier class for the `sm` breakpoint. Notice that we will also generate the modifier class `.timeline-horizontal`, which will display the component in the horizontal version for all screen sizes.

The modifier classes can be added to our HTML in the following way:

part-3/chapter-10/examples/custom-component/index.html

```html
<ul class="timeline timeline-horizontal-sm">
  <li class="timeline-item">
    <div class="timeline-time">2022</div>
    <p class="timeline-text">Lorem ipsum dolor sit amet,
      consectetur adipiscing elit. Duis convallis velit
      quis sapien sollicitudin ultrices.</p>
  </li>
  [More timeline items here]
</ul>
```

When viewing this example in a browser, you can see how the different timeline components turn into horizontal versions at various breakpoints.

In this section, we have seen how to create a custom component using the approach recommended by the team behind Bootstrap. We have created a timeline component, but the method can be used to create any kind of custom component that you want.

Using Bootstrap 5 CSS custom properties

Bootstrap 5 includes many CSS custom properties in its compiled CSS file (`bootstrap/dist/css/bootstrap.css`). This gives us global access to values for colors, typography, and borders, as well as local access to various values for most components and some utilities when the Bootstrap 5 CSS is loaded. With these CSS custom properties, we can do customization without having to recompile the Sass code using a CSS preprocessor.

> **CSS custom properties or CSS variables?**
>
> CSS custom properties are also often referred to as CSS variables. This is also the way the Bootstrap team refers to them in the official documentation, but in this chapter, I will refer to them as CSS custom properties, to better distinguish them from Sass variables.

Groups of CSS custom properties

In Bootstrap 5, there are three major groups of CSS custom properties:

- Root CSS custom properties
- Component CSS custom properties
- Utility CSS custom properties

Root CSS custom properties

The root CSS custom properties are added to the `:root` pseudo-class, which is equal to the `<html>` element in an HTML document. This placement gives us global access to them from all other HTML elements on our page. They are located before all other code in the compiled Bootstrap 5 CSS (`bootstrap/dist/css/bootstrap.css`).

The root custom properties are generated from the `_root.scss` file. The first part of the file generates CSS custom properties for various colors by using a Sass loop for the `$colors`, `$grays`, `$theme-colors`, and `$theme-colors-rgb` map as well as a few other CSS custom properties. The next part of the file generates CSS custom properties for various typography styles, such as the font stacks and the base styles for the `<body>` element, as well as a CSS custom property for the default `$gradient`. The last part of the file generates CSS custom properties for borders and the border radius. Most of the CSS custom properties for typography are used by the `_reboot.scss` file to style the `<body>` element, and the CSS custom properties for borders and the border radius are used for generating border and border radius utilities and within a few components. Finally, the CSS custom properties for colors are simply made globally available to use for customization.

Here's an example of how to change the primary, secondary, and success color by overriding the following CSS custom properties:

```
:root {
  --bs-primary: red;
  --bs-secondary: green;
  --bs-success: blue;
  --bs-primary-rgb: #{to-rgb(red)};
  --bs-secondary-rgb: #{to-rgb(green)};
  --bs-success-rgb: #{to-rgb(blue)};
}
```

This should be placed somewhere after the compiled Bootstrap 5 code to work. The example has not been implemented on our website but is just shown here as an example of how to use the root CSS custom properties.

Component CSS custom properties

The component CSS custom properties are locally scoped to the individual components of Bootstrap 5. Since they are local, they can only be accessed by the element where they are defined and not globally like the root custom properties. All components, except the scrollspy and close button components, have CSS custom properties.

In a partial .scss file for a component, the technique of using Sass variables and CSS custom properties is as follows:

- CSS custom properties are added to the parent (or main) class of the component
- Sass variables from _variables.scss are assigned as values to the CSS custom properties
- CSS custom properties are used as values for the regular CSS properties

Here's the source code of the badge component that shows this technique (comments have been removed):

bootstrap/scss/_badge.scss

```
.badge {
  --#{$prefix}badge-padding-x: #{$badge-padding-x};
  --#{$prefix}badge-padding-y: #{$badge-padding-y};
  @include rfs($badge-font-size, --#{$prefix}badge-font-
size);
  --#{$prefix}badge-font-weight: #{$badge-font-weight};
```

```scss
  --#{$prefix}badge-color: #{$badge-color};
  --#{$prefix}badge-border-radius: #{$badge-border-radius};

  display: inline-block;
  padding: var(--#{$prefix}badge-padding-y) var(
    --#{$prefix}badge-padding-x);
  @include font-size(var(--#{$prefix}badge-font-size));
  font-weight: var(--#{$prefix}badge-font-weight);
  line-height: 1;
  color: var(--#{$prefix}badge-color);
  text-align: center;
  white-space: nowrap;
  vertical-align: baseline;
  border-radius: var(--#{$prefix}badge-border-radius, 0);
  @include gradient-bg();

  &:empty {
    display: none;
  }
}
```

And here's the compiled CSS for that component:

bootstrap/dist/css/bootstrap.css line 4809-4829

```css
.badge {
  --bs-badge-padding-x: 0.65em;
  --bs-badge-padding-y: 0.35em;
  --bs-badge-font-size: 0.75em;
  --bs-badge-font-weight: 700;
  --bs-badge-color: #fff;
  --bs-badge-border-radius: 0.375rem;
  display: inline-block;
  padding: var(--bs-badge-padding-y) var(--bs-badge-
    padding-x);
  font-size: var(--bs-badge-font-size);
  font-weight: var(--bs-badge-font-weight);
```

```
    line-height: 1;
    color: var(--bs-badge-color);
    text-align: center;
    white-space: nowrap;
    vertical-align: baseline;
    border-radius: var(--bs-badge-border-radius, 0);
}
.badge:empty {
    display: none;
}
```

We can see that the component has six different CSS custom properties, which are not used out of the box. Instead, they are available to us for customizing this component. We will make use of that by increasing the horizontal and vertical padding with the following lines of code:

part-3/chapter-10/website/scss/_custom-styles.scss line 74-77

```
.badge {
  --bs-badge-padding-x: 1em;
  --bs-badge-padding-y: 0.7em;
}
```

When we have compiled our CSS, we will now see these CSS custom property overrides taking effect with increased padding on the badge component.

Utility CSS custom properties

The utility CSS custom properties are defined for the background, color, and border utilities, and they are locally scoped like the component CSS custom properties. Using these CSS custom properties, we can, for example, control the alpha transparency value of rgba() colors.

If we take the background utility as an example, the .bg-primary utility has the following CSS styles:

bootstrap/dist/css/bootstrap.css line 8402-8405

```
.bg-primary {
  --bs-bg-opacity: 1;
  background-color: rgba(var(--bs-primary-rgb), var(--bs-
    bg-opacity)) !important;
}
```

We can see that the utility has the `--bs-bg-opacity: 1` CSS custom property, which is used by the `background-color` property to specify the a part of the `rgba()` color function. We can now add, for example, the class `.bg-opacity-25` or `.bg-opacity-50` to the same element to change the opacity from `1` to `0.25` or `0.5`. If we want the opacity to be somewhere in between, we can overwrite the CSS custom property, for example, like so:

HTML

```
<div class="bg-primary" style="--bs-bg-opacity: 0.33">Primary
background with an opacity of 0.33</div>
```

Limitations of CSS custom properties for customization

You can do powerful customization with CSS custom properties. However, you can't just replace the usage of Sass variables in all situations. As an example of this, let's consider the global styling for border radiuses. These are initially defined as six different Sass variables in the `_variables.scss` file:

bootstrap/scss/_variables.scss line 495-500

```
$border-radius: .375rem !default;
$border-radius-sm: .25rem !default;
$border-radius-lg: .5rem !default;
$border-radius-xl: 1rem !default;
$border-radius-2xl: 2rem !default;
$border-radius-pill: 50rem !default;
```

These Sass variables are then used to generate the CSS custom properties for border radius in the `_root.scss` file like so:

bootstrap/scss/_root.scss

```
--#{$prefix}border-radius: #{$border-radius};
--#{$prefix}border-radius-sm: #{$border-radius-sm};
--#{$prefix}border-radius-lg: #{$border-radius-lg};
--#{$prefix}border-radius-xl: #{$border-radius-xl};
--#{$prefix}border-radius-2xl: #{$border-radius-2xl};
--#{$prefix}border-radius-pill: #{$border-radius-pill};
```

If we now use the compiled Bootstrap 5 CSS and we want to change the border radius of buttons, we can target the .btn in our own CSS and override the CSS custom property for border radius like so:

```
.btn {
  --bs-btn-border-radius: 0.75rem;
}
```

The limitation here is that we can't define the $border-radius Sass variable, which is used across many components, using a CSS custom property. So, in our example, the border radius of button elements will change, but not the border radius of input elements, even though they use the same border radius value in the Sass code:

bootstrap/scss/_variables.scss line 774 and 835

```
$btn-border-radius: $border-radius !default;
$input-border-radius: $border-radius !default;
```

As we can see, this is a limitation. So, even though customization with CSS custom properties is powerful and we don't need to use a CSS preprocessor, we can't do the same kinds of customizations as we can using Sass. Nonetheless, we will now take a look at a few more examples of how we can use CSS custom properties for customization.

The dark color theme

We previously saw how to create styles for a dark color theme using the color-scheme mixin and color variables. It's also possible to create the same dark color theme styles using a media query and CSS custom properties. The necessary CSS code for this is as follows:

part-3/chapter-10/website/css/darkmode.css

```
@media (prefers-color-scheme: dark) {
  body {
    background-color: var(--bs-dark);
    color: var(--bs-light);
  }
  .bg-light, .jumbotron {
    background-color: var(--bs-dark) !important;
  }
  .bg-dark {
    background-color: var(--bs-gray-700) !important;
```

```
  }
  .accordion-button,
  .accordion-item,
  .card,
  .list-group-item {
    background-color: var(--bs-dark);
  }
  .accordion-button,
  .breadcrumb-item.active,
  .figure-caption,
  .list-group-item,
  .navbar-light .navbar-brand,
  .navbar-light .navbar-nav .nav-link {
    color: var(--bs-light);
  }
}
```

To use it, you simply include the darkmode.css file in the <head> somewhere after the compiled Bootstrap 5 CSS file; for example, like this:

```
<link rel="stylesheet" href="css/style.css">
<link rel="stylesheet" href="css/darkmode.css">
<link rel="stylesheet" href="icons/bootstrap-icons.css">
```

Since we have already created the dark color theme for our website with Sass, we will keep that and not update our code to use the darkmode.css file, but it's included in the css folder for you to use if you want to. If you choose to use it, remember to remove the styling for the dark color theme in the _custom-styles.scss file.

Breadcrumb

We previously changed the breadcrumb divider by overriding the $breadcrumb-divider variable in the _default-variable-overrides.scss file. We can use the --bs-breadcrumb-divider CSS custom property for this instead since the Sass variable is actually just a fallback to the CSS custom property.

To make this update to our website, we will first remove our Sass customization for the breadcrumb divider:

part-3/chapter-10/website/scss/_default-variable-overrides.scss

```
// Breadcrumb
$breadcrumb-divider: quote("-");
```

Instead, we will now use the CSS custom property by assigning a value to it in an inline style on the `<nav>` element wrapping the breadcrumb component on the **Shop** and **Product** pages, which are the only places we're using that component:

part-3/chapter-10/website/shop.html line 216-222

```
<nav aria-label="Breadcrumb navigation" style="--bs-breadcrumb-
divider: '-';">
  <ol class="breadcrumb mb-2 mb-lg-0">
    <li class="breadcrumb-item"><a href="#">Shop</a></li>
    <li class="breadcrumb-item"><a
      href="#">Category</a></li>
    <li class="breadcrumb-item active" aria-
      current="page">Subcategory</li>
  </ol>
</nav>
```

We won't see any visual change in the browser, which means that we have successfully updated our code.

Helper

We previously added a new ratio helper class with the aspect ratio 5x3 by creating a `$custom-ratio` map and merging it with the default `$aspect-ratios` map. This required several lines of code at the end of our `_variable-value-using-variable.scss` file. We can use the `--bs-aspect-ratio` CSS custom property for this instead since the Sass code for the ratio helper is already using the values in the `$aspect-ratios` map to set the value of that CSS custom property.

To make this update to our website, we will first remove our Sass customization for the ratio helper:

part-3/chapter-10/website/scss/_variable-value-using-variable.scss

```
// Ratio
// Create custom ratio map
```

```
$custom-ratio: (
  "5x3": calc(3 / 5 * 100%)
);
// Merge "$aspect-ratios" and "$custom-ratio"
$aspect-ratios: map-merge($aspect-ratios, $custom-ratio);
```

Instead, we will now use the CSS custom property by assigning a value to it in an inline style on the ratio helper wrapping the <iframe> with the Google Maps map on the **Contact** page, which is the only place we're using the ratio helper:

part-3/chapter-10/website/contact.html line 177-179

```
<div class="ratio ratio-5x3" style="--bs-aspect-ratio: 60%;">
  <iframe src="https://www.google.com/maps/
    embed?pb=!1m18!1m12!1m3!1d3022.6175453420647!2d-
    73.98784413479707!3d40.748440379327945!2m3!1f0!2f
    0!3f0!3m2!1i1024!2i768!4f13.1!3m3!1m2!1s0x89c259a9aeb
    1c6b5%3A0x35b1cfbc89a6097f!2sEmpire+State+Building
    %2C+350+5th+Ave%2C+New+York%2C+NY+10118%2C+USA
    !5e0!3m2!1sda!2sdk!4v1491841211721"
    allowfullscreen></iframe>
</div>
```

To keep it short and simple, we're using the value 60%, which is simply the result of calc(3 / 5 * 100%). The aspect ratio will now stay the same when we view the page with the updated code in the browser.

Prefix for CSS custom properties

By default, all Bootstrap 5 CSS custom properties are prefixed with bs- (the double hyphen -- in front of the prefix bs- is how you declare a CSS custom property, and this can't be omitted). Should you wish to change this prefix, it can be done by overriding the $prefix variable defined on line 357 in the _variables.scss file. The default value for this variable is bs-.

Deprecated variable for the CSS custom property prefix

The variable to specify the CSS custom property prefix used to be $variable-prefix, but from version v5.2.0 of Bootstrap, this will be deprecated and replaced by the shorter $prefix. So, in this current version, v5.2.0, both variables are found in the code.

Using the RFS Sass plugin

RFS is officially described as a "unit resizing engine" that "automates responsive resizing." In other words, RFS is a collection of Sass mixins and functions for calculating automated responsive CSS values based on the width of the viewport. Being an abbreviation for *Responsive Font Sizes*, it was originally developed for font resizing, but it's now capable of resizing almost any value for any CSS property with units. RFS can be downloaded from its official website at GitHub at github.com/twbs/rfs/ or through NPM with the command npm install rfs. As you can see from the GitHub URL, the repository lives side by side with Bootstrap, since RFS is a side project from the team behind Bootstrap. In fact, RFS comes packaged with Bootstrap 5 as the file _rfs.scss in the vendor folder, and it's used for resizing font sizes. This is most apparent in headings. RFS is enabled by default by the global option $enable-rfs and can therefore also be disabled by setting that variable to false, as we saw in *Chapter 4, Bootstrap 5 Global Options and Colors*.

The syntax for RFS is as follows:

```
@include rfs([max-value], [property])
```

[max-value] is the value you would like for the specified [property] on large screens. RFS will use this value when the width of the viewport is 1200px or larger (so from the xl breakpoint and up). Below that, the value will dynamically scale in relation to the width of the viewport, until it reaches the base value of 1.25rem, after which it will no longer scale. These two options can be customized using the $rfs-breakpoint and $rfs-base-value variables along with other options.

There are also the following shorthand mixins for font size, padding, and margin we can use, so we don't need to specify the property explicitly:

bootstrap/scss/vendor/_rfs.scss

```scss
// Shorthand helper mixins
@mixin font-size($value) {
  @include rfs($value);
}

@mixin padding($value) {
  @include rfs($value, padding);
}
@mixin padding-top($value) {
  @include rfs($value, padding-top);
}
```

```scss
@mixin padding-right($value) {
  @include rfs($value, padding-right);
}
@mixin padding-bottom($value) {
  @include rfs($value, padding-bottom);
}
@mixin padding-left($value) {
  @include rfs($value, padding-left);
}
@mixin margin($value) {
  @include rfs($value, margin);
}
@mixin margin-top($value) {
  @include rfs($value, margin-top);
}
@mixin margin-right($value) {
  @include rfs($value, margin-right);
}
@mixin margin-bottom($value) {
  @include rfs($value, margin-bottom);
}
@mixin margin-left($value) {
  @include rfs($value, margin-left);
}
```

Now, let's see an example where we're using RFS to set the padding of a box. In the HTML, we first have a box using RFS for padding and then another box using a spacing utility for padding:

part-3/chapter-10/examples/rfs/index.html

```html
<!DOCTYPE html>
<html>
  <head>
    <meta charset="utf-8">
    <meta name="viewport" content="width=device-width,
      initial-scale=1">
    <title>RFS</title>
```

```html
      <link rel="stylesheet" href="css/style.css">
    </head>
    <body>
      <div class="container mt-3">
        <p>Box with RFS used for padding</p>
        <div class="box border mb-3">
          <h1 class="m-0">Heading</h1>
        </div>
        <p>Box with spacing utility used for padding</p>
        <div class="p-5 border">
          <h1 class="m-0">Heading</h1>
        </div>
      </div>
    </body>
  </html>
```

Then, in our Sass, we first import Bootstrap 5 and then use the shorthand mixin for padding on our .box class like so:

---

part-3/chapter-10/examples/rfs/scss/style.scss

```scss
// Bootstrap 5
@import "../../../../../bootstrap/scss/bootstrap.scss";


.box {
  @include padding(3rem);
}
```

We're using the value 3rem, which is the same value that's used by the .p-5 class on the first box. In that way, it's easy to see what difference the RFS makes. Following are two screenshots showing the difference, and I also suggest that you view the example in a browser, where you can better see the automatic calculations done by RFS when resizing the width of the browser.

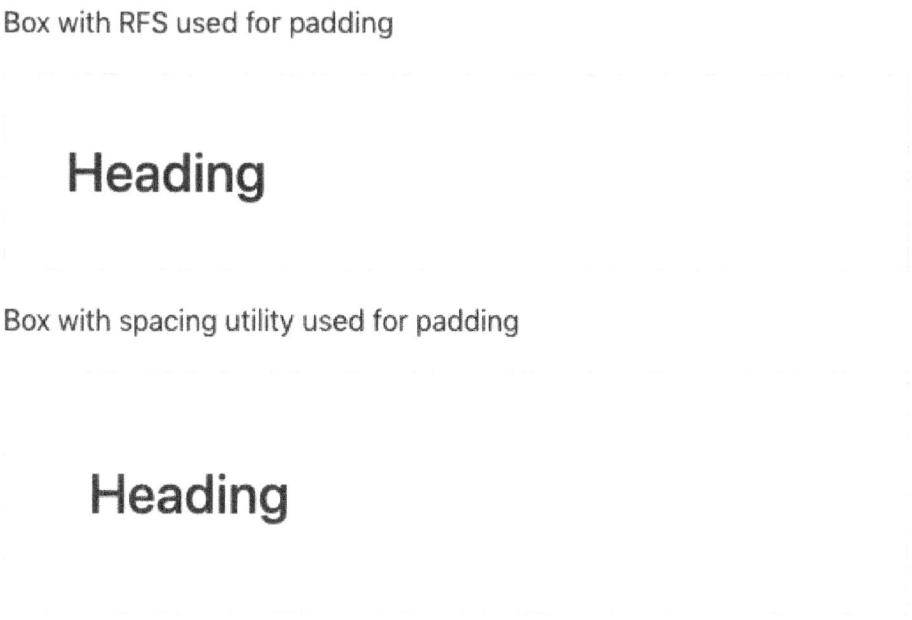

Box with RFS used for padding

Heading

Box with spacing utility used for padding

Heading

Figure 10.10 – Viewed on a small device (576px): calculated value is being used for padding

Box with RFS used for padding

Heading

Box with spacing utility used for padding

Heading

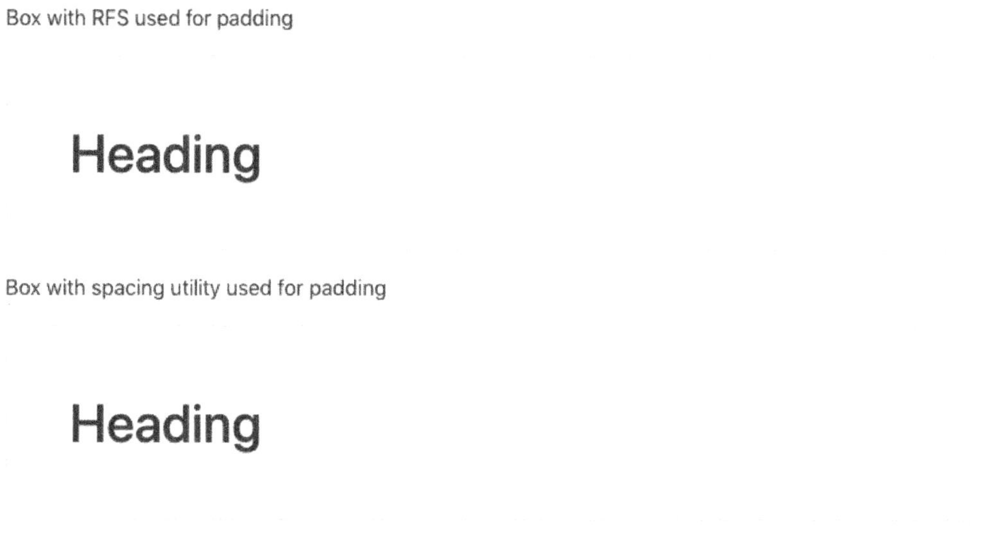

Figure 10.11 – Viewed on an extra large device (1200px): the max value is being used for padding

Summary

In this chapter, we have had a look at various advanced Sass and CSS features related to Bootstrap 5. We first saw how we could use various Bootstrap 5 mixins and functions and how to use the extend feature for various purposes. We then learned about the recommended approach to creating custom components using the Bootstrap 5 variables, mixins, and functions. After that, we saw how to use the Bootstrap 5 CSS custom properties to create a dark color theme and to customize a component and a helper. Finally, we learned how to use Bootstrap's side project, RFS, to calculate automated responsive CSS values.

In the next chapter, we will take a closer look at the JavaScript features of Bootstrap 5.

Using Bootstrap 5 with Advanced JavaScript Features

In this chapter, we will learn about some advanced JavaScript features that can be used with the interactive components of Bootstrap 5. First, we will get a quick overview of the interactive components and see which requirements they have in common in terms of dependencies and initialization. Then, we will see how we can initialize interactive components with either data attributes or JavaScript. Following this, we will see how we can define options with either data attributes or JavaScript, and finally, we will take a closer look at how we can use JavaScript for methods and events.

In this chapter, we're going to cover the following main topics:

- Interactive components of Bootstrap 5

- Initializing interactive components

- Defining options for interactive components

- Using JavaScript methods

- Using JavaScript events

Technical requirements

To preview the examples, you will need a code editor and a browser. The source code for all code examples can be found here:

`https://github.com/PacktPublishing/The-Missing-Bootstrap-5-Guide`

Interactive components of Bootstrap 5

We will start this chapter by getting an overview of the interactive components of Bootstrap 5. For each component listed here, we will see which JavaScript file is being used, whether it requires custom initialization, which options, methods, and events it has, whether it has any dependencies, and for some of them also some additional information. In the following sections, we will then look closer at initialization, options, methods, and events, so this should just be regarded as an overview. At the end of the list, there's also a summary to highlight the most important differences.

Accordion

This component is built using the collapse component described later.

Alert

JavaScript file: `alert.js`

Custom initialization: No

Options: None

Methods: `close, dispose, getInstance, getOrCreateInstance`

Events: `close.bs.alert, closed.bs.alert`

Dependencies: None

This component can be dismissed with the close button component.

Button

JavaScript file: `button.js`

Custom initialization: No

Options: None

Methods: `toggle, dispose, getInstance, getOrCreateInstance`

Events: None

Dependencies: None

Carousel

JavaScript file: `carousel.js`

Custom initialization: No

Options: `interval, keyboard, pause, ride, wrap, touch`

Methods: `cycle`, `pause`, `prev`, `next`, `nextWhenVisible`, `to`, `dispose`, `getInstance`, `getOrCreateInstance`

Events: `slide.bs.carousel`, `slid.bs.carousel`

Dependencies: None

Collapse

JavaScript file: `collapse.js`

Custom initialization: No

Options: `parent`, `toggle`

Methods: `toggle`, `show`, `hide`, `dispose`, `getInstance`, `getOrCreateInstance`

Events: `show.bs.collapse`, `shown.bs.collapse`, `hide.bs.collapse`, `hidden.bs.collapse`

Dependencies: None

Dropdown

JavaScript file: `dropdown.js`

Custom initialization: No

Options: `boundary`, `reference`, `display`, `offset`, `autoClose`, `popperConfig`

Methods: `toggle`, `show`, `hide`, `update`, `dispose`, `getInstance`, `getOrCreateInstance`

Events: `show.bs.dropdown`, `shown.bs.dropdown`, `hide.bs.dropdown`, `hidden.bs.dropdown`

Dependencies: Popper

This component requires the external third-party library Popper for positioning. It must be included before `bootstrap.js` or by using `bootstrap.bundle.js`, which contains Popper.

List group

This component uses `tab.js` to create tab navigation based on list groups. Please refer to the details for navs and tabs, which use the same JavaScript file.

Modal

JavaScript file: `modal.js`

Custom initialization: No

Options: `backdrop, keyboard, focus`

Methods: `toggle, show, hide, handleUpdate, dispose, getInstance, getOrCreateInstance`

Events: `show.bs.modal, shown.bs.modal, hide.bs.modal, hidden.bs.modal, hidePrevented.bs.modal`

Dependencies: None

Navs and tabs

JavaScript file: `tab.js`

Custom initialization: No

Options: None

Methods: `show, dispose, getInstance, getOrCreateInstance`

Events: `show.bs.tab, shown.bs.tab, hide.bs.tab, hidden.bs.tab`

Dependencies: None

The JavaScript file used by this component is also used by the list group component.

Offcanvas

JavaScript file: `offcanvas.js`

Custom initialization: No

Options: `backdrop, keyboard, scroll`

Methods: `toggle, show, hide, getInstance, getOrCreateInstance`

Events: `show.bs.offcanvas, shown.bs.offcanvas, hide.bs.offcanvas, hidden.bs.offcanvas`

Dependencies: None

Popover

JavaScript file: `popover.js`

Custom initialization: Yes

Options: `animation`, `container`, `content`, `delay`, `html`, `placement`, `selector`, `template`, `title`, `trigger`, `fallbackPlacements`, `boundary`, `customClass`, `sanitize`, `allowList`, `sanitizeFn`, `offset`, `popperConfig`

Methods: `show`, `hide`, `toggle`, `dispose`, `enable`, `disable`, `toggleEnabled`, `update`, `getInstance`, `getOrCreateInstance`

Events: `show.bs.popover`, `shown.bs.popover`, `hide.bs.popover`, `hidden.bs.popover`, `inserted.bs.popover`

Dependencies: `tooltip.js`, Popover

This component requires `tooltip.js` as a dependency. It also requires the external third-party library Popper for positioning. The latter must be included before `bootstrap.js` or by using `bootstrap.bundle.js`, which contains Popper.

Scrollspy

JavaScript file: `scrollspy.js`

Custom initialization: No

Options: `rootMargin`, `smoothScroll`, `target`

Methods: `refresh`, `dispose`, `getInstance`, `getOrCreateInstance`

Events: `activate.bs.scrollspy`

Dependencies: None

Toast

JavaScript file: `toast.js`

Custom initialization: Yes

Options: `animation`, `autohide`, `delay`

Methods: `show`, `hide`, `dispose`, `getInstance`, `getOrCreateInstance`

Events: `show.bs.toast`, `shown.bs.toast`, `hide.bs.toast`, `hidden.bs.toast`

Dependencies: None

Tooltip

JavaScript file: `tooltip.js`

Custom initialization: Yes

Options: `animation`, `container`, `delay`, `html`, `placement`, `selector`, `template`, `title`, `trigger`, `fallbackPlacements`, `boundary`, `customClass`, `sanitize`, `allowList`, `sanitizeFn`, `offset`, `popperConfig`

Methods: `show`, `hide`, `toggle`, `dispose`, `enable`, `disable`, `toggleEnabled`, `update`, `getInstance`, `getOrCreateInstance`

Events: `show.bs.tooltip`, `shown.bs.tooltip`, `hide.bs.tooltip`, `hidden.bs.tooltip`, `inserted.bs.tooltip`

Dependencies: Popover

This component requires the external third-party library Popper for positioning. It must be included before `bootstrap.js` or by using `bootstrap.bundle.js`, which contains Popper.

The `tooltip.js` file is required by the popover component as a dependency.

We just ran through a list of all of the 15 components that use JavaScript in some way or another. Now, we will summarize this and highlight the most important differences among the components. Under the next four headings, we will therefore see which components stand out from the crowd.

Requires initialization

Components: Popover, toast, tooltip

These components can't be initialized with the use of data attributes due to performance reasons. Hence, they must instead be initialized using custom JavaScript. We will see how in the *Initializing interactive components* section.

Has dependencies

Components: Dropdown, popover, tooltip

These components all require the external third-party library Popper for positioning. It must be included before `bootstrap.js` or by using `bootstrap.bundle.js`, which contains Popper.

In addition to this, the popover component also requires the `tooltip.js` JavaScript file from the tooltip component as a dependency.

Has no options

Components: Alert, button, navs, and tabs

These components don't have any options.

Has no events

Component: Button

This component doesn't have any events.

Initializing interactive components

In this section, we will see how we can initialize interactive components in two different ways. First, we will see how we can do it with data attributes in the HTML, which is the default way, which you might have already been using. Then, we will see how we can do it with JavaScript instead. We can initialize most of the interactive components that come with Bootstrap 5 using data attributes and without adding any extra JavaScript code ourselves, while some of them we must initialize with our own JavaScript.

Initializing interactive components using data attributes

We can initialize most of the interactive components that come with Bootstrap 5 using data attributes and without adding any extra JavaScript code ourselves. For most components, we use the data-bs-toggle data attribute, with the value being the name of the component, like so:

HTML

```
<button type="button" class="btn btn-primary" data-bs-
toggle="button">Button</button>
```

However, for the carousel component, we must use data-bs-ride="carousel", for the scrollspy component we must use data-bs-spy="scroll", and, to dismiss the alert or offcanvas component, we must use data-bs-dismiss="[alert/offcanvas]".

> **Other required data attributes**
> Various other data attributes are required for some components to make them work. The data attributes mentioned above are just the ones used to initialize them.

Initializing interactive components using JavaScript

As we saw in the list at the beginning of this chapter, we must initialize some of the interactive components with our own JavaScript code.

As an example, we want to create a tooltip component for the following badge component:

HTML

```
<div class="badge bg-secondary" title="Tooltip for badge">Badge
with tooltip</div>
```

The `<div>` tag has the `title` attribute that is used by the tooltip component.

Syntax

We can initialize an interactive component by using the constructor function in JavaScript to create and initialize an object instance of a class using the `new` keyword.

The syntax for this is as follows:

JavaScript

```
var tooltip = new bootstrap.Tooltip(element, options)
```

Here, `element` can be either a DOM element or a CSS selector and `options` is an object and is optional. Options can still be defined using data attributes, even though we are initializing a component with JavaScript. We will learn more about options in the *Defining options for interactive components* section.

Using a DOM element

To initialize an interactive component using a DOM element, we must first store it in a variable, and then use that variable as a reference to the DOM element. Here's an example of how to do this:

part-3/chapter-11/examples/initialization/index.html line 14

```
<div class="badge bg-secondary" title="Tooltip for badge"
id="tooltipDOM">Badge with tooltip</div>
```

part-3/chapter-11/examples/initialization/js/script.js line 1-2

```
var tooltipDOMelement = document.getElementById('tooltipDOM');
var tooltipDOM = new bootstrap.Tooltip(tooltipDOMelement);
```

In the previous code, we stored the element with `id="tooltipDOM"` in the `element` variable, which we then passed as an argument to the constructor function. We didn't pass any options since we will take a closer look at that later in this chapter.

Using a CSS selector

To initialize an interactive component using a CSS selector, we can simply pass it as the argument to the constructor function. The element is then found using the querySelector() method. Here's an example of how to do this using the ID of the <div> element as the selector:

part-3/chapter-11/examples/initialization/index.html line 19

```
<div class="badge bg-secondary" title="Tooltip for badge"
id="tooltipCSS">Badge with tooltip</div>
```

part-3/chapter-11/examples/initialization/js/script.js line 4

```
var tooltip = new bootstrap.Tooltip('#tooltipCSS');
```

Initializing multiple components

The various JavaScript plugins for the interactive components only support a single element. So, to initialize multiple elements, we can call the constructor function for each element in a list or an array. We will now see two different examples of how we can do just that.

Using a for loop

For the first example, we will use the following HTML with three identical badge components that all have the same tooltipLoop class:

part-3/chapter-11/examples/initialization/index.html line 24-26

```
<div class="badge bg-secondary tooltipLoop" title="Tooltip for
badge">Badge with tooltip</div>
<div class="badge bg-secondary tooltipLoop" title="Tooltip for
badge">Badge with tooltip</div>
<div class="badge bg-secondary tooltipLoop" title="Tooltip for
badge">Badge with tooltip</div>
```

When using a for loop, we first store all <div> elements in the tooltipLoopElements variable. Then, we loop through this NodeList and call the constructor function for each element:

part-3/chapter-11/examples/initialization/js/script.js line 6-9

```
var tooltipLoopElements = document.querySelectorAll('.
tooltipLoop');
```

```
for (var i = 0; i < tooltipLoopElements.length; i++) {
  new bootstrap.Tooltip(tooltipLoopElements[i])
}
```

Using the map method

For the second example, we will use the following HTML with three identical badge components that all have the same `tooltipMap` class:

part-3/chapter-11/examples/initialization/index.html line 31-33

```
<div class="badge bg-secondary tooltipMap" title="Tooltip for
badge">Badge with tooltip</div>
<div class="badge bg-secondary tooltipMap" title="Tooltip for
badge">Badge with tooltip</div>
<div class="badge bg-secondary tooltipMap" title="Tooltip for
badge">Badge with tooltip</div>
```

When using the map() method, we first store all `<div>` elements in the `tooltipMapElements` variable. However, this time we use the `slice()` and `call()` methods to turn the NodeList into an array. Then, we create a new array using the map() method and store it in the `tooltipMap` variable. For every element in the array, we call the constructor function like before:

part-3/chapter-11/examples/initialization/js/script.js line 11-14

```
var tooltipMapElements = [].slice.call(document.
querySelectorAll('.tooltipMap'));
var tooltipMap = tooltipMapElements.
map(function(tooltipMapElement) {
  return new bootstrap.Tooltip(tooltipMapElement)
});
```

> **Data attribute required for the dropdown component**
>
> Even if you choose to initialize the dropdown component using JavaScript, the `data-bs-toggle="dropdown"` data attribute is still required on the trigger element for the dropdown.

We have now learned how to initialize interactive components in various ways. We will continue to learn how to define options for interactive components.

Defining options for interactive components

In the list at the beginning of this chapter, we saw which options were available for interactive components. In the official documentation of Bootstrap 5, you will find a table describing all of the available options (if any) for each component. In this table, you will find the name, type, default value, and description for each option. You can access the components in the official documentation through this link: `getbootstrap.com/docs/5.1/components`.

Default options for all components of a type and common options for a group of components can be set via JavaScript, while options for individual components can be passed either via data attributes or via JavaScript. Let's now see how this is done.

Defining default options

You can change the default value for an option for a component by using the following syntax:

JavaScript

```
bootstrap.[component name].Default.[option name] = [option
value];
```

As an example, we can set our tooltip components to have a default delay of 1,000 milliseconds in the following way:

JavaScript

```
bootstrap.Tooltip.Default.delay = 1000;
```

Defining options using data attributes

To define options using data attributes, we append the option name to `data-bs-`, and the case type of the option name should be changed from *camelCase* to *kebab-case*.

Now, let's see how we can initialize a tooltip component with an option for how to trigger it. For this purpose, we can use the `trigger` option, which accepts a value of the `string` type. The default is `'hover focus'`, and the possible values are `'click | hover | focus | manual'`. We will make the tooltip trigger on click only using the following code:

HTML

```
<a href="#" id="tooltip" title="Tooltip for link" data-bs-
trigger="click">Link</a>
```

The tooltip will now only be triggered on click for both showing and hiding – just like the popover component. Keep in mind that the previous code on its own will not initialize the tooltip component. As we just learned, this must be done with our own JavaScript code:

> **Options that can't be set using data attributes**
>
> The following options used by the popover and tooltip components can't be set using data attributes due to security reasons: `sanitize`, `sanitizeFn`, and `allowList`. These are all related to using HTML in the content of the tooltip or popover.

Defining options using JavaScript

As mentioned earlier in this chapter, it's possible to pass an optional `options` object to the constructor when initializing an interactive component with JavaScript. To repeat, the syntax looks like this:

```
var tooltip = new bootstrap.Tooltip(element, options)
```

To define an option with an object, we simply use the option name as a property of the object and then give it a valid value depending on the type of option. Initializing the same tooltip component as before, with the `trigger` option set to `click`, will then look like this:

HTML

```
<a href="#" id="tooltip" title="Tooltip for link">Link</a>
```

JavaScript

```
var tooltip = new bootstrap.Tooltip('#tooltip', { trigger:
'click' })
```

The tooltip will now only be triggered on click for both showing and hiding.

Defining default, common, and individual options

As mentioned previously, we can define default, common, and individual options for components using JavaScript and data attributes. This is useful if you want to define some default options for all components of a type, options with the same value for a group of components, and individual options with different values for each instance of a component.

We will now see an example where we make use of all of this. In our HTML, we have four badge components to which we want to add a tooltip component. On each of the <div> elements, we define the placement for the tooltip using the data-bs-placement data attribute:

part-3/chapter-11/examples/options/index.html

```
<div class="badge bg-secondary tooltipOnClick" title="Tooltip
on top" data-bs-placement="top">Badge with tooltip on top</div>
<div class="badge bg-secondary tooltipOnClick" title="Tooltip
on bottom" data-bs-placement="bottom">Badge with tooltip on
bottom</div>
<div class="badge bg-secondary tooltipOnClick" title="Tooltip
on left" data-bs-placement="left">Badge with tooltip on left</
div>
<div class="badge bg-secondary tooltipOnClick" title="Tooltip
on right" data-bs-placement="right">Badge with tooltip on
right</div>
```

Then, in our JavaScript, we first define the default option for delay and set it to 1000 milliseconds. After that, we initialize the components using JavaScript with the trigger option set to 'click':

part-3/chapter-11/examples/options/js/script.js

```
bootstrap.Tooltip.Default.delay = 1000;

var tooltipElementList = document.querySelectorAll('.
tooltipOnClick');
for (var i = 0; i < tooltipElementList.length; i++) {
    new bootstrap.Tooltip(tooltipElementList[i], { trigger:
        'click' })
}
```

The four badge components will now have a tooltip component each that will trigger on click with a delay of 1,000 milliseconds. The tooltips will be placed at the top, bottom, left, and right respectively.

> **Using data attributes and JavaScript for the same option**
>
> If you specify the same option with both a data attribute and using JavaScript, the JavaScript setting will take precedence.

Using JavaScript methods

In the list at the beginning of this chapter, we saw that all interactive components have methods. In the official documentation of Bootstrap 5, you will find a table describing all of the available methods for each component. In this table, you will find the name and description for each method. You can access the components in the official documentation through this link: `getbootstrap.com/docs/5.2/components`.

Now, we will see some examples of how to use specific methods for the tooltip component. In our example page, we first have a default tooltip component for comparison. The HTML for this is as follows:

part-3/chapter-11/examples/methods/index.html line 15

```
<div class="badge bg-secondary" id="tooltipDefault"
title="Default tooltip">Badge with default tooltip</div>
```

The tooltip has the `id="tooltipDefault"` attribute, which we use to initialize it with the following JavaScript:

part-3/chapter-11/examples/methods/js/script.js line 1

```
var tooltipDefault = new bootstrap.Tooltip('#tooltipDefault', {
placement: "bottom" });
```

As we can see, the tooltip is placed at the bottom using the `placement` option. This is simply to make the example page better visually.

For the next tooltip component on the example page, we want it to show when the page loads and, at the same time, disable triggering on hover and focus. The HTML is as follows:

part-3/chapter-11/examples/methods/index.html line 21

```
<div class="badge bg-secondary" id="tooltipOnLoad"
title="Tooltip triggered on load">Badge with tooltip triggered
on load</div>
```

The tooltip has the `id="tooltipOnLoad"` attribute, which we will use for initialization. The JavaScript code looks like this:

part-3/chapter-11/examples/methods/js/script.js line 3-4

```
var tooltipOnLoad = new bootstrap.Tooltip('#tooltipOnLoad', {
trigger: "manual", placement: "bottom" });
tooltipOnLoad.show();
```

The tooltip is placed at the bottom using the `placement` option and the method to trigger the tooltip is set to `manual`. This means that the tooltip will be triggered programmatically using JavaScript, which is exactly what we do in the line below where we call the `show()` method on the initialized tooltip component.

For our final tooltip component on the example page, we want to toggle its visibility when we click a button placed elsewhere on the page. The HTML for this is as follows:

part-3/chapter-11/examples/methods/index.html line 27-28

```
<button type="button" id="triggerForTooltip" class="btn btn-
secondary mb-4">Trigger for tooltip</button><br>
<div class="badge bg-secondary" id="tooltipOnButtonClick"
title="Tooltip toggled on button click">Badge with tooltip
toggled on button click</div>
```

The button has the `id="triggerForTooltip"` attribute, which we will use to attach an event listener, and the tooltip has the `id="tooltipOnButtonClick"` attribute, which we will use for initialization. The JavaScript code looks like this:

part-3/chapter-11/examples/methods/js/script.js line 6-10

```
var tooltipOnButtonClick = new bootstrap.
Tooltip('#tooltipOnButtonClick', { trigger: "manual",
placement: "bottom" });
var triggerForTooltip = document.
getElementById('triggerForTooltip');
triggerForTooltip.addEventListener('click', function() {
  tooltipOnButtonClick.toggle();
})
```

The first line is similar to the previous example: the tooltip is placed at the bottom using the `placement` option and the method to trigger the tooltip is set to `manual`. Below that, we first get the button element and then attach a `click` event to it and execute the `toggle()` method when the button is clicked. This will show and hide the tooltip.

Asynchronous methods and transitions

It's important to know that all methods are asynchronous and start a transition. As soon as that transition is started, they return to the caller. This means that a method call on a component that is currently transitioning is ignored. Take the following example, which will show the modal, but not hide it, since the `hide()` method is called immediately after `show()` and therefore before the transition to show that the modal is finished:

JavaScript

```javascript
var modalElement = document.getElementById('modal');
var modal = bootstrap.Modal.getOrCreateInstance(modalElement);
modal.show();
modal.hide();
```

Instead, if we want to execute some code when the transition is finished, we need to listen to the corresponding event, like so:

JavaScript

```javascript
var modalElement = document.getElementById('modal');
var modal = bootstrap.Modal.getOrCreateInstance(modalElement);
modal.show();

modalElement.addEventListener('shown.bs.modal', function
(event) {
  modal.hide();
})
```

Now, the modal will first show and then hide again when the modal's `shown` event is fired. In the next section, we will see another example of how to use Bootstrap 5 events.

Using JavaScript events

In the list at the beginning of this chapter, we saw that most interactive components have events. In the official documentation of Bootstrap 5, you will find a table describing all of the available events for each component. In this table, you will find the event type and description for each method. You can access the components in the official documentation through this link: `getbootstrap.com/docs/5.2/components`.

Now, we will see an example of how to use a specific event for the tooltip component. In our example page, we have a button that triggers a modal component. In the modal footer, we have a **Confirm** button on which we want to show a tooltip when the modal is shown and the transition is finished.

Here's what the HTML looks like:

part-3/chapter-11/examples/events/index.html

```html
<button type="button" class="btn btn-primary" data-bs-
toggle="modal" data-bs-target="#modal">Open modal</button>
<div class="modal fade" id="modal" tabindex="-1" aria-
labelledby="modalTitle" aria-hidden="true">
  <div class="modal-dialog">
    <div class="modal-content">
      <div class="modal-header">
        <h5 class="modal-title" id="modalTitle">Modal
          title</h5>
        <button type="button" class="btn-close" data-bs-
          dismiss="modal" aria-label="Close"></button>
      </div>
      <div class="modal-body">
        <p>Lorem ipsum dolor sit amet, consectetur
          adipiscing elit. In laoreet pellentesque lorem
          sed elementum. Suspendisse maximus convallis ex.
          Etiam eleifend velit leo.</p>
      </div>
      <div class="modal-footer">
        <button type="button" class="btn btn-primary"
          id="tooltip" title="Click here to
          confirm">Confirm</button>
        <button type="button" class="btn btn-secondary"
          data-bs-dismiss="modal">Close</button>
      </div>
    </div>
  </div>
</div>
```

The tooltip has the `id="tooltip"`, which we will use for initialization, and the content for the tooltip is placed in a `title` attribute. In the JavaScript code, we first store the DOM element of the modal in a variable and initialize the tooltip component. Then, in an event listener attached to the modal, we listen to the `shown.bs.modal` event and call the `show()` method on the tooltip component when it fires. The JavaScript code for this is as follows:

part-3/chapter-11/examples/events/js/script.js

```
var modal = document.getElementById('modal');
var tooltip = new bootstrap.Tooltip('#tooltip');

modal.addEventListener('shown.bs.modal', function (event) {
    tooltip.show();
})
```

This example will now show the tooltip exactly when the transition for the modal is finished.

Events with properties

The two events for the carousel component have the following additional properties: `direction` (`"left"` or `"right"`), `relatedTarget` (DOM element), `from` (index number), and `to` (index number).

Summary

In this chapter, we have learned about some advanced JavaScript features that can be used with the interactive components of Bootstrap 5. First, we got a quick overview of the interactive components and saw which requirements they have in common in terms of dependencies and initialization. Then, we saw how we can initialize interactive components with either data attributes or JavaScript. Following this, we saw how we can define options with either data attributes or JavaScript, and finally, we took a closer look at how we can use JavaScript for methods and events.

In the next and final chapter of this book, we will learn how to optimize the compiled Bootstrap 5 CSS and JavaScript code.

12
Optimizing Bootstrap 5 CSS and JavaScript Code

In this chapter, we're not going to use Bootstrap 5 to create any new user interfaces or customize any existing ones. We won't even look at any of the source code contained in the Bootstrap 5 files. Instead, we will see how we can optimize our compiled Bootstrap 5 CSS and JavaScript code after we have finished creating our website.

We will first concentrate on optimizing our stylesheet by only including the Bootstrap 5 Sass partials we actually use and removing all the helpers and utilities that we don't use. Then we will use Node.js, NPM, and Laravel Mix to set up a build process to automate some tasks that will help us bundle only the JavaScript that our components actually use and minify both our compiled CSS and bundled JavaScript.

In this chapter, we're going to cover the following main topics:

- Including the Sass partials for the used components only
- Removing unused helpers and utilities
- Setting up a build process using Node.js, npm, and Laravel Mix
- Using a module bundler to optimize JavaScript
- Minifying our compiled CSS and bundled JavaScript

Technical requirements

- To preview the examples, you will need a code editor and a browser. The source code for all code examples can be found here: `https://github.com/PacktPublishing/The-Missing-Bootstrap-5-Guide`.

- To compile Sass to CSS, you will need either of the following:

  - **Node.js**, if you prefer a **command-line interface** (**CLI**) using Terminal (Mac) or Command Prompt (Windows)

  - **Scout-App**, if you prefer a **graphical user interface** (**GUI**)

  - **Visual Studio Code**, if you prefer to use an extension from the Visual Studio Code Marketplace

  All these approaches are explained in *Chapter 2, Using and Compiling Sass*.

To use Laravel Mix, you will need **Node.js** installed on your computer and then follow the instructions to download the required packages from npm.

Including the Sass partials for the used components only

In this section, we will see how we can optimize our compiled CSS by only including the Bootstrap 5 Sass partials that are actually used by the components in our HTML code. On the website that we created earlier in this book, we have used all of the Bootstrap 5 components except for the Placeholder, Popover, and Scrollspy components. Scrollspy is a JavaScript-only component, so we will remove the Sass partials belonging to the Placeholder and Popover components. In our `styles.scss` file, we have a long list of `// Optional Bootstrap CSS`, which among other things contains the Sass partials for all components. So, this is where we want to carefully consider which partial files we can remove. In the following code snippet, you will see the long list of `// Optional Bootstrap CSS` where the lines that import the Sass partials for the Placeholder and Popover components have been commented out. You could also choose to delete those lines, but by keeping them commented out it's easy to uncomment them if you add any of these components to the website at a later stage, and they will anyway be removed automatically when the Sass is compiled:

part-3/chapter-12/website/scss/style.scss

```scss
// Optional Bootstrap CSS
@import "../../../../bootstrap/scss/reboot";
@import "../../../../bootstrap/scss/type";
@import "../../../../bootstrap/scss/images";
@import "../../../../bootstrap/scss/containers";
@import "../../../../bootstrap/scss/grid";
@import "../../../../bootstrap/scss/tables";
```

```scss
@import "../../../../bootstrap/scss/forms";
@import "../../../../bootstrap/scss/buttons";
@import "../../../../bootstrap/scss/transitions";
@import "../../../../bootstrap/scss/dropdown";
@import "../../../../bootstrap/scss/button-group";
@import "../../../../bootstrap/scss/nav";
@import "../../../../bootstrap/scss/navbar";
@import "../../../../bootstrap/scss/card";
@import "../../../../bootstrap/scss/accordion";
@import "../../../../bootstrap/scss/breadcrumb";
@import "../../../../bootstrap/scss/pagination";
@import "../../../../bootstrap/scss/badge";
@import "../../../../bootstrap/scss/alert";
@import "../../../../bootstrap/scss/progress";
@import "../../../../bootstrap/scss/list-group";
@import "../../../../bootstrap/scss/close";
@import "../../../../bootstrap/scss/toasts";
@import "../../../../bootstrap/scss/modal";
@import "../../../../bootstrap/scss/tooltip";
// @import "../../../../bootstrap/scss/popover";
@import "../../../../bootstrap/scss/carousel";
@import "../../../../bootstrap/scss/spinners";
@import "../../../../bootstrap/scss/offcanvas";
// @import "../../../../bootstrap/scss/placeholders";
```

When we compile our Sass code, the compiled CSS stylesheet will now be slightly smaller since the CSS for the Popover and Placeholder components have been removed.

Dependencies across Sass partials

There are some dependencies across the various Sass partial files, so it might not be easy to simply remove a file for a specific component. Make sure that you test your website carefully.

Removing unused helpers and utilities

The helpers and utilities of Bootstrap 5 are something that we use in addition to components, sometimes on specific code inside of a component, and sometimes as part of our own HTML code. Therefore, it can also be considered which of these we actually use, and make sure to not include the ones that we don't use.

Removing unused helpers

In our code for the website, we have used the following helpers: Ratio, Position, Visually hidden, and Stretched link. The Bootstrap 5 code for these helpers is imported in our `style.scss` file using the following code:

---

part-3/chapter-12/website/scss/style.scss

```scss
// Helpers
@import "../../../../bootstrap/scss/helpers";
```

This will import the `_helpers.scss` file containing `@import` statements for the individual helpers. The content of that file is as follows:

---

part-3/chapter-12/website/bootstrap/scss/_helpers.scss

```scss
@import "helpers/clearfix";
@import "helpers/colored-links";
@import "helpers/ratio";
@import "helpers/position";
@import "helpers/stacks";
@import "helpers/visually-hidden";
@import "helpers/stretched-link";
@import "helpers/text-truncation";
@import "helpers/vr";
```

We might now think that we simply need to uncomment the @import statements for the helpers that we don't use, just as we did with the components in the previous section. This will work here and now, but if we choose to update Bootstrap 5 at a later point, our changes will be gone, since the _helpers.scss file will be replaced. This is because this file is part of the Bootstrap 5 source code that is replaced when you update Bootstrap 5. If you know you won't update Bootstrap 5 at a later point or know that you will remember to make the same edits to the _helpers.scss file again after updating, you can do it like this:

part-3/chapter-12/website/bootstrap/scss/_helpers.scss

```
// @import "helpers/clearfix";
// @import "helpers/colored-links";
@import "helpers/ratio";
@import "helpers/position";
// @import "helpers/stacks";
@import "helpers/visually-hidden";
@import "helpers/stretched-link";
// @import "helpers/text-truncation";
// @import "helpers/vr";
```

But to do it in a better and more maintainable way, we can change our @import statement in the styles.scss file and import only the individual helper partial files that we need instead of importing the _helpers.scss file. So, we will ignore that file (even though it's part of the Bootstrap 5 source code) and instead implement our own way of importing the helpers.

The code will then look like this:

part-3/chapter-12/website/scss/style.scss

```
// Helpers
// @import "..//../../../bootstrap/scss/helpers/clearfix";
// @import "..//../../../bootstrap/scss/helpers/colored-links";
@import "..//../../../bootstrap/scss/helpers/ratio";
@import "..//../../../bootstrap/scss/helpers/position";
// @import "..//../../../bootstrap/scss/helpers/stacks";
@import "..//../../../bootstrap/scss/helpers/visually-hidden";
@import "..//../../../bootstrap/scss/helpers/stretched-link";
// @import "..//../../../bootstrap/scss/helpers/text-
truncation";
// @import "..//../../../bootstrap/scss/helpers/vr";
```

I have chosen to keep the unused imports in our file but have them commented out. Then, it's easier to uncomment them in the future if the need arises, and it will anyway be removed when compiling the Sass and hence not take up any space. Just like the way we did with the imports of the component partial files.

Removing unused utilities

To remove unused utilities, we will need to take a different approach than what we have seen with components and helpers. We now need to use the utility API, which we learned about in *Chapter 6, Understanding and Using the Bootstrap 5 Utility API*. In the `_utilities.scss` file of Bootstrap 5, we see a total of 80 defined utility classes that have different settings and values. For each of them, we can see what the class or class prefix will be, and we can use that to search through our code to see which ones we actually use. If we do this, we will see that we roughly use half of them. To be precise, we need to remove the following 37 utility classes that are not being used:

```
align, opacity, overflow, shadow, start, translate-middle,
max-width, viewport-width, min-viewport-width, max-height,
viewport-height, min-viewport-height, flex, flex-grow, flex-
shrink, flex-wrap, gap, align-content, align-self, order,
margin, margin-start, padding-x, padding-end, padding-start,
font-family, word-wrap, text-opacity, bg-opacity, gradient,
user-select, pointer-events, rounded-top, rounded-end, rounded-
bottom, rounded-start, visibility
```

The negative margin utilities (`negative-margin`, `negative-margin-x`, `negative-margin-y`, `negative-margin-top`, `negative-margin-end`, `negative-margin-bottom`, and `negative-margin-start`) are not included in the list, since they are disabled by default, and we haven't enabled them through the `$enable-negative-margins` option in our own Sass code.

To remove all of the unused utilities so that they are not generated through the utility API, we use the following code:

part-3/chapter-12/website/scss/_utilities.scss

```scss
// Remove unused utilities
$utilities: map-merge(
  $utilities,
  (
    "align": null,
    "opacity": null,
    "overflow": null,
```

```
    "shadow": null,
    "start": null,
    "translate-middle": null,
    "max-width": null,
    "viewport-width": null,
    "min-viewport-width": null,
    "max-height": null,
    "viewport-height": null,
    "min-viewport-height": null,
    "flex": null,
    "flex-grow": null,
    "flex-shrink": null,
    "flex-wrap": null,
    "gap": null,
    "align-content": null,
    "align-self": null,
    "order": null,
    "margin": null,
    "margin-start": null,
    "padding-x": null,
    "padding-end": null,
    "padding-start": null,
    "font-family": null,
    "word-wrap": null,
    "text-opacity": null,
    "bg-opacity": null,
    "gradient": null,
    "user-select": null,
    "pointer-events": null,
    "rounded-top": null,
    "rounded-end": null,
    "rounded-bottom": null,
    "rounded-start": null,
    "visibility": null,
  )
);
```

After compiling the Sass code, the resulting CSS file (in the expanded Sass output format) will now be 1,513 lines smaller, which is equal to 25,485 bytes saved.

Specifying used utilities

Another way to optimize the usage of utilities is to specify the utilities that are *being used* instead. There are a total of 39 utilities being used in our project, and we can generate just these by using the map-get-multiple() Sass function provided by Bootstrap 5 in the _functions.scss file. With this function, we can get multiple keys from a Sass map and thus overwrite the $utilities variable as follows:

SCSS

```scss
$utilities: map-get-multiple(
  $utilities,
  (
    "float",
    "display",
    "position",
    "top",
    "bottom",
    "end",
    "border",
    "border-top",
    "border-end",
    "border-bottom",
    "border-start",
    "border-color",
    "border-width",
    "width",
    "height",
    "flex-direction",
    "justify-content",
    "align-items",
    "margin-x",
    "margin-y",
    "margin-top",
    "margin-end",
```

```
    "margin-bottom",
    "padding",
    "padding-y",
    "padding-top",
    "padding-bottom",
    "font-size",
    "font-style",
    "font-weight",
    "line-height",
    "text-align",
    "text-decoration",
    "text-transform",
    "white-space",
    "color",
    "background-color",
    "rounded",
    "utility",
  )
);
```

No matter whether you choose to specify which utilities to remove or which are being used, the result will be the same.

Trimming used utilities

If you want to go that extra mile, it's also possible to trim any used utilities. By that, I mean that we remove any variations of a utility that we are not using by editing the values of that utility.

Say that we want to edit the text-align utility since we are only using the .text-center class in our project. So, we want to remove the .text-start and .text-end variations as well as disable the responsive variations of this utility. To accomplish this, we can use the following code:

SCSS

```
$utilities: map-merge(
  $utilities,
  (
    "text-align": map-merge(
      map-get($utilities, "text-align"),
```

```
        ( values: (
            center: center,
        ),
        responsive: false
    ),
),
)
);
```

Now, we will only generate the `.text-center` class, which is the only one we use for text alignment.

Alternatively, this can also be done by using the following code, where we overwrite the code for the text alignment utility and, therefore, must also specify `property` and `class`:

SCSS

```scss
$utilities: map-merge(
  $utilities,
  (
    "text-align": (
      property: text-align,
      responsive: false,
      class: text,
      values: (
        center: center,
      )
    )
  )
);
```

This was just an example. I have not used this method of trimming used utilities for the project, since it's a rather big task. But if you go that extra mile, it will be possible to save some lines and bytes of code.

In the next section, we will set up a build tool using Node.js, npm, and Laravel Mix. We will do that to be able to optimize our usage of JavaScript and automate tasks for Sass compiling and general minifying.

Setting up a build process using Node.js, npm, and Laravel Mix

In *Chapter 2, Using and Compiling Sass*, we already learned how to use Node.js and npm to set up a script that would compile our Sass to CSS. In this setup, we will use Laravel Mix, which is a wrapper around Webpack. In short, Webpack is a module bundler that prepares JavaScript and assets for the browser. By using Laravel Mix, we get a simple API for setting the Webpack configuration without any prior experience with Webpack.

If you haven't already installed Node.js, then please go back and take a look at *Chapter 2* and the *Compiling Sass* section. Now, here's a step-by-step guide on how to set up Laravel Mix using Node.js and npm. This will, in the end, generate a `package.json` file, a Laravel Mix configuration file, as well as a folder, and some empty files.

> **Skip setting up Laravel Mix**
>
> If you want, you can choose to skip the manual setup of Laravel Mix and simply use the Laravel Mix template provided with this book in the code related to this chapter. Then, simply go to the next section.

Before we start setting up Laravel Mix, we must open the Terminal (Mac) or Command Prompt (Windows) and navigate to our project folder. Then, we can follow these eight steps:

1. Generate an empty npm project with the default settings:

    ```
    npm init -y
    ```

2. Install the latest version of Bootstrap 5:

    ```
    npm install bootstrap@5.2.0 --save-dev
    ```

    `--save-dev` is used to specify that it is a development dependency. Change the version number if you want another version.

3. Install Popper, which is a dependency for the Dropdown, Popover, and Tooltip components:

    ```
    npm install @popperjs/core --save-dev
    ```

4. Install Laravel Mix:

    ```
    npm install laravel-mix --save-dev
    ```

5. Create the `webpack.mix.js` file in the root folder of the project. This is a configuration file for Laravel Mix.

6. In the root folder of the project, create the `src` folder with the empty `js` and `scss` folders inside. Create the `script.js` file in the `js` folder and the `style.scss` file in the `scss` folder. The file and folder structure should look like this:

```
src
|- js
    |- script.js
|- scss
    |- style.scss
```

We will put some code in those files in just a moment.

7. Add the following code to the configuration file (`webpack.mix.js`) to import `mix` and define our build:

```
let mix = require('laravel-mix');
mix.js('src/js/script.js', 'js/').sass(
    'src/scss/style.scss', 'css/');
```

Laravel Mix has now been instructed to do the following:

I.   Bundle the JavaScript in `src/js/script.js` and output it to the `js` folder.

II.   Compile the Sass in `src/scss/style.scss` and output it to the `css` folder.

8. Run the following command to install additional dependencies:

npx mix

This command should only be necessary to run once.

Using the Laravel Mix template

If you haven't followed the manual steps to set up Laravel Mix, you can also grab the Laravel Mix template from the `part-3/chapter-12/laravel-mix/template` folder. In this case, you should simply place the content of that template folder inside your project folder and run the following command:

npm install

This will install Bootstrap 5, Popper, and Laravel Mix, as well as all dependencies. You don't have to run the `npx mix` command to install additional dependencies.

Using Laravel Mix

The code in our project should now look like this:

```
src
|- js
   |- script.js
|- scss
   |- style.scss
package-lock.json
package.json
webpack.mix.js
```

Be aware that we haven't put any code inside the `script.js` and `style.scss` files just yet, and neither have we added any HTML files or other assets to the project. We will do that in just a moment. First, let's take a look at two of the most useful commands.

To trigger the Webpack build, which we defined in the `webpack.mix.js` file, we simply run the following command:

`npx mix`

This will now compile the files and build the bundle.

To watch the filesystem for changes and automatically recompile the files and rebuild the bundle, we can use the following command:

`npx mix watch`

Webpack will now run every time we save changes to a JavaScript or Sass file in our project folder.

> **No code was added to** `script.js` **and** `style.scss` **yet**
>
> The Laravel Mix commands currently don't produce any results, since we haven't added any code to our `script.js` and `style.scss` files in the `src` folder. We will do that now.

Adding the website code to the build process

We have to make some changes to our project, since it's not compatible with the way we want to use Laravel Mix. Because of this, we won't make changes to the existing project in `part-3/chapter-12/website`, but instead, make a copy to `part-3/chapter-12/laravel-mix/setup` and make our changes there. . Please note that all the changes described in this section has already been applied to the code on GitHub.

Here are the steps we need to make in order to restructure and update our project:

1. **Move JavaScript and Sass to the `src` folder**:

    First, we have to move our `js` and `scss` folder into the new `src` folder and delete the `bootstrap.bundle.min.js` file. The Bootstrap 5 JavaScript code will be compiled and bundled by Laravel Mix and then placed in another folder.

2. **Update HTML**:

    Since we have now deleted the `bootstrap.bundle.min.js` file in the previous step, we can now delete the following line of code from all HTML files:

HTML

```
<script src="js/bootstrap.bundle.min.js"></script>
```

Then, in the files that previously had only the `bootstrap.bundle.min.js` file and not the `script.js` file, we must add this file, so that all HTML pages, in the end, have only the following `script` tag:

```
<script src="js/script.js"></script>
```

So, the bottom part of each HTML file should look like this with few exceptions:

```
    </footer>
  <script src="js/script.js"></script>
  </body>
</html>
```

3. **Update Sass**:

    Now, we need to update the file path of the imports of the Bootstrap 5 Sass partials in the `style.scss` file. We need to replace `../bootstrap/scss/` with `~bootstrap/scss/` (or simply `../` with `~`) to make sure we get the source code directly from the `node_modules` folder. The tilde character, `~`, is a reference to that folder.

    Our top part of the `style.scss` file should now look like this:

part-3/chapter-12/laravel-mix/website/src/scss/style.scss

```
// Required
@import "~bootstrap/scss/functions";


// Default variable overrides
@import "default-variable-overrides";
```

```
// Required
@import "~bootstrap/scss/variables";

// Variable value using existing variable
@import "variable-value-using-variable";

// Required
@import "~bootstrap/scss/maps";
@import "~bootstrap/scss/mixins";
@import "~bootstrap/scss/root";
```

We will keep the rest of our Sass files untouche4.

1. **Update JavaScript**:

When we load Bootstrap 5 via a `<script>` tag, we use the `bootstrap` namespace when initializing JavaScript components as follows:

JavaScript

```
new bootstrap.[component]([element])
```

To import the Bootstrap 5 JavaScript source code to make it work with our own current JavaScript code, we must do it in the following way at the top of our `script.js` file:

part-3/chapter-12/laravel-mix/setup/src/js/script.js

```
import * as bootstrap from 'bootstrap';
```

This will import all Bootstrap 5 JavaScript source files, which is similar to what we had before when we used the `bootstrap.bundle.min.js` file in a `<script>` tag.

Now, to actually trigger the Webpack build, compile the Sass, and bundle the JavaScript, we can use the Laravel Mix commands from before to run it once:

npx mix

Or we can use the following command to run it every time we save changes to a JavaScript or Sass file in our project folder:

npx mix watch

We have now learned how to set up a build process using Node.js, npm, and Laravel Mix. However, we are importing all of the JavaScript code even though we don't use it all. Next up, we will see how we can optimize the JavaScript import.

Using a module bundler to optimize JavaScript

We can optimize our usage of JavaScript files when using a module bundler. Instead of importing all the Bootstrap 5 JavaScript source files like we just did before, we can import only the ones we need.

In the source code of Bootstrap 5, we have the `bootstrap/js/dist` folder, which contains the source code for the individual JavaScript components, as well as the `base-component.js` file and the `dom` folder, with some more general code related to working with the DOM (the Document Object Model of the page).

We might imagine that we can just add one of these files in a `<script>` tag in our HTML as follows:

HTML

```
<script src="node_modules/bootstrap/js/dist/modal.js"></script>
```

However, this won't work. We'll get an error in the browser console. We have to reference these files in our `script.js` file and use a module bundler.

As an example, if we only import the `bootstrap/js/dist/modal.js` file, it will also import the `bootstrap/js/dist/base-component.js` file and all the DOM-related files in the `bootstrap/js/dist/dom` folder.

If we instead only import the `bootstrap/js/dist/tooltip.js` file, it will also import the `bootstrap/js/dist/base-component.js` file, all the DOM-related files in the `bootstrap/js/dist/dom` folder, and all the necessary files from the Popper npm package, since the tooltip component relies on this library for positioning.

Before we proceed, please note that we won't make more changes to the code in `part-3/chapter-12/laravel-mix/setup`, but instead, make a copy of that code to `part-3/chapter-12/laravel-mix/optimize-js` and make our changes there. Please note that all the changes described in this section has already been applied to the code on GitHub.

On our website, we use all of the JavaScript components, except for Button, Popover, and Scrollspy (however, we still use Button as a regular component using HTML and CSS). Now, to optimize the usage of JavaScript files, we will add the following lines of code to our `script.js` file to only include the components we actually use:

part-3/chapter-12/laravel-mix/optimize-js/src/js/script.js

```
import Alert from 'bootstrap/js/dist/alert';
import Carousel from 'bootstrap/js/dist/carousel';
import Collapse from 'bootstrap/js/dist/collapse';
import Dropdown from 'bootstrap/js/dist/dropdown';
```

```
import Modal from 'bootstrap/js/dist/modal';
import Offcanvas from 'bootstrap/js/dist/offcanvas';
import Tab from 'bootstrap/js/dist/tab';
import Toast from 'bootstrap/js/dist/toast';
import Tooltip from 'bootstrap/js/dist/tooltip';
```

As mentioned in the previous section, when we load Bootstrap 5 via a `<script>` tag, we use the `bootstrap` namespace when initializing JavaScript components, as follows:

JavaScript

```
new bootstrap.[component]([element])
```

Since we're now using a bundler, the window object will not be defined, so we must initialize components in the following way:

JavaScript

```
new [component]([element])
```

Because of this, we need to make some changes to our `script.js` file. We need to replace the new `bootstrap.[component]` code with new `[component]` everywhere we're using it. As an example, in the code where we initialize all tooltips, we must make the following change:

part-3/chapter-12/laravel-mix/optimize-js/src/js/script.js

```
const tooltipTriggerElements =
  document.querySelectorAll('[data-bs-toggle="tooltip"]');
for (let i = 0; i < tooltipTriggerElements.length; i++) {
  new bootstrap.Tooltip(tooltipTriggerElements[i])
}
```

Now, we can run the same Laravel Mix commands as mentioned before again.

Please note, that we must also run the command:

npm install

if it hasn't been run already. This command will create the `node_modules` folder and download all necessary dependencies (including the source code for Bootstrap 5) to that.

Minifying our compiled CSS and bundled JavaScript

To optimize our code even further, we want to minify the compiled CSS and bundled JavaScript. We can do this with Laravel Mix simply by running the following command:

```
npx mix --production
```

The `--production` flag is used to indicate that we want to minify the compiled and bundled files.

Summary

We have now learned how we can optimize the compiled Bootstrap 5 CSS and JavaScript code. First, we learned how to optimize our stylesheet by only including the Bootstrap 5 Sass partials we actually used and removing all the helpers and utilities that we didn't use. Then, we learned how to use Node.js, npm, and Laravel Mix to set up a build process to automate some tasks, which helped us bundle only the JavaScript that our components actually used and minify both our compiled CSS and bundled JavaScript.

Even though the methods and techniques described in this chapter don't alter the look and feel of the website, they will optimize your final code and thus provide better performance and a faster load time for the user.

Throughout this book, we have learned how to work with Bootstrap 5 in various new ways. From only knowing about the HTML structure and class names for the various Bootstrap 5 components with the default style, we have learned how to change the global options and the color palette, how to understand and navigate the Sass source code, how to customize various Bootstrap 5 elements with the use of Sass variables, and how to use the powerful utility API. On top of that, we have learned how to use Bootstrap 5 with more advanced Sass, CSS, and JavaScript features, and finally, how to optimize the compiled CSS and JavaScript (including using a module bundler). We are now well equipped as Bootstrap 5 developers to solve more advanced tasks and be more creative with the usage of the Bootstrap 5 source code.

Thanks for reading!

Index

Other Books You May Enjoy

If you enjoyed this book, you may be interested in these other books by Packt:

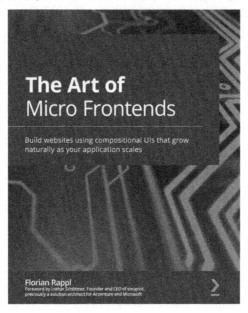

The Art of Micro Frontends

Florian Rappl

ISBN: 978-1-80056-356-8

- Understand how to choose the right micro frontend architecture
- Design screens for compositional UIs
- Create a great developer experience for micro frontend solutions
- Achieve enhanced user experiences with micro frontends
- Introduce governance and boundary checks for managing distributed frontends
- Build scalable modular web applications from scratch or by migrating an existing monolith

A Frontend Web Developer's Guide to Testing

Eran Kinsbruner

ISBN: 978-1-80323-831-9

- Choose the ideal tool or combination of tools for testing your app
- Continuously monitor the market and ensure that your developers are using the right tools
- Advance test automation for your web app with sophisticated capabilities
- Measure both code coverage and test coverage to assess your web application quality
- Measure the success and maturity of web application quality
- Understand the trade-offs in tool selection and the associated risks
- Build Cypress, Selenium, Playwright, and Puppeteer projects from scratch
- Explore low-code testing tools for web apps

Packt is searching for authors like you

If you're interested in becoming an author for Packt, please visit authors.packtpub.com and apply today. We have worked with thousands of developers and tech professionals, just like you, to help them share their insight with the global tech community. You can make a general application, apply for a specific hot topic that we are recruiting an author for, or submit your own idea.

Share Your Thoughts

Now you've finished *The Missing Bootstrap 5 Guide*, we'd love to hear your thoughts! Scan the QR code below to go straight to the Amazon review page for this book and share your feedback or leave a review on the site that you purchased it from.

https://packt.link/r/180107643X

Your review is important to us and the tech community and will help us make sure we're delivering excellent quality content.